D0083075

Black Men in Interracial Relationships

Black Men in Interracial Relationships

What's Love Got to Do with It?

Kellina M. Craig-Henderson

Transaction Publishers
New Brunswick (U.S.A.) and London (U.K.)

This book is printed on acid-free paper that meets the American National Standard for Permanence of Paper for Printed Library Materials.

Library of Congress Catalog Number: 2005054948
ISBN: 0-7658-0309-7
Printed in the United States of America

Library of Congress Cataloging-in-Publication Data

Craig-Henderson, Kellina M.
  Black men in interracial relationships : what's love got to do with it? /
Kellina M. Craig-Henderson.
     p. cm.
  Includes bibliographical references.
  ISBN 0-7658-0309-7 (alk. paper)
  1. Interracia ldating—United States. 2. Interracial marriage—United States. 3. African American men—Attitudes. 4. Man-woman relationships. I. Title.

HQ801.8.C73   2005
306.84'608996073—dc22   2005054948

To African American women who have wondered
what love has to do with it.

Contents

Acknowledgements

There were many people who helped me throughout this project including the women and men who suggested referrals to me, as well as the men I interviewed. I am grateful to each of them.

On a more personal note, there were also several special people who provided me support and encouragement without which I could not have completed this project. Foremost among them, my mother, who continues to be my greatest fan. My support network also included several other family members, as well as a few very good friends who believed in this project from the beginning. In fact, they were there when I began asking them about what I perceived to be an absence of Black women from many Black men's lives. Their encouragement has been invaluable. Last but by no means least, I thank my husband—a very special man—whose love has been there for me throughout much of this project. God continues to bless me.

1

Why Look at Black Men in
Interracial Relationships?

Not long ago I lived in a small, Midwestern town about 135 miles
south of Chicago. At that time, I was on the faculty of a large re-
search-oriented university where Black professors were rare. In my
primary department, which regularly boasted a faculty of 70 to 75
Ph.D.s, I was one of three people of color and the only African
American.[1] Indeed, there were so few Black professors present at
that university that when more than one person was present the topic
of conversation invariably turned to our dismal representation on
the faculty and our less than optimal lives away from work in that
very small, White, Midwestern town. Aside from our academic ap-
pointments, there was little in the way of cultural or social activities.
Many of us relied heavily on the functions sponsored by the Black
studies unit on campus to meet and greet others with similar interests, histories, and experiences. On one of these occasions, I be-
friended a petite, attractive woman, "Carla," who had recently joined
the faculty of the law school at the university.

We became good friends, and periodically joked about the fact
that we were both single and had pretty limited social lives. At those
times, we consoled ourselves by reminding each other that we had
good jobs and were employed at a top-ranking institution. For us, as
well as the many other academics employed at prestigious universi-
ties in the United States, there was a bitter irony to our relative successes.[2] On the one hand, the assistant, associate, and full professo-
rial, dean and headship positions African Americans occupied at the
university reflected our superior scholarly achievements and professional competencies. In all of these respects, we decidedly saw
ourselves as equal to any one of our majority (i.e., White) class of
colleagues. On the other hand, it was not possible to overlook the

1

fact that our numbers on the campus of that university were in no way comparable to that of our White colleagues, nor were they in any way reflective of the percentage of African Americans in the U.S. population. For the most part, we were present as "solos."[3]

Carla and I got together frequently for conversation and laughs. During one of these times, we discussed who among the men on the faculty was Black, single, and "straight." There weren't many, and by the time we identified each of them, we realized we both knew about one particular man who had recently obtained an appointment as an associate professor in the engineering school. I knew of him only because I had seen his photograph in a campus publication of new faculty. It was a good picture, and "Paul" had an engaging and warm smile. His complexion was dark chestnut brown, and his attractive smile showed off a beautiful set of teeth. In all respects, his photograph was flattering. I remembered it well and immediately hunted out the issue of the faculty publication in which it appeared for Carla.

As it turned out, although she had never seen him before looking at the picture I showed her, Carla's knowledge of Paul went well beyond awareness of his good looks and marital status. Apparently, one of her female colleagues, "Susan," fancied herself a matchmaker. Carla was friendly with Susan, and when Susan made repeated overtures to introduce her to Paul, a good-looking professor she'd met recently at the gym, she always declined. On more than one occasion, Susan encouraged her to consent to the introduction. Eventually Carla gave in, and although she had never seen Paul, she agreed to allow Susan to "hook her up." After all, she reasoned, Susan swore he was intelligent, attractive, single, heterosexual, and socially skilled. How could she pass up an opportunity to meet this guy? Even if it wasn't a "love connection," it would at least be a chance to make a new friend. After giving Susan permission to make the introduction, she anxiously awaited word from her.

About a week later, Susan came to Carla with some rather sobering news. She explained she had, indeed, caught up with Paul at the gym and told him of her desire to introduce him to her friend and colleague. She said she had described her as a single, youthful, attractive Black woman who was also new to the area. Susan told Carla not only had Paul declined the chance to meet her, but he had asked out Susan instead! Susan was White. According to Susan, when she expressed surprise at his response, Paul explained he had nothing in common with Black women, and he was not particularly interested in meeting, much less dating, any of them. Susan was already involved with someone else and did not take him up on his invitation. Carla never questioned Susan's motives, and as for Susan, she never brought up the subject of matchmaking again.

After getting over my own disappointment with Paul and his remark, I thought about the implications of what he had said and the extent to which it may or may not have been echoed by other similarly educated and employed Black men. I really did not understand what he meant about not having anything in common with Black women, and I plied Carla with a host of questions about her own reactions to what he had said. Together, we began to consider the implications of his remark in earnest. Here was a man of African descent who was clearly identifiable as such by anybody's classification system. That is to say, he had a dark complexion and features characteristic of people whose ancestry can be visibly traced to Africa. Yet, he consciously and explicitly chose not to have anything to do with women who, no doubt, looked a lot like any one of the women in his own family, or for that matter, his own birth mother. What could account for this? Since that time, I have struggled to come up with a reasonable explanation.

Life continued for us in that small town, and we went on with our daily routines. I didn't think much more about Paul, and I don't recall us ever discussing him or his remark again. I did, however, tuck that exchange away somewhere in my memory. What he had said was inexplicable to me. How could he have ruled out the possibility of intimacy with any one of the more than 15 million Black women in the United States? Hadn't he heard about the ever-expanding cadre of Black women who were professionally employed, economically independent, and upwardly mobile? Did he not realize young Black women increasingly populated college and university classrooms and women who were once just like them could now be found within the ranks of America's CEOs, elected public officials, surgeons, and television talk show hosts? Did he overlook the fact Black women come in all sizes, shapes and hues, and while some enjoy jazz, others like hip-hop, and still others love opera? How could he have failed to realize Black women play tennis, ski, go to movies, line-dance, travel, and visit museums?

I was at a loss to explain how a seemingly intelligent Black man could commit so grave an error and do so in such a way as to legitimize his request for a date with a White woman. I suspected my contempt for him was as much a matter of the fact he had said what he had said, as it was he had said this to a White woman. Admittedly, had I overheard him saying the very same thing to another Black man, or even to a Black woman, I probably would not have felt so strongly about it nor would I have taken his remark so personally. No doubt the acerbity of his remark was enhanced as a consequence of his having said it to Susan.

And what about Susan? She had unwittingly become the bearer of bad news (that Paul chose to reject Carla sight unseen!), as well as the target of unexpected racial sentiment. This sentiment, she surely reasoned, was not intended to offend her. However, given Carla's description of her, I suspect she nevertheless, found the situation unpleasant. That she would then voluntarily serve as a conduit for the transmission of that sentiment to Carla, someone for whom that sentiment would surely offend, seemed terribly insensitive.

Although I never quite forgot Paul's remark, only when I began this project did the complete recollection of it return to me. Back then, it never really occurred to me to give it any more thought than to simply "write off" Paul. At the time when Carla and I talked about it, I never seriously considered the social psychology of interracial intimacy,[4] much less did I think of actually writing about Black men in interracial relationships. Only after I resigned from my position at that university and moved to the west coast did I decide to do so. At that time, Paul's remark would begin to resonate with more than a few of my own personal observations.

For example, I began to notice that many within the ranks of America's Black male elite were coupled with women who were not Black. I started wondering why. Why was it successful Black men— Black men who were "at the top of their games" in the arts, entertainment, politics and athletics—were more apt to be married to or dating a woman who was not an African American? In addition to their celebrity status, which includes wide-spread popularity and wealth, Black men like Charles Barkley, James Earl Jones, Michael Jackson, Scotti Pippen, Quincy Jones, Sidney Poitier, Charles Moose, Taye Diggs, Clarence Thomas, Berry Gordy, Cuba Gooding, Jr., Kobe Bryant, "Ice-T," Russell Simmons, Walter Mosley, Bryant Gumbel, Karl Malone, "The Rock," Gordon Parks, Melvin Van Peebles, Bill Lee, Wayne Brady, Dennis Haysbert, B.J. Armstrong, Randy Jackson, Yaphet Koto, and Wesley Snipes share something in common that also characterizes the experiences of more than 250,000 less well-known Black men in the United States. Each of these heterosexual Black men happens to have been involved in an intimate interracial relationship.

Today, more Black men than ever are involved in intimate interracial relationships and marriages. As race and gender relations in U.S. society have improved, the rates of interracial intimate relationships have also increased. The outcomes of the various liberation strategies and protest movements that occurred during the latter half of the twentieth century (e.g., civil rights and equal rights) have involved increased contact between groups of people who were previously prohibited from interacting. Consider that today's public school classrooms are increasingly manned by White women whose pupils are overwhelmingly Black and "brown." This was certainly not the case in earlier years.[5] Changes in the labor force have also occurred as a result of the relatively recent entry of large numbers of White women and, to a lesser degree, men and women of color. If social progress is regarded as the elimination of discriminatory barriers, then some measure of social progress has certainly been achieved within the last fifty years. Of the many outcomes of the protest movements of the 1950s and the 1960s, the access of Black men to women of other races and ethnicities is surely one of the more noticeable and potentially meaningful ones.

The number of Black men who are involved in interracial relationships far exceeds that of Black women. Although it is true more Black women are involved in intimate interracial relationships than as recently as twenty years ago, it is also true the rate of their involvement in these relationships pales in comparison to Black men. Today Black men are more than twice as likely as Black women to be involved in an interracial relationship.[6] Yet, at the same time, Blacks as a group are less likely than other minorities to be involved with people from other races and ethnicities. Are current rates of interracial intimacy to be expected as signs of progress, or is there a different explanation for Black men's increased involvement in interracial relationships?

Many well-respected theorists in various social science disciplines have pointed to trends such as these in debates about whether and to what extent race has declined as a variable in determining an individual's life chances.[7] Think about it. Less than fifty years ago, most public schools were segregated, less than 10 percent of African Americans could be categorized as "middle class," and interracial relationships were forbidden. Indeed the consequences of transgression in either public schooling or interpersonal relationships at that time might have even been fatal. Children who dared to break the color barrier by attending formerly all-White schools were intimidated and physically assaulted, and Black men who were accused of having had sexual relations with White women were sometimes murdered. Public schools are now prohibited from barring students because of their racial or ethnic status, and although some opposition to interracial relationships continues to flourish, it is illegal to discriminate against individuals because of their involvement in these types of relationships. Clearly, significant changes in race relations have occurred.

In the last year, two events, especially relevant to this discussion, have occurred which are worth mentioning here. The first concerns the celebratory context in which discussions about the fiftieth anniversary of the *Brown v. the Board of Education* Supreme Court case have taken place. Across America, public and private institutions and officials have explicitly acknowledged the value and important consequences of the landmark decision to desegregate the public schools. The other event, which is also relevant, concerns the recent announcement by the U.S. Department of Justice of its decision to re-open the murder case of Emmett Till.[8] Though some might argue public discussions about the *Brown v. Board* decision as well as the reopening of the Till case are more symbolic than anything else, it is impossible to overlook their significance. Events such as these reflect an era when Blacks were second-class citizens, and the fact legislation resulting from them is now accepted, indeed taken for granted, is a significant indicator of social progress.

No doubt the current number of Black men in interracial relationships reflects these changes. What is less clear, however, is the degree to which the personal motives of Black men are responsible for this particular trend. Given the substantially lower rate of involvement by Black women in interracial relationships and given what appears to be a tendency towards interracial intimacy among Black male elites, the question arises as to whether these trends are merely a result of large-scale changes in race relations. Is it really just a matter of racial progress?

Bearing Witness to Current Trends

In the summer of 1997, I resigned from my faculty position at that particular Midwestern university for several reasons. To be sure, I was still committed to a career in the academy, but after four years, I recognized certain basic quality of life issues about which I was no longer willing to compromise. I was no longer satisfied with the two-hour commute north in order to interact with other African Americans in cultural, professional and social settings. And I was tired of my perpetual "solo status." What's more, I missed the energy and diversity inherent to the cities I'd previously called home, and I had never really acquired the uniquely Midwestern sensibilities of that particular small town. Although I was fully aware of the professional risks involved in a move such as the kind I prepared to undertake,[9] I also recognized the importance of personal fulfillment. The latter I knew was a necessary aspect of my ability to remain disciplined and focused. Given the autonomous nature of academia, discipline and motivation are essential to any type of professional work one engages in outside of the classroom (e.g., research, advising, publishing). I knew in order to continue to maintain an active level of research productivity and to remain committed to my teaching responsibilities, I needed to be happy, or at least not miserable. I repeated this line of reasoning to myself at various times during my move west and throughout the first six months while living there.

One of the impressions that first struck me when I arrived in California was the abundance of highly visible interracial, heterosexual couples.[10] They seemed to be everywhere. More often than not, I noticed Black men in almost every possible age group with women who appeared to be of Asian, Indian, Mexican, and European descent. I knew because I had spent the previous four years suffering through the homogeneity characteristic of small town middle America, I was especially sensitive to displays of interracial intimacy. When I saw a Black man in an interracial relationship, I looked perhaps a moment longer than I would have had the man and the woman both been Black, or White, or Hispanic. But what was most striking to me was the apparent absence of Black women. At public and social gatherings and events, I searched for Black men who were accompanied by Black women, but rarely did I see them.

I became obsessed with what seemed to me to be an absence of Black women, and I began seriously to consider not only the cause of this state of affairs, but I also began to speculate about its implications. During outings and while running errands, I was acutely aware of the presence of Black men who were accompanied by women who were not Black. Initially, I attributed this perceptual imbalance to the distinctiveness of the neighborhood I now called home. I reasoned because I had settled into a relatively high-income section of a city of about 500,000 and because a majority of my new neighbors were White, the probability of seeing any African Americans, men or women, was small. Consequently (and prematurely), I concluded this accounted for my failure to see Black men and Black women together.

But as I became more familiar with my surroundings and began to make new friends, the geographical radius of my "stomping ground" expanded. I began to travel well beyond the neighborhood that included my home and my new job. While shopping, eating out, attending concerts, or simply walking along the beach, I began to think of a much greater area as my own. At these times, I anticipated seeing more Black couples. Yet I still did not see great numbers of Black men with Black women, or numbers that were comparable to the rates of pairings of Black men with women from other racial backgrounds. I was curious about this and wondered aloud to friends and family. On more than one occasion, I found myself asking others where the Black women were, whom they dated, loved and married.

More often than not, my questions went unanswered. Furthermore, I found the answers I did receive addressing the apparent absence of Black women from the lives of Black men were unsatisfying and incomplete. Indeed, the more people I talked to and the more I learned about the various patterns of interracial intimacy in the region, the more perplexed I became. I considered the fact that although intimate interracial relationships occurred in other parts of the country, in no other place and at no other time had they seemed to be so prevalent to me. But was this simply a matter of my perception, or are more people, particularly Black men, involved in interracial relationships today?

As a social psychologist, I was intellectually intrigued about just what aspect of contemporary race, gender, and socioeconomic relations was responsible for increases in interracial intimate relationships. At that time, however, as a single, heterosexual Black woman, I was somewhat uneasy. Something about Black men's pursuit of and subsequent coupling with women who were not Black did not sit particularly well with me. Although I considered my observations might have reflected, in fact, a new and improved era in race relations, I wasn't convinced this alone was the answer. What accounted for Black men's involvement in intimate interracial relationships?[11]

While there is no shortage of hyperbole to answer this question, informed analysis and systematic efforts to address the question accurately are rare. Although more popular books and magazine articles increasingly mention interracial relationships, they tend to do so in a brief and often undeveloped manner. In fiction, for example, the interracial relationship exists as "a problem" for its protagonist and the plot involves description of the course through which resolution occurs—either through extraction from the relationship or deeper commitment to it. In nonfiction texts and articles, the attention is generally focused on self-help remedies or inspirational affirmations.[12]

Public discourse in recent years about one well-known interracial couple has also fueled speculation about intimate interracial relationships in general, and those involving Black men in particular. Writers and self-appointed experts have routinely cited O.J. Simpson and the late Nicole Brown Simpson as the prototype for the Black male/White female interracial couple. Indeed, according to one writer, public reaction to the Simpsons reflected America's longstanding preoccupation and paranoia with Black male sexuality.[13]

O.J. Simpson's celebrity status made him unique and certainly not representative of the typical Black man in an interracial relationship. However, it is worth noting the sensationalism that surrounded his wife's murder and the ensuing celebrity status of everyone who was even remotely associated with the couple was a consequence of her status as a White woman. During the investigation, a number of people within the Black community speculated about the likelihood that the disproportionate media and public attention directed at the case was *because* Nicole Brown Simpson was White and not Black. That the alleged villain was a Black man only served to further fuel the public's fanatical obsession with the case.[14]

One writer who sought to make sense out of the Black community's response to the O.J. trial articulates this point eloquently:

...[B]oth Nicole Brown Simpson's and OJ Simpson's race and gender matter. Simpson represents first and foremost Black male sexuality, which White America finds threatening and seeks to control. His status as an athlete, his physicality, makes this image of him all the more compelling: he is buff and Black and uncontrollably sexual, particularly in the presence of White women.... . Nicole Brown Simpson, on the other hand, represents innocent, White female sexuality, which White America seeks to protect from Black male sexual aggression. [15]

Current Rates of Interracial Relationships

In the past thirty years, rates of interracial marriages in the United States have nearly quadrupled. Not surprisingly, rates of interracial dating and intimacy have also increased at even greater rates. Most analysts who forecast trends predict with the continued erosion of racial barriers, we can expect continuing increases in rates of interracial intimacy. In large cities and small towns, more than ever before, men and women from different racial backgrounds are getting together.

Today there are nearly 1,500,000 interracial marriages in the United States,[16] and although Asians, Hispanics, and Whites are more likely to marry each other interracially, more than 325,000 of existing interracial marriages are between Blacks and Whites.[17] But people involved in interracial relationships are not the only ones with favorable opinions about these types of relationships. As a matter of fact, results of a 1997 Gallup poll provide evidence of Americans' generally increasing tolerance for interracial marriages. Touted as "one of the most substantial race-related changes ever noted in a Gallup poll," a majority of Black and White Americans expressed acceptance of interracial marriage. According to one article describing these data,[18] whereas only 25 percent of Whites approved of interracial marriage in 1972, 61 percent noted their approval in 1997. A change was evidenced among Blacks such that although 61 percent noted their approval in 1972, 77 percent did so in 1997. More than anything else, these findings show acceptance for interracial marriages has generally increased.

Yet, differences in rates of participation for men and women within certain racial groups are perplexing. For example, census data available for rates as recent as 1992 reveal marriages between Black men and White women comprised 66 percent of the interracial Black/White marriages occurring that year, and almost twice as many as the numbers of marriages involving Black women and White men. Of the

246,000 Black/White marriages that took place in 1992, more than half, 163,000, were between Black men and White women.[19] Clearly, these numbers suggest Black men are more likely to be in interracial relationships (at least marriages) than are women.

Whereas men and women from other racial backgrounds tend to be equally as likely to participate in interracial relationships, this is not the case among Black men and women today, nor was it ever the case in the decades during which records have been compiled. Consider the findings from one study which examined actual trends in Black/White marriages drawing from census data for 1970 and 1980.[20] Important and of particular relevance here, the authors of the study concluded, "The percentage of Blacks marrying Whites has been increasing since 1960 particularly among Black males and White females."[21] One other study that reviewed marriage certificates filed in the non-Southern states found in the 1980s approximately 10 percent of Black men who were married, married White women.[22] How do today's rates compare with previous eras? The following figure depicts rates of interracial marriage between Blacks and Whites during the latter half of the twentieth century and clearly shows among Black the greatest increase has occurred in marriages between Black men and White women.[23]

Figure 1.1

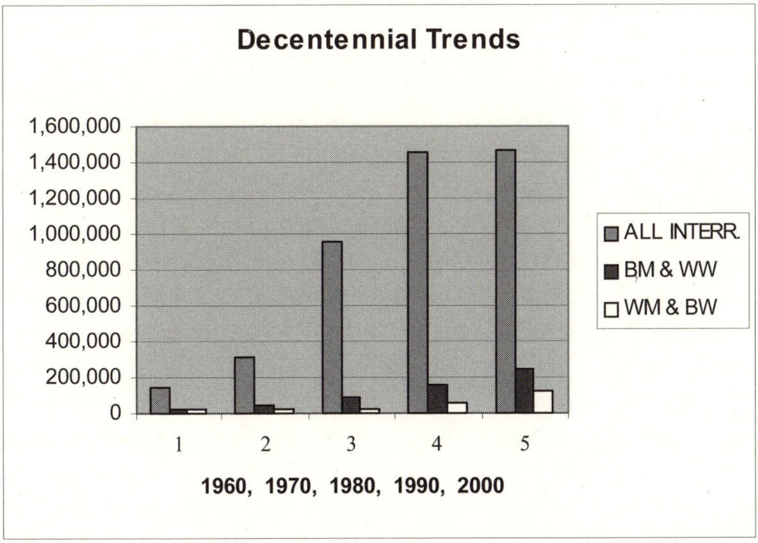

Decentennial Trends

1,600,000
1,400,000
1,200,000
1,000,000
800,000
600,000
400,000
200,000
0

1   2   3   4   5

1960, 1970, 1980, 1990, 2000

■ ALL INTERR.
■ BM & WW
□ WM & BW

So what is really going on with Black men in interracial relationships? This book and the material included here represent one small effort aimed at unraveling the mystery behind Black men's greater involvement in interracial relationships today. Why are there as many men involved in interracial relationships as there are? And, why are there more Black men involved in these types of relationships than Black women? How do men in these relationships explain their own personal experiences? As a way of getting at the answers, over the course of several years, I interviewed a small group of Black men who were involved in interracial relationships. The men to whom I spoke lived in different regions of the country. Among other things, they provided their ideas about interracial relationships. Many of the men's detailed remarks are included on the following pages.

In this book, I have chosen to focus on men in interracial relationships. Admittedly, I could have examined the experiences of White or Black women, or for that matter, women of any racial background who have been in relationships with Black men. But there were two reasons why I chose to focus exclusively on men. First, I was most concerned with what I perceived to be the absence of Black women. I thought by exploring the personal ideas of heterosexual men about their own relationships with women of other races, I could better understand the apparent absence of women from the lives of Black men. What better way to tackle this issue than to ask men directly?

The second reason for looking at Black men in interracial intimate relationships has to do with the way heterosexual relationships are initiated. Because intimate heterosexual relationships continue to be more frequently initiated by the male rather than the female,[24] the pressure to initiate a relationship seems to lie more with men than women. If Black men and women are not getting together and establishing intimate relationships, then Black men are largely (though not entirely, of course) responsible for not initiating the relationship. In order to understand Black men's choices with respect to mate selection asking a sample of Black men these questions seemed practical. I reasoned the only way to really understand the factors associated with the involvement of Black men in interracial intimacy was to speak directly and candidly with them.

My aim here was to prompt an extensive discussion about interracial intimacy with a particular focus on relationships involving Black men. Because of the way race and gender are conceptualized in the United States, an understanding of the factors associated with the choices of Black men in mate selection can illuminate connections between individual behaviors and forces occurring within the greater social context. While it is true individuals act freely and create their own circumstances, there is also a degree to which their behaviors are restricted, or in some cases, instigated by the very environment in which they find themselves. For example, no matter how much one particular individual might wish to establish an interracial intimate relationship, if that individual exists in a completely homogenous environment lacking any interaction with people of different racial backgrounds, it would be impossible actually to have an intimate interracial relationship. Conversely, although others might wish to establish relationships with individuals of their own race, because of geographic or professional constraints, they might very well find themselves with little or no opportunity to interact with those of similar racial backgrounds.[25]

Both of these cases represent extremes, and one might argue increasingly unlikely given the relative mobility and connectedness of today's society. However, as examples they highlight the unique way individual behaviors, though freely chosen, can be restricted by greater social forces. Most of the men I spoke to during this project fall somewhere in between these extremes. As a result, it is more challenging to understand these more normative cases and careful analysis is necessary.

This discussion, peppered with interview responses throughout the pages, tells only part of the story of interracial intimacy in contemporary America. The complete story requires the inclusion of the responses of each of the men's mates, as well as an examination of the responses of the many people who comprise the alternate forms that interracial intimate, heterosexual relationships may assume in the United States today (e.g., Black woman/Asian man). However, this discussion represents an exploratory effort that is limited to the comments of Black men and their perspectives on interracial intimacy. Hopefully, these responses will not only illuminate some of the motives and circumstances surrounding the involvement of Black men in interracial relationships, but will also provide a better understanding of the dynamics of interracial intimacy in general.

Final Note on Terminology

I believe it is important to note although I am in agreement with most social scientists that regard "race" as a fairly meaningless category whose importance is limited to social categorization, [26] I do recognize that to the extent it continues to demarcate people in society it is "more than a notion." Were it not, this discussion and the material included here could not exist.[27] To the extent that life chances and opportunities continue to be determined in large part by race, [28] the significance some people may attach to this variable when thinking about and selecting a mate is worth considering.

Race has been an important determinant of movement, policy, and personal identities within the United States. Though it is not a fixed, concrete possession or attribute such as an individual's automobile or age, it is far more meaningful in that it represents a culmination of meanings, perceptions, and experiences.[29] Race is fluid in that racial identities and the meanings ascribed to them have not only shifted with the passage of time, but they have also prompted changes over time. Its significance cannot be overlooked. According to sociologists Omi and Winant,

> How one is categorized is far from a merely academic or even personal matter. Such matters as access to employment, housing or other publicly or privately valued goods, social program design and the disbursement of local, state, and federal funds, or the organization of elections (among many other issues) are directly affected by racial classification and the recognition of "legitimate" groups. [30]

Notes

1. Throughout this discussion, I have used the terms "Black" and "African American" interchangeably. This practice not only reflects my own tendency when speaking, but it is also a reflection of the terminology used by the people with whom I spoke whom I'll describe shortly. It is important to note, however, not all "Blacks" self-identify or are classified as African Americans because of a variety of reasons. For example, in some cases, Blacks who were born in the U.S. and have lived in other countries for long periods of time are sometimes less enthusiastic about identifying themselves as African Americans. Moreover, foreign-born "Black" people living in the United States do not regard themselves as African Americans. Some Blacks who were born and raised in the U.S. and who, because of the time period in which they came of age or because of particular concerns about identity, do not claim either of the two terms.

2. Several authors have written about the strange predicament of professionally employed African Americans. They speak of the "tax" levied against them and note the anger and disillusionment they experience when they come to terms with the fact that their success does not protect them from certain forms of discrimination and prejudice, or as was the case for my colleagues and I, isolation. For more discussion of this problem, see Ellis Cose's *Rage of a Privileged Class* (NY: HarperCollins Publishers, 1993) and Derrick Bell's *Faces at the Bottom of the Well: The Permanence of Racism* (NY: BasicBook, 1992).

3. The term "solo" refers to the person who is distinctive within a particular setting. This distinctiveness results from the salience of an ascribed primary feature such as

their race, gender, or age. Social psychologists have argued solo status is associated with performance pressures, self-consciousness, and stereotyping for the solo. See the research report by Kellina Craig and Karen Feasel titled "Do Solo Arrangements Lead to Attributions of Tokenism?" *Journal of Applied Social Psychology 28* (1998): 1810-1836 for an empirical test of solo status.

4. I use the term "interracial" rather than, for example, "biracial," because my interests include relationships involving men and women from multiple racial groups.

5. For an extensive discussion on the role of race in schooling in northern and southern regions of the United States, see the chapter by James Andersen on literacy and education of African Americans, "Literacy and Education. The African American Experience," in *Literacy Among African-American Youth*, edited by Vivien L. Gadsen & Daniel A. Wagner, Creskill, N.J.: Hampton Press, 1995.

6. U.S. Bureau of the Census (2003): Hispanic origin and race of coupled households.

7. Theorists from an array of disciplines and political orientations have debated the veracity of the claim that the significance of race is declining, including, though not limited to, William J. Wilson in his aptly titled book *The Declining Significance of Race,* as well as Cornel West in *Race Matters.*

8. Emmett Till was a teenager who was brutally murdered by White men while visiting relatives in Mississippi in 1956.

9. When I announced my decision to leave the university, I was warned by many well-meaning friends (and a few acquaintances whose motives I considered questionable) about the perils of leaving a full-time position in such a well-respected department and university.

10. My attention throughout this text is on heterosexual men. However, it should be noted at least some of factors associated with intimate interracial, heterosexual relationships might operate similarly in gay, bi-sexual, and lesbian relationships.

11. According to the report *The State of America 2001* by the National Urban League, recent analyses of the data from the 2000 Current Population Survey show Black men are three times more likely to marry someone of a different race than are women.

12. In the case of the latter, see Kimberly Hohman's *The Color of Love: A Black Person's Guide to Interracial Relationships.*

13. Earl Ofari Hutchinson described public reaction to the Simpson murder and trial in *Beyond OJ. Race Sex and Class Lessons for America.*

14. As evidence of this, criminal justice statistics reveal rape convictions continue to be correlated with the race of both the perpetrator and victim such that the swiftest and severest punishment is exacted when the rape victim is a White woman and the alleged perpetrator is a Black man. This phenomenon does not occur in the case of the rape victim who is a woman. Nor is punishment as sure when the alleged perpetrator is White and his victim a or White woman. The writer Earl Ofari Hutchison describes the study by the *Dallas Herald* that found when a Black male was convicted of raping a White woman, the average sentence was ten years. In contrast, when the victim was a woman, the average sentence was two years.

15. See Devon W. Carbado's chapter "The Construction of O.J. Simpson as a Racial Victim" in his text *Black Men on Race, Gender and Sexuality: A Critical Reader* (New York: New York University Press, 1999).

16. U.S. Bureau of the Census, (2000). *Report on Characteristics of the Black Population.*

17. See the chapter by Stanley Gaines and William Ickes, "Perspectives on Interracial Relationships," in the edited volume *Handbook of Personal Relationships.*

18.   See the online article by Charlotte Astor discussing results of a 1997 Gallup poll "Gallup Poll: Progress in /White Relations, but Race Is Still an Issue," *U.S. Society & Values, USIA Electronic Journal 2* (August 1997): online.

19.   The figures are available in the report from U.S. Bureau of the Census (1996). *Current Projections of the Population Make-Up of the U.S.*

20.   See the research report by James Gadberry and Richard A. Dodder, "Educational Homogamy in Interracial Marriages: An Update," *Journal of Social Behavior and Personality 8* (1993): 155-163.

21.   Ibid.161.

22.   Interestingly, results of this analysis revealed the rate for African American women marrying White men was about half that figure.

23.   Importantly, it should be noted although rates of interracial marriage have increased with each decade that records have been compiled, these marriages constitute only a small percentage of the marriages that occur each year in the United States.

24.   For more about the way psychological processes have evolved to facilitate mate selection and sexual reproduction see the book by David Buss' *The Evolution of Desire: Strategies of Human Mating* (N.Y.: BasicBooks, 1994).

25.   Social psychologists have speculated about the factors contributing to the likelihood of relationship formation. For example, the Social Contextual Model suggests social norms influence not only the pool of potential eligible people with whom one interacts but also members of a person's social network.

26.   For discussion about the significance of and meaning of "race" see the article "Addressing Psychology's Problems with Race," by Yee, Fairchild, Weizman, and Wyatt (*American Psychologist 48* (1993): 1132-1140). Also see the article by Zuckerman, "Some Dubious Premises in Research and Theory on Racial Differences: Scientific, Social and Ethical Issues," *American Psychologist 45* (1990): 1297-1303.

27.   For this reason, a number of writers have advocated the use of the term "ethnicity" as it implies information about nationality, language, and cultural traditions. This is agreeable, but I think it is less well known by laypersons. Moreover, to the extent the individuals referred to in the present discussion identify themselves as "American," they share the same ethnicity. Their differences are, therefore, limited to their skin color and all of what is associated with these differences. Consequently, I use "race" and "racial differences" reluctantly throughout this discussion. The anthropologist Roger Sanjek makes a similar distinction in the chapter "Intermarriage and the Future of the Races in the United States," in *Race* by Steven Gregory and Roger Sanjek. For an informative discussion about the relative superiority of the term "ethnicity" over "race," see Itabari Njeri's chapter (1993), Sushi and Grits: Ethnic Identity and Conflict in a Newly Multicultural America, in *Lure and Loathing*, edited by Gerald Early.

28.   Scholar and author Cornel West eloquently describes the continuing significance of "race" as a social variable, as well as its interactive effects with economic class status in his book *Race Matters.*

29.   For a helpful essay about the way race is socially constructed, see Paul Spickard's "The Illogic of American Racial Categories," in *Racially Mixed People in America,* ed. M.P. Roost (Newbury Park, Calif.: Sage, 1992), 12-23.

30.   From Michael Omi and Howard Winant's *Racial Formation in the United States. From the 1960s to the 1980s* (New York: Routledge & Kegan Paul, Inc.), 3-4.

2

What's New and What's Not about Blacks and Interracial Intimacy

Not long after settling in California, I decided to carry out a study so that I could speak directly with Black men who were involved in interracial relationships about their experiences. Because of my own training, I fantasized about conducting a flawless, systematic, qualitative analysis of Black men who were involved in these types of relationships. Yet, I realized at the outset that not only was I going to have difficulty getting men to speak to me about so private an issue as their choice of a mate, but I also realized at the outset that this type of study would probably engender a number of negative reactions from a variety of audiences.

As far as Black audiences go, the popular admonition is to refrain from "airing dirty laundry in public," which has censored many well-intentioned debates about important issues affecting African Americans.[1] This is understandable when you consider that, as a group, African Americans have consistently found themselves under attack from mean-spirited and formidable adversaries. Consequently, a great deal of collective energy has focused on defending "the race."

This defensive strategizing that is apparent in the reluctance of African Americans to engage in critical self-reflection is particularly noticeable when it comes to discussions about Black men. Not surprisingly, the pressure to refrain from directing anything that resembles criticism at Black men also serves to stifle critical analysis of gender relations within the Black community. This tendency results from the current outlook for Black men that continues to be bleak and, some would argue, necessitates a degree of protective discourse where they are concerned.

Consider that, according to the U.S. Department of Justice, Black men between the ages of twenty-five and twenty-nine are almost eight times as likely as their White counterparts to be incarcerated.[2]

Furthermore, 10 percent of Black males in this age group are incarcerated compared to 1.29 percent of Whites and 2.9 percent of Hispanic males.[3] The rates of unemployment, though less disparate, still reveal an almost 5 percent difference such that although the unemployment rate for White men in 2003 was 4.5 percent, the rate for Black men was 8.8 percent. [4]

But what may be the most startling evidence of "at risk" status for Black men is provided by the U.S. National Center for Health Statistics that compiles mortality rates for specific race and gender categories. The rates of Black and White men who are victims of homicide each year are very different; Black men have a life expectancy of 68.6 years compared with 75 years for White men.[5] These conditions are especially alarming when one considers the long-term consequences of this state of affairs for the African American community and Black families. According to the former head of the U.S. Commission on Civil Rights, Dr. Mary Frances Berry, these conditions are extremely disturbing. She has noted that, "this crisis has broad implications for the future of the race."[6]

Given these alarming facts, the tendency to avoid criticism of Black men is understandable and when it is not constructive, certainly justified. But regardless whether the criticism is warranted or not, one risks being labeled a "traitor," a "sell-out," or a "man-hater," particularly when attempting a critical examination of Black men with respect to Black women.[7] Any degree of potentially critical analysis of gender relations within the African American community is generally discouraged. I realized early on that my attempt at initiating a discussion about Black men who seek, date, have sex with, love and marry women who aren't Black would not be palatable for many readers of the African American community and might, in some cases, generate a degree of enmity.

Yet the understanding of this very aspect of contemporary interpersonal and sexual relations among Blacks (i.e., why Black men are increasingly involved in interracial intimate relationships) can better our understanding of current trends within the African American community, as well as help to unravel the mystery concerning Black women's absence from many Black men's lives. To understand the factors associated with Black men's affiliation with women who are not Black is to begin to understand at least some of the problems currently facing the African American community, the development of Black female identity, and the socialization of Black youth. An understanding of these factors can also illuminate the sometimes subtle ways in which social progress and the elimination of social barriers can have unintended and unexpected consequences.

By looking at the responses of Black men who are intimately involved with women who are not Black, one can learn more about trends within the African American community as well as the larger American society. These trends can be especially revealing because of the animosity that White America has historically directed at interracial relationships involving Black men.[8] The reflections of Black men on the conditions leading up to and affecting their interracial relationships can actually serve as a barometer for the state of race relations in U.S. society. By examining these reactions of Black men to trends in interracial relationships, we can learn about the conditions leading up to these changes. An examination of the current trends in interracial relationships involving Black men suggests volumes about today's race relations in comparison to earlier eras.

What is perhaps most striking about any examination of interracial relationships over time within the United States is the extent to which public reactions to them have mirrored other types of societal trends and changes. The fact that rates of interracial relationships are related and, to some extent, influenced by large scale changes was not lost on the men that I interviewed. Each of the men I spoke to had some ideas about the way that contemporary social forces had affected their own interracial relationships. For example, J.J. specifically noted the way that these trends had not only affected the likelihood of his own involvement in an interracial relationship, but had also increased the likelihood that other Blacks would be involved in interracial relationships. J.J., who was forty-one years old when I spoke with him, explained that within the last couple of years, he had divorced his wife of seventeen years who was "a beautiful Black woman." At the time of the interview, he was living with "Lisa" who was White and who was fifty-two years old. He described how they had gotten together, and noted that he had known "Lisa" for more than eighteen years. His wife, in fact, introduced him to her. He spoke about the different reactions to his interracial relationships he remembered getting over the years.

> When I was in high school my girlfriend was White. Not that I dated only White women, but my girlfriend, that's what she was. She was kind, very consumed with my needs, very affectionate...Before it was like, if you saw a brother and a White girl together, everybody was shocked ... and now, everybody else is used to it because its been happening so long.

He went on to say:

> The reactions have changed from the seventies, to the eighties, and to the nineties. Now it's more accepted, it's more acceptable. Lisa, my girl, knows a lot of people too. And a lot of times if we go somewhere, someone either knows me, or knows her. Nowadays I don't feel that uncomfortableness, it's not like somebody staring. But then if they are [staring] I really don't give a damn. Like in a restaurant, if they're staring at us that's taking time away from their meal to worry about something that they cannot control, and I just pray for them.

I scheduled my interview with J.J. on a sunny afternoon at the football field of a local community college in Los Angeles. It was the spring of 1999. He showed up shortly thereafter in an open-air, jeep—the quintessentially rugged and stylish vehicle for Southern California. J.J. was an attractive, physically fit brown-skinned man who stood about 6'3". He had retired some years earlier from a thirteen-year successful stint in the NFL. Previously, he had played varsity football and accrued its highest rankings. He now served as a football coach for the community college where I met him. He was charming and somewhat flirtatious throughout the interview. It was clear that he enjoyed being interviewed.

At one point while talking about rates of interracial relationships involving Black men and White women compared to those with Black women and White men (a point he brought up), he said,

> It's changing to where now you can see more Black women with White men, or Black women with something even different. Ummm … and its shocking to me because I'm not used to it. Now I put the shoe on the other foot, and I can imagine what the Black women, the "sisters" were thinking about when all the "fellas" were all going to, when it seemed like all the brothers were going to a White woman, or someone other than their own race.

When I asked him to talk about his reactions to what he saw as an increase in the numbers of Black women in interracial relationships he said,

> You do look when you see it. I know I do...It's more now than in the seventies. Because it's a new generation...the nineties is just a new breed. In the nineties you find more…the nineties is just different...

To what extent were J.J.'s perceptions consistent with other Black men's perceptions? Were his observations a function of his particular age cohort? Do Black men in interracial relationships today perceive their interracial relationships to be an indication of social progress?

Blacks with Whites: Still More Rare

Although public reactions to intimate interracial relationships have generally become more positive with the passage of time, it is important to realize that interracial marriages between Blacks and Whites continue to occur less frequently than mixed marriages involving Asians, Hispanics, and others with Whites.[9] Blacks are less likely to marry outside of their racial group for a variety of reasons. Social taboos still regulate interracial marriages, and their influence is greatest in marriages involving Blacks and Whites. The reason has to do with the unique character of relations between Blacks and Whites in the United States. Contemporary relations between Blacks and Whites must be viewed in conjunction with the history of slavery, legalized segregation, and anti-miscegenation laws; all of which were powerful obstacles to marriage as well as any other form of intimacy. The legacy of each of these proscriptions is a continuing influence upon contemporary interpersonal relations between Blacks and Whites. So while it is true that more African Americans enjoy economic and political opportunity than ever before, the effects of America's earliest treatment of Blacks linger.[10]

Just how much the past can influence present relationships is especially apparent when one considers patterns of interaction among adolescents and teenagers. In their quest to define their own identities, adolescents must consider the dictates of their parents and peers and, at the same time, independently navigate themselves through an increasingly diverse society. Adolescents who date interracially often report hostile reactions from their families, friends and even strangers. In one article reporting interviews with adolescents who attended a large racially diverse high school on the West Coast, a number of students who had dated interracially reported experiencing problems with parents as well as peers.[11] The problems these students described occurred because they were involved with a person whose race was different from their own, but according to students and experts alike, they were most extreme when their partner was Black.

That reactions to interracial relationships involving African Americans are most extreme is not surprising given the unique quality of relations between Blacks and Whites in the United States, as well as the unique status Blacks have had in the United States over the years. Since this country's inception, African Americans have had the du-

bious distinction of being the most consistently negatively stereo-
typed minority group. According to San Rafael marriage counselor
Joel Crohn, "The reason that Blacks and Whites remain the most
controversial of mixed matches is that America's history of slavery,
segregation and bans on interracial marriages has made it difficult
for many to forgive and forget..."[12] This point is particularly complicated given that it would seem that because Blacks have been the
actual targets of America's racism, they would be the ones who would
have the most difficulty in forgiving and forgetting. Yet it is those
who have been the greatest perpetrators of America's racism—White
Americans—who seem to have the greatest difficulty in "getting over
it" i.e., checking their own racial prejudices.

According to one writer whose recent book addresses the different perceptions and experiences of Blacks and Whites, these differences in perceptions that are based on longstanding racial antagonism fuel contemporary miscommunications. Unlike most White
Americans "Black America generally lives with a different memory,
one that feels the reverberations of slavery, yearns for roots, searches
for pride and reaches back to grasp at ancient uncertainties."[13] Ironically, as a group, African Americans tend to express more sanguine
reactions than Whites to interracial intimate relationships.

Surveys examining people's racial attitudes provide convincing
evidence of these types of racial differences. When asked, most White
Americans publicly endorse non-prejudiced attitudes. They indicate little to no opposition with abstract issues associated with racial
equality and integration, but when asked about their own specific
behaviors and attitudes, their responses reveal somewhat less than
charitable feelings for Blacks. Several years ago, the National Opinion Research Council, located at the University of Chicago, conducted a study that included a full-scale probability sample.[14] In the
study, involving telephone interviews of more than 5000 Americans,
the researchers noted a decline in blatant expressions of racial bigotry from that of previous years. However, at the same time and in
response to different attitude questions, many White Americans still
privately expressed racial ambivalence for African Americans. Most
of the White respondents "paid lip-service" to the principles of equality in the abstract but oftentimes fell short in supporting polices that
would ensure equal opportunity for minorities.[15]

Consider the recent New York Times Poll of over 2000 adults
randomly sampled in the United States.[16] Results revealed continu-

ing differences in opinions between Blacks and Whites. In the matter of interracial relationships, these differences were especially apparent. For example, in response to the question, "Do you approve or disapprove of marriage between people of different races?" almost 30 percent of Whites stated that they were opposed to such relationships, and this was compared to 15 percent of Blacks who felt similarly. According to this survey, almost twice as many Whites than Blacks continue to oppose interracial relationships.

These differences aside, it is impossible to overlook the fact that contemporary reactions to interracial relationships are substantially more favorable today than they were in the not so distant past. Generally speaking, interracial marriages between Blacks and Whites were expressly prohibited in a majority of the states until as late as June 1967. As noted in a recent text examining the history of interracial relationships and adoption, "the race bar at the altar has a long history in America."[17]

Laws prohibiting interracial marriages were enacted in the early American colonies as early as 1661 in order to ensure legitimacy and position within the existing social order. Within this hierarchy, land-owning White men had the greatest status. The earliest laws prohibiting mixed marriages came about as a result of White opposition to marriages between White female servants and Black male slaves.[18] These laws expanded as the racial justification for slavery developed. Because a person's position within the social order was based first on race and followed by class, the children of interracial unions were a source of grave concern.[19]

The chastity of White women, women of the dominant social group, had to be guarded in order to protect their virtue from men in the lower social positions as well as to ensure clear separation between racial groups. Therefore, any form of sexual relations between White women and Black men was strictly prohibited and resulted in the severest of penalties.[20] This prohibition was not the case for relations between White men and Black women, which though covert, exceeded rates of Black male/White female liaisons and often involved either rape or other forms of coercion.[21]

Although prohibitive statutes existed and prevented the widespread occurrence of mixed marriages, these laws did not prevent "miscegenation."[22] That is, even though it was illegal for Blacks and Whites to marry, children of sexual unions between Blacks and Whites were conceived.[23] As interracial intimacy continued to transpire (however covertly), the ranks of mixed-race offspring grew.[24] Some writers have suggested that it was this particular artifact of interracial intercourse that prompted the most vociferous opposition by Whites to unions between Blacks and Whites.[25]

This latter point is particularly revealing as it "underscores the unique status of 'color' in American life."[26] According to law professor Randall Kennedy, although early Americans openly discriminated against an array of "others" (e.g., Jews and certain European ethnics like the Irish or Italians), it was fear about the color line (i.e., miscegenation) that prompted the mobilization of state authorities as well as the enactment of numerous anti-miscegenation laws.

In response to concerns about interracial relationships, all but a small minority of the states enacted anti-miscegenation laws.[27] Historians and writers have noted that opponents to interracial marriage and miscegenation often couched their opposition in rhetoric about "racial dilution" and "racial purity." Whether opposition to mixed marriages stemmed entirely from such concerns is difficult to determine conclusively. Yet, there is good reason to believe that such thoughts about "racial dilution" and "purity" weighed heavily in eighteenth- and nineteenth-century discussions about interracial intimacy.[28]

In its most lethal form, public disapproval of Black men's relationships with White women assumed the form of deadly assaults known as "lynchings." Lynchings typically involved "mutilation, castration, skinning, roasting, burning and hanging" of a Black man and were public affairs attended by large numbers of Whites who, usually in response to a public notice advertising the spectacle, came from far and wide.[29] Woe to the Black man accused of having had relations with a White woman. These attacks occurred most frequently during the latter half of the nineteenth century in the post-Reconstruction South and were prompted by accusations about a Black man's impropriety. Interestingly, lynching was relatively rare before the civil war, and it occurred most frequently in the period between 1892-1900; a time when many Whites opposed the newly freed class of African Americans.

Concerns about racial purity and the chastity of White women continued to be articulated during the more recent twentieth century as well. For example, early in the century, the noted social scientist and writer Gunnar Myrdal observed that White resistance to Black progress was linked to fears of Whites about interracial sex, specifically that which occurs between Black and White Americans.[30] According to Myrdal, "[S]ex and race fears are the main defense for segregation and, in fact, the whole caste order."[31] Having been reared outside of the United States, Myrdal was aptly poised to see the hypocrisy of America's democratic ideals given its staunch subjugation one of its oldest class of "immigrants"...African Americans.[32]

In the infamous Scottsboro case, White racism based on fears about interracial sex fueled the charges of rape that were levied against nine innocent teenage boys in an earlier period of the twentieth century. In 1931, nine African American teenage boys were accused of having raped two White women in Scottsboro, Alabama. The boys were tried, convicted, and sentenced to death. Their convictions were eventually overturned on procedural grounds. Though their lives were spared, the case highlights the threat that White accusations of Black rape posed for African American men.[33]

Almost twenty-five years after the Scottsboro case, Money, Mississippi was the setting for one of the most heinous manifestations of White fears about Black and White sex in the 20th century.[34] In 1955, at least two White men brutally beat and murdered fourteen-year-old Emmett Till, a Black teenager from Chicago who was visiting family members in Mississippi. Ostensibly, the murder occurred because the two White men believed that Emmett had whistled at the White woman manning the candy store he had just patronized. The White woman was the wife of one of Till's murderers and the sister-in-law of the other. Following perjured eyewitness identification and testimony in the case in which the murderers were tried, the two were later acquitted by an all-White and all-male jury.

Fortunately, this type of brutality in response to reports of Black men's involvement with White women declined in the twentieth century. Murder and lynching resulting from White antipathies toward Black men and White women were replaced in large part in the twentieth century with threat, harassment, and intimidation. [35] This type of response to interracial relationships permitted the post-Civil War republic to retain its ideals of democracy and liberty, while simultaneously sustaining a fear-laden atmosphere intended to maintain the racial inequalities of the previous slave-based economy. Consider, for example, the well-known case of harassment involving the heavyweight champion Jack Johnson. Johnson's longstanding affection for White women may not have been the only instigator of the Mann Act of 1910, but his openly visible interracial relationships likely accounted for some measure of enthusiasm among federal prosecutors who charged him with violation of this law.[36] The Mann Act, formerly known as the White Slave Traffic Act of 1910, was ostensibly established to regulate prostitution. The law, which made it a crime for anyone to transport a female across state lines for "immoral" purposes, was principally applied to activities associated with brothels. However, because of public opposition to Johnson's flagrant affairs with White women, this law formed the basis of the government's case against him and the subsequent prison sentence he later received.

A Pivotal Case

No historical description of interracial marriage in the United States, however brief, would be complete without mention of the case that resulted in the Supreme Court's decision to judge laws forbidding marriage between individuals from different races as unconstitutional. Ironically, this case involved what is perhaps the least common form that Black/White interracial marriages assume today: the marriage of a White man and a Black woman. The case, which was recently depicted in a television movie, involved the Lovings—Richard, a White man, and Mildred, a Black woman. The two married in 1958 in Washington, D.C., and they moved to their home state, Virginia. Upon arrival, they were promptly charged with violation of Virginia's ban on interracial marriages.

On January 6, 1959, the Lovings pleaded guilty to the charge and were sentenced to one year in prison. Their sentence was suspended for twenty-five years on the condition that they permanently leave Virginia. The Lovings moved to the District of Columbia and, in 1963, filed a motion to vacate the Virginia judgment against them. They contested the judgment on the grounds that the statutes they were convicted of violating were inconsistent with the 14th Amendment of the U.S. Constitution.[37] After a number of lower court battles, the Supreme Court eventually decided upon the Lovings' case. The Court ruled that the statutes barring the Lovings' marriage were in violation of the 14th Amendment. Furthermore, the Court determined that the freedom to marry was one of the "vital personal rights" ensured by the Amendment.

Even though historical records of the day-to-day life of interracial marriages between Blacks and Whites are scarce, some evidence does exist for a few states. Previous studies have provided data on interracial marriage occurring in Michigan, Connecticut, Rhode Island, Boston, Philadelphia, and New York. Additional evidence is also provided by several authors who have noted that the majority of documented interracial marriages in the early part of the twentieth century were between Black men and White women.[38]

From a historical perspective, what is less well known, however, is the extent to which these unions involved individuals with similar status, or whether one person had substantially greater economic status than the other.[39] Some evidence suggests that, during one period, the bulk of White women who married Black men were of a lower socioeconomic status.[40] These relationships involving Black men and White women have been labeled "hypogamous." According to this perspective, Black men have a lower social status in society relative to White women because of their race and can "trade" certain assets like money, fame, or physical attractiveness for the status they receive as a result of coupling with a White woman. Presumably, the Black man provides certain assets in exchange for the higher social status he now receives from being affiliated with a White woman. Based on this line of thinking, early social science researchers advocated a theory of hypogamy in explaining Black male/White female unions.[41] The noted anthropologist Melville Herskovits was among the first to characterize these unions in this way. Herskovits suggested that successful Black men were more likely to marry White, or lighter complexioned Black women than they were to marry Black, or dark complexioned women.[42] The theory of hypogamy suggested that these Black men offered their success in exchange for the greater social value of White, or in some cases, lighter skin.

In general, existing research on interracial marriage is scarce, and what does exist is largely focused on Black-White marriages. Not surprisingly, this is especially so for the periods preceding the twentieth century. A review of the existing studies on Black-White interracial relationships and marriages reveals that writers and researchers in this area have focused on the rates of occurrence of Black-White relationships,[43] the characteristics and personalities of those who marry outside of their racial groups,[44] the unique problems associated with mixed marriages,[45] the psychosocial development issues for children,[46] treatment by the larger community and kinship networks,[47] and, to some degree, the way that the occurrence of interracial relationships reflects societal-level changes.[48] Furthermore, it should be noted that a number of older, small-scale studies document specific aspects of interracial marriages according to state and regional trends.[49]

Notes

1.   Nathan McCall attributes this to what he calls "colored logic" in *What's Going On*. According to McCall, "The colored logic dictates that we Black people put on our best and most dignified, unified, and glorified face for White America, even if such an image misrepresents the truth. The colored logic argues that if we African Americans –er, colored people -air our dirty laundry, if we reveal the worst of what's going on among us, White folks will use that information to confirm the ugliest stereotypes they already hold…" (p. 17).
2.   United States Department of Justice. Report: Prisoners in 2001. Washington, D.C.: Bureau of Justice Statistics, 2001.
3.   See the report prepared by Paige M. Harrison and Allen J. Beck called "Prisoners in 2001" for U.S. Department of Justice, Bureau of Justice Statistics Bulletin, 2002.
4.   See data contained in the Current Population Survey provided by the U.S. Bureau of Labor in its report *Characteristics of the Unemployed*, 2004.
5.   See report prepared by Elizabeth Arias and Betty Smith of the Division of Vital Statistics *Deaths: Preliminary Data for 2001,* Hyattsville, M.D.: National Center for Health Statistics, Division of Vital Statistics.
6.   This quote attributed to Dr. Berry comes from a Washington Post article by M.A. Fletcher, on April 17, 1999 titled "Crisis of Black Males Gets High-Profile Look." Additionally, the issue is addressed extensively in Haki Madhubuti's *Black Men: Obsolete, Single, Dangerous? (*Chicago, Ill.: Third World Press, 1990). The latter discusses, among other subjects, the relative imbalance between the sexes within the African American community and the relative status of the African American male.
7.   For a discussion of the tendency to indict African American feminist writers, see the chapter by Deborah McDowell called "Reading Family Matters," in *Changing Our Own Words: Essays on Criticism, Theory and Writing by Black Women,* edited by Cheryl Ward (New Brunswick, NJ: Rutgers University Press, 1989).
8.   For a historical discussion of the evolution of White hostility to Black male/White female intimacy, see the book by Martha Hodes, *White Women, Black Men: Illicit Sex in the 19th Century South*. The author's discussion is as fascinating as it is informative. Hodes locates the origins of White hostility to Black male/White female unions in the post-bellum (i.e., post Civil War) period.
9.   This is evident in the graph included early on in the preceding chapter. Although it is limited to marriages only and does not reflect the many intimate relationships that do not involve marriage, it makes clear the fact that interracial relationships involving African Americans are more rare than the many other forms that interracial relationships can assume.
10.   See Michael E. Dyson's *Race Rules* for an extensive discussion about this point (New York: Vintage Books, 1997).
11.   The article "Interracial Dating Becoming More Common" appeared in the July 27, 1998, *San Francisco Chronicle* and was authored by Yumi Wilson.
12.   Ibid.
13.   See David Shipler's *A Country of Strangers. Blacks and Whites in America*. Shipler covers a broad spectrum of topics in trying to discuss how and what race means to African Americans and Whites today (New York, NY: Alfred A. Knopf, 1997).
14.   See the chapter "Context Effects in the General Social Survey" by Tom W. Smith based on a National Opinion Research Center survey cited in *Measurement Error in Surveys*, edited by Paul Biemer et al. (New York: John Wiley & Sons, 1991).
15.   For extensive discussion of this see the article by Joe Feagin "The Continuing Significance of Race: Anti-Black Discrimination in Public Places," *American So-*

ciological Review 56 (1991): 101-116; also the chapter by J.K. Morland, "Token Desegregation and Beyond," in *Minority Problems*, edited by Arnold M. Rose and Caroline B. Rose, 229-238 (New York: Harper & Row, 1965).

16. Results and commentary about the poll appear in *How Race Is Lived in America* by the Correspondents of the *New York Times*.

17. This quote appears in chapter 5 of the book *Interracial Intimacies* by Harvard Law Professor Randall Kennedy (New York: Pantheon Books, 2003). Among other things, the book provides an in-depth, historical view of statutes and laws enacted in response to interracial intimacy.

18. See the article by Ernest Porterfield, "Black-American Intermarriage in the United States," *Marriage and Family Review 5* (1982): 17-34.

19. See the provocative chapter titled "The Hybrid and the Problem of Miscegenation" by Louis Wirth and Herbert Goldhammer in Otto Klineberg's 1969 text *Characteristics of the American Negro* as evidence of such concerns.

20. In 1883, the Supreme Court ruled that sexual intercourse between a Black man and a White woman was illegal.

21. See Paul Spickard's *Intermarriage and Ethnic Identity in Twentieth Century America* (Madison, Wisc.: University of Wisconsin Press, 1989).

22. According to historian Martha Hodes, author of *White Women, Black Men*, the term was "coined during the presidential campaign of 1864 by the Democratic Party in order to cast aspersions on Abraham Lincoln's Republican Party" (New Haven, CT.: Yale University Press, 1997).

23. This has led historian Winthrop Jordan, author of *White Over Black,* to conclude that proportionately more interracial mating occurred in the colonial era than at any other time in American history (New York: Norton, 1968).

24. See Martha Hodes' *White Women, Black Men, Illicit Sex in the19th Century South.*

25. For examples see the following selections: Robert Merton "Intermarriage and Social Structure: Fact and Theory," *Psychiatry 4* (1941): 361-374; Roger Sanjek, "Intermarriage and the Future of the Races in the United States," in *Race*, ed. Steven Gregory and Roger Sanjek, (pp. 103-130). (New Brunswick, NJ: Rutgers University Press), 103-130; and Frances C. Welsing, *The Isis Papers* (Chicago: Third World Press, 1989).

26. See p. 219 in *Interracial Intimacies* by Randall Kennedy (New York: Pantheon Books, 2003).

27. Those states that have never had anti-miscegenation laws include Connecticut, New Hampshire, New Jersey, New York, Vermont, Kansas, Illinois, Iowa, Minnesota, Alaska, Hawaii, and Washington, and the District of Columbia.

28. Within the colonies, interracial marriages though extremely rare, did occur and more often than not assumed the form of Black men with White women. Historians note however that the most frequent form of interracial mating took place "under cover" and was between Black women and White men. Given Black women's state of bondage, these relationships often involved coercion, threat, and/or rape.

29. See Martha Hodes' book, *White Women, Black Men, Illicit Sex in the19th Century South* (New Haven, Conn.: Yale University Press, 1997).

30. Myrdal's observations were recorded in his 1944 seminal text *An American Dilemma: The Negro Problem and American Democracy* (New York: Harper & Brothers, 1944).

31. Ibid.

32. A similar observation was made earlier by the African American writer James Weldon Johnson who wrote in his autobiography, "In the core of the heart of the American race problem the sex factor is rooted, rooted so deeply that it is not always recognized when it shows on the surface." See *Along This Way: The Autobiography of James Weldon Johnson* (New York: Penguin Books, 1933).

33.   *Stories of Scottsboro* by James Goodman describes the way that beliefs about Black male and White female sexuality have affected the civil rights of young Black men in certain places and at certain times in our nation's history (New York: Vintage Books, 1995).

34.   For a complete discussion of the incident, see Stephen Whitfield's *A Death in the Delta: The Story of Emmett Till* (New York: Free Press, 1988).

35.   It is worth mentioning that as recently as 2003, an eighteen-year old African American high school student found himself on the receiving end of a rape charge following (what was later determined to be) consensual sex with a fifteen-year-old White school mate. Ostensibly, the case was about Georgia's statutory rape and child molestation statutes that require a minimum of a ten-year prison term. Supporters of the young man contend that had he not been Black, neither the charge nor the conviction of statutory rape would have occurred. This incident reminds us of a not so distant past. In this case, many of the past antipathies towards interracial sex (particularly between a Black man and a White woman) were once again made painfully salient.

36.   See the book *Jack Johnson* by Robert Jakoubek. (New York: Chelsea House Publishers, 1990).

37.   The 14th Amendment was proclaimed on July 28, 1868, and ensures equal protection and due process under the laws for all Americans. Among other things, it ostensibly provided African Americans with rights to citizenship that were previously withheld from them.

38.   See for example, Ernest Porterfield's *Black and White Mixed Marriages*. (Chicago: Nelson-Hall, 1978).

39.   Although the case can be made for some of these marriages occurring because the White woman did not know her betrothed was "Black," typically these oversights do not appear to account for the greater frequency of Black man/White woman pairings than Black woman/White man pairings.

40.   For discussion of this, see Paul Spickard's *Intermarriage and Ethnic Identity in Twentieth Century America* (Madison, Wisc.: University of Wisconsin Press, 1989).

41.   For example, see Robert Merton's early paper "Intermarriage and Social Structure: Fact and Theory," *Psychiatry 4* (1941): 361-374.

42.   See the book by Melville Herskovits, *The American Negro*. (Bloomington, IN: Indiana University Press, 1968).

43.   See the article by Peter Blau, Terry Blum, & Joseph Schwartz, "Heterogeneity and Intermarriage," *American Sociological Review 47* (1982): 45-62.

44.   See the article by James Gadberry & Richard Dodder, "Educational Homogamy in Interracial Marriages: An Update," *Journal of Social Behavior and Personality 8* (1993): 155-163; and Doris Wilkerson's *Black Male/White Female: Perspectives on Interracial Marriage and Courtship* (Cambridge, MA: Schenkman Publishing Co., 1975); as well as the article by Stanley Gaines & Diana Rios, "Romanticism and Interpersonal Resource Exchange among African American-Anglo and Other Interracial Couples," *Journal of Black Psychology 25* (1999): 461-490.

45.   See the article by Jeanette R. Davidson, "Theories about Black-White Interracial Marriage: A Clinical Perspective," *Journal of Multicultural Counseling and Development 20* (1992): 150-157.

46.   See the book by Susan Benson, *Ambiguous Ethnicity: Interracial Families in London* (London: Cambridge University Press, 1981); as well as the comprehensive treatise which argues for interracial adoption by Randall Kennedy, *Interracial Intimacies* (New York: Pantheon Books, 2003).

47.   See the article by Kris Kouri & M. Laswell, "Black-White Marriages: Social Change and Intergenerational Mobility," *Marriage and Family Review, 19* (1993): 241-255.

48. See the article by M. Belinda Tucker & Claudia Mitchell-Kernan, "New Trends in Black American Interracial Marriage: The Social Structural Context," and also the article by Robert M. Hauser & David L. Featherman, "Socioeconomic Achievements of U.S. Men, 1962-1972," *Science 185* (1974): 325-331.

49. Some examples include the article by Ray E. Baber, "A Study of 325 Mixed Marriages," *Sociological Review 2* (1937): 705-716; and the book by W.E.B. DuBois *The Philadelphia Negro: A Social Study*.

3

The Men Who Were Interviewed for This Study

Conversations about the way that race and sex affect us are not only emotionally charged but also provocative. Not surprisingly, I encountered a number of difficulties in just getting a sample of Black men involved in interracial relationships to talk with me. To begin with, I had to justify my reasons for wanting to talk with them. After I had convinced them of my intentions, I was then faced with the challenge of getting them to respond openly and honestly to my frank questions. Of course, I also knew that because I was a Black woman, some men were probably going to be uncomfortable with talking about these issues to me. It's fair to question whether they actually gave honest answers to my questions. Can I be certain of the veracity of the men's responses? No, I cannot say, unequivocally, that all of the men were always truthful. I had only their testimony to go on. On a few occasions, I was able to validate (or invalidate) their remarks with those of the person who referred me to them. I am grateful for this help, but I am also cautious in attempting to interpret any differences in the men's reports from those of the referrals.

For the most part, friends, associates, and family members put me in touch with men to speak to and interview. From the very beginning, after having heard of my interests and intentions in carrying out this project, most people that I knew were enthusiastic about providing me with referrals.[1] I asked only that they give the men to which they referred me some descriptive information about the study before I contacted them. This allowed the men gracefully to decline participation without any pressure. Occasionally, even after I had compiled the sample of men for this study, I received telephone calls and emails from people who continued to offer referrals to me.

Sometime after I had finished most of the interviewing, a friend who introduced me to two of the men I interviewed also forwarded me an email message that had apparently been circulating in a number of chat-rooms in cyberspace. The actual message contained the copy of a letter that had been sent as a "letter to the editor" of the March 2000 issue of a magazine called *Sister 2 Sister*. After reading the email, I decided to get my own copy of the magazine. In the magazine section of a supermarket, I saw the following that appeared at the top of the magazine's cover: "White Woman Says Black Women Cause Black Men to Run to Them!" Underneath in a slightly smaller text was the following: "Stella's Answer for Black Women!!" According to the inside cover's list of magazine staff, "Stella,"—Stella Foster—was one of twelve writers for the magazine. I turned to the two pages reserved for letters to the editor and read the following:

Dear Jamie,

I'm sorry but I would like to challenge some of your Black male readers. I am a White female who is engaged to a Black man –good-looking, educated and loving. I just don't understand a lot of Black females' attitudes about our relationship. My man decided he wanted me because the pickings amongst Black women were slim to none. As he said it they were either too fat, too loud, too mean, too argumentative, too needy, too materialistic and carrying too much baggage…

For the sake of brevity, I have included only the first paragraph of the letter signed "Disgusted White girl somewhere in Virginia." The rest of the letter continued in a similarly contentious tone, and at one point referred to some of today's well-known athletes, entertainers, and celebrities as evidence of Black men's preference for White women. Because the writer closed the letter by stating "If I'm wrong, Black men, let me know," one can assume that at least one of the letter writer's intentions in writing the letter was to hear from Black men. However, because of the blatant hostility and unabashed derogation she directed at Black women, it is also probably safe to assume that the writer intended to insult the magazine's Black female readership.

Sister 2 Sister is a magazine that appears to target a decidedly urban, hip hop audience, and because it features an ensemble of trivia, articles, and advertisements for and about African Americans, it clearly casts itself as a "Black" magazine; that is, a magazine purchased primarily by Black people. After reading this letter, I was anxious to read "Stella's" response. But I was quickly disappointed because there was no response to this letter contained in the issue.

However, in an entirely different section of the magazine, another piece by Stella titled "Oh Boy! Ain't she opinionated, you bet I am" appears as a response to a previous letter writer who presumably took issue with a point made by Stella in an earlier issue. This, I quickly realized, was what the subtitle appearing on the cover, "Stella's answer for Black women!!" foreshadowed.

In the earlier issue (which I did not read) Stella had apparently taken issue with Michael Jackson's choice of marrying White women on two occasions. In response, another letter writer called her a "racist" and suggested she realize "that if someone is happy, and isn't hurting anyone, then more power to them... " Stella acknowledged the writer's right to call her a racist and went on to describe the many ways that she believes that Black men's affiliation with women from other races hurts the "Black family structure." After reading her response, as well as the widely distributed initial letter (which prompted me to purchase the magazine), I understood why it had attracted so much attention in cyberspace. Stella's response mirrored the responses of any one of the Black women with whom I happened to discuss the purpose of this project.

For many heterosexual Black women who expressed these types of reactions and who were opposed to Black men being in interracial relationships, the matter was far more complex than them simply being racists. Because of the heightened visibility of Black men like James Earl Jones, Clarence Thomas, Sidney Poitier, and Scottie Pippen who have interracial marriages these women tended to assume that all successful Black men were in some way at risk of being in an interracial relationship. Even well known Black men who were married to Black women were regarded as having this "at risk" status. When one considers that these perceptions are predicated on ideas about the shortage of available Black men,[2] Black women's concerns about any one Black man's susceptibility to interracial intimacy appear reasonable. Moreover, given the disproportionate numbers of Black men who, for any number of reasons, cannot or do not reach their full potential, such reactions by Black women to highly visible successful Black men who marry non-Black women are not surprising.

In *Divided Sisters*,[3] authors Kathy Russell and Midge Wilson include a brief discussion of the way that the politics of interracial dating and marriage influence relationships between Black and White women. They describe how reactions of Black women to White women's involvement with Black men are often of anger and disdain, and they include an excerpt from a 1992 article written by the best-selling novelist Bebe Campbell-Moore appearing in the *New York Times*.[4] In that article, Campbell-Moore described an incident during which she was dining out with girlfriends at a trendy restaurant in Los Angeles. As the group of women were eating, a well-known, attractive, and successful Black actor who was accompanied by a White woman walked in to be seated. There was a collective reaction to the couple expressed by the women at the table. According to Campbell-Moore, it was a one of utter disappointment and anger. Later, she thought about why it bothered them so much to see this actor with a woman who wasn't Black. She wrote,

> For many African American women, the thought of Black men, particularly those who are successful, dating or marrying White women is like being passed over at the prom by the boy we consider our steady date, causing us pain, rage and an overwhelming sense of betrayal and personal rejection… . For sisters, the message that we don't measure up is the nightmare side of integration.

Without doubt, I was not only aware of these kinds of reactions, but I, too, had experienced them. Indeed, my reaction several years earlier to "Paul's" dismissal of the invitation to meet my friend "Carla" was evidence of this. Consequently, I knew that reactions such as these often played a role in the enthusiasm of the individual Black women who assisted me in identifying potential men to interview.[5] Were the men that I interviewed aware of any of this? In one case, in response to the question about whether and to what extent friends and family expressed unique reactions to his relationship, one of the men discussed the less than positive reactions of his friend, the Black woman, who referred me to him.

Who Were the Men Interviewed?

The men in this study hailed from a number of different regions throughout the U.S. They lived in California (14), New York (4), Pennsylvania (1), Indiana (1), Virginia (1), Illinois (3) and Missouri (1), with the greatest number coming from California. That most of them were from California was as much a result of the fact that I was able to make direct contact with potential participants as it was a result of the fact that the rates of interracial intimacy in that state surpass rates in the other states from which the men came.[6] Most of the interviews were conducted in person, but when this was not pos-

sible the interview took place over the course of at least two telephone conversations (and emails). When I met with the men face-
to-face, the taped interviews were conducted in a variety of settings
including office cafeterias, coffee shops, and restaurants.

Most of the men were happy to talk with me and took some de-
light in being interviewed. A few approached the interview skepti-
cally or defensively, and in those cases, it was necessary for me to
spend some time explaining in detail the purposes of the study. In
the end, however, all of the men who initially began the interview
with some reticence later disclosed their satisfaction with having
participated. In some cases, these men explicitly indicated their desire for anonymity. In order to satisfy them, I have used initials to
refer to them throughout the text. In the case of those men who gave
me permission to identify them in the text, I have used an altered
form of their first name.

Because some people have suggested that Black men in interracial relationships are more heavily represented in one economic class
than in another, I tried to include men from different socioeconomic
backgrounds. Consequently, I have included the responses of a professional musician, several attorneys, a gardener, a retired professional athlete, as well as someone who was currently unemployed,
and in one case, presently incarcerated. These very distinctive men
differed from one another in predictable ways, but they often described having had similar experiences in dealing with other people's
reactions to their relationship. The following table includes a description of each of the men interviewed along with relevant demographic information about each of them and their partners.

This discussion and analysis of Black men in interracial relationships is based upon the comments of a diverse (though small) group
of Black men who were currently or had been recently involved in a
long-term interracial relationship. The average length of the relationship reported by the men was six years, and the average age of
the men was thirty-eight years old with partners' average age being
thirty-four years. The men typically reported annual income levels
substantially higher than their partners. Indeed, in very few instances
(four) did any of the men indicate that their partners' incomes sur-
passed their own. More than half of the men (n = 18) noted that they
were employed in "White-collar" jobs, and this was slightly less than
the number (n = 19) reporting that their partners were also employed
in these types of jobs. Overall, the men were slightly more educated

Table 3.1

	State	R-age	R-educ.	R-occu.	R-inc.	P-age	P-educ.	P-occu.	P-inc.	P-eth.
Carlton	CA	42	JD	Attorney	20-30k	36	MBA	Asst. St. treasurer	>100k	White
David	CA	30	BA	Admin. Asst.	20-30k	21	BA	Loan processor	20-30k	White
MB	CA	31	BS	PersonalTrainer	31-35k	28	BA	Actress	10-20k	White
Chester	IN	29	BA	Financial Analyst	35k	29	HS diploma	Part-time	<10k	White
AD	CA	36	BA	Salesman	>100k	32	BA	Part-time	10-20k	White
WG	CA	37	BA	Manager	>100k	35	BA	Manager	51-60k	White
BH	NY	23	BS	Student	<10k	22	BA	Admin.Asst.	20-30k	PuertoRican
Gary	VA	40	Assoc	Manager	80-100k	42	MBA	Sales	71-80k	White
JH	NY	58	BFA	Actor	50k	46	BFA	Agent	70k	White
Barry	NY	47	HSDiploma	Musician	20-30k	33	HSDiploma	SalesClerk	10-20k	Asian
RL	NY	35	Assoc	FederalClerk	51-69k	30	BA	AdminAsst.	20-30k	Asian
Warren	CA	47	HSDiploma	Part-timeGardener	10-20k	48	HSDiploma	Telecom.Clerk	20-30k	White
DM	CA	44	Assoc	Fireman	>100k	41	HSDiploma	AirlineRep.	31-35k	White
EM	CA	25ish	BA	Ins.Sales	35k	35ish	HSDiploma	DentalTech.	35k	ElSalvad.
LG	PA	34	MA	Account.	51-60k	30	BA	n/a	n/a	Indian
Peyton	IL	34	HS	SecurityGuard	36-40k	36	HSDiploma	Military	20-30k	Mex.
CR	CA	38	HSDiploma	Comp.Program	61-70k	27	HSDiploma	SalesClerk	20-30k	White
J.J.	CA	41	BA	FootballCoach	>100	50ish	HSDiploma	Entrepeneur	>100	White
OS	CA	46	BA	Entrepeneur	80-100k	40	HS Diploma	n/a	n/a	White
Brian	CA	51	JD	Attorney	>100	30	HSDiploma	AdminAsst.	20-30k	All
Keith	IL	39	HSDiploma	Janitor	36-40k	39	HSDiploma	CityClerk	20-30k	White
Derrick	CA	23	HSDiploma	Ins. Rep.	20-30k	22	HSDiploma	Purchsg.Agent	10-20k	Mex.
Damon	MO	48	MA	Psychther.	50k	42	MA	DirectorH. Serv.	50k	White
KF	CA	37	BA	Musician	51-60k	27	n/a	LoanProcessor	46-50k	Phil.
WA	IL	47	JD	Attorney	85k	42	BA	Teacher	45k	White

than their partners. Sixteen of them had college degrees or more; whereas, only eleven of their partners did.

I began the interviews by asking them their ideas about interracial relationships in general. This was followed by a discussion describing the very first time that they were involved in this type of a relationship. I organized the interviews around several themes, which represent recurrent issues that were mentioned by at least a third of the men interviewed. For example, one theme addressed family and friends and the degree to which they had encouraged, or in some cases discouraged, the relationship. Here discussions focused on conflicts and specific challenges. This yielded a variety of responses including perceptions of Black women's hostility and in-laws' reactions. Another theme tapped ideas about beauty, and the role of the media, and another addressed their ideas about race relations in general in the United States. One other theme addressed the experiences of the partners of the men, and the way that the different racial backgrounds (e.g., whether their partner was Asian or White) were associated with the reactions of other people.

The chapter that follows provides a discussion of existing academic and popular explanations for interracial intimacy, and comments of some of the men are interspersed throughout this section. Taken together, these explanations attempt to explain the various forces of attraction, psychological and otherwise, that influence the likelihood of an interracial relationship occurring as well as the likelihood of it continuing. For example, some theories attempt to explain the formation of interracial relationships by focusing on aspects of the individual's social environment. According to this type of theory, the demise of legal prohibitions against interracial relationships is one of the main reasons for Black men's involvement in interracial relationships. Alternatively, some theories posit that individuals involved in interracial relationships actively seek out mates who have a different racial status from their own. According to these theories, Black men in interracial relationships are motivated in large part by their own preferences or insecurities.[7] Each of the different types of theories is discussed and a model that includes relevant variables is outlined at the end of this section.

Chapter 5 examines the impact of the media and its effects on the men's beliefs about beauty and ideas about physical attractiveness and interracial relationships. The media represents a powerful socializing agent with an almost omnipotent ability to influence.

Whether we are aware of its effects and correspondingly believe ourselves to be immune from its allure, or even if we have never even thought about it, the media affects our ideas and beliefs about what is attractive, what is right, and what is good. It influences us in many different ways, including the movies we pay money to view and the music videos whose adolescent pop stars earn millions. No less influential are the supermodels and pop-culture trivia appearing in magazines, the protagonists and plots in books we read, and the daytime and evening television shows to which we regularly tune in.

Almost all of the men interviewed provided their thoughts about the influence of the media on the development of their perceptions of beauty as well as their beliefs about its current effects upon them. This elicited discussion about the stereotypic portrayals of Black men and women. Stereotypes about Black men and women differ and reflect their different positions and power in American society.[8] Consequently, examination of the way that Black men and women are represented in the media can be instructive. Some of the men also discussed media stereotypes about interracial relationships and the way that these types of relationships have typically been portrayed when one partner is an African American man.

Writers and social commentators have rarely addressed this latter point, but it is particularly important to consider within the context of the present discussion. To the extent that images of Black male masculinity and sexuality have been widely distributed to mainstream American consumers in recent years, Black men have now been deemed desirable and attractive, potential mates for heterosexual females. Consequently, Black male sexuality is sought after by females of all races and copied by other males in a way unlike ever before. This has not been the case for Black females who continue to occupy the lowest rung on mainstream America's hierarchical ladder of attractiveness and desirability. In short, because of the successful marketing of well-known Black male athletes and entertainers to mainstream American audiences, there now exists a collective fascination and appreciation with that which reflects the images of these Black men. Whereas images of Black male sexuality now enjoy iconic status, images of Black female sexuality continue to either be absent or denigrated.[9]

I was interested in the extent to which Black men in interracial relationships were aware of this state of affairs or had thought about images of Black male sexuality vis-à-vis Black female sexuality. I asked the men to explain what makes a woman beautiful to them, that is, what physical attributes most attract them to a woman and what characteristics most attracted them to their partner. Not surprisingly, the men differed substantially in their descriptions. Whereas some men opted to provide me with graphic descriptions of the physical qualities they were most attracted to in women, others completely downplayed the significance of physical characteristics in their selection of a mate.

In the next chapter, chapter 6, a typology of the different characterizations of interracial relationships with Black men is presented. This typology came about only after all of the interviews for the text had been conducted. Subsuming the relationships into a typology provides one way of simplifying the process of identifying similarities and differences across the relationships described by the men who were interviewed. Admittedly, however, this involves a trade-off. While it is true that this approach permits a certain ease in categorizing the men because it allows one to gloss over the minor ways in which the men differed, it is also true that because of the unique distinguishing characteristics of each of the relationships, and because of the individuality of the men interviewed, many of the nuances are lost as a result of this very process of categorization. Consequently, a typology is useful only up to a point. That said, the typology presented in chapter 6 provides the reader with one way of thinking about Black men in interracial relationships. But it does so cautiously by reminding the reader of the extent to which a few details, some more important than others, are potentially lost. Moreover, although the present typology consisting of five types captures well the responses of the twenty-five men interviewed in the present study, the possibility that additional typologies might be delineated should not be overlooked.

The names I used to refer to the different relationship types were consistent with the most distinguishing feature of each relationship described by the men introduced at that point. For example, in the case of one man who suggested that there was only one race (the human race) and that "love knows no colors," the label "color blind" seemed appropriate. The resulting typology included the "rebellious relationship," "the obsessive relationship," "the color blind relationship," "the retreatist's relationship," and the "lonely hearts relationship."

Deriving a typology required close attention to each of the men's remarks and explanations as well as their interpretations of specific events. For example, one such question, "what were the circumstances surrounding the initiation of your relationship?" Or, stated another way, "how did you and your partner "hook up?" elicited particularly illuminating responses. I reasoned that a relationship in which a man reported becoming involved with his partner because "love is blind" was qualitatively different from one in which the man reported that he became involved with his partner because he did not have anything in common with Black women. Similarly, I expected that a relationship in which a man reported <u>never</u> having had a relationship with a Black woman would, in fact, be different from one in which a man, who though currently in an interracial relationship or marriage, had had on at least one occasion been intimately involved with a Black woman. Frank and sometimes surprising remarks of the men are presented throughout this section.

In chapter 7, I have presented the responses of some of the men who spoke at length about the reactions of other people. Here the men described the unique ways that members of their own families and kinship networks have reacted to their interracial relationships. Not surprisingly, for those men who were not married, there were fewer reports of family reactions. As for their friends, several of the men noted specific problems with their friendships with Black women, which they attributed to their intimate interracial relationship. In this part of the interviews it becomes especially clear that Black men in these types of relationships may choose to or be forced to change their friendships or acquaintanceships with others.

Most of the married men in the sample revealed that although some of the interactions with their own families were tumultuous at times, they generally found acceptance and support from them. In one particular case, DAMON, who was living in St. Louis, Missouri, spoke at length about the effect that his decision to marry a White woman had had on his mother. At that time, Damon's mother was not only unhappy about her son's impending interracial marriage but also unwilling to accept it. Although Damon was sympathetic to his mother's concerns, he was also in love with his fiancée. The two married in the absence of his mother and for some time he neither heard from nor spoke to his mother. Later, after about a year, she came around. Damon and his wife have been married for sixteen years, and with the exception of the one-year absence instigated by his mother's reaction, he has enjoyed a close relationship with both his mother and his wife.

In contrast, several of the men chose to focus on the reactions of their mate's family. More often than not they spoke of nonacceptance and sometimes even downright hostility from their mates' families. GARY, a manager who was recently divorced from his ex-wife who was White, described the way that her mother reacted to him and to their union. According to Gary, his wife had had several siblings, and each of their wedding pictures were prominently displayed throughout his mother-in-law's house. But his mother–in-law chose not to display a single one of his wedding pictures. At the time that I met with Gary, he had been divorced for a little over a year and was preparing to marry another woman whose parents were also in a mixed marriage. But even at the time of the interview nearly a year after his divorce, Gary continued to express anger at his former mother-in-law.

After reading this particular section (with the exception of DAMON), it becomes clear that the men generally received the greatest support from their own families. This support was substantially greater than what their partners received from their own families, or that which the men could recall having received from their partners' families. Here the reader is encouraged to consider why the men tended to find relatively more acceptance from their families than their partners'. A discussion about the reactions of strangers is also included at this point.

In chapter 8, a discussion of the men's ideas about race relations in the United States is presented. This includes a consideration of their thoughts about the existence of racism and its effects, if any, upon them. At this point in the interviews, the men described some of their most poignant experiences. When these experiences are viewed collectively, they paint a rather somber picture about the nature of contemporary race relations. According to even the most optimistic of the men interviewed, racism and its effects continue to operate. Where the men differed was in their beliefs about whether and to what extent it had personally affected them or their families. The men also differed in the extent to which they chose to identify racism as the primary culprit or merely one of any number of injustices they perceived themselves to have experienced.

This chapter also details the specific challenges associated with interracial relationships that Black men and their mates must face.

Although each of the men had a unique story to tell, it was possible to identify similarities in their stories. What is perhaps most interesting about the comments presented in this section is the extent to which the men were able to recall the actual difficulties they faced that they attributed to their interracial relationship, and, at the same time, still remain committed to that very relationship, their partner, and in some cases, their offspring. Indeed, in some of the cases, the men seemed to find this type of adversity to be empowering and motivating.

But for every man who was empowered by these challenges, there was another who clearly expressed an air of resignation in dealing with these problems. The problems ranged from the mundane —as when they suspected a waiter's delay in service was more a matter of his disapproval over the interracial nature of their relationship than it was a matter of staffing inadequacies, to the extreme—as when a man reported having been verbally harassed and threatened by strangers on the street. Yet, not one of the men suggested the dissolution of their relationship as a possible remedy to the problems they encountered. This was the case even for the two men who though now divorced from their White wives spoke retrospectively about the challenges they had encountered because theirs was an interracial marriage.

In the next section of the text, chapter 9, I have suggested a number of ways that the experience of being in an interracial relationship differs as a result of the racial status of the men's mates. That is, after talking with each of the men at length, I could identify differences that were associated with the race and cultural background of their partners. For example, DERRICK, who married a Mexican American woman, described having had the obvious difficulties in communicating with some of his in-laws because of the language barrier. At the same time, he described other types of problems that had to do with the relationship between his mother and his wife. His mother, a devout Baptist, could not understand his Catholic wife's laissez-faire approach to matters of the church. His wife, who showed up for religious services in tattered jeans and halter-tops, did not practice her brand of Christianity with the same fervor that his mother practiced hers. The two could not see eye-to-eye.

In contrast, A.D., a man who married a foreign born White woman, said that he believed his parents approved of her *because* she was foreign-born. He believed that had she been an American White woman, they would have vehemently contested his decision to wed. When I asked him about how his parents, who had emigrated from Haiti in their youth, would have reacted to him having married an African American woman, he said that they would have reacted similarly. That is, they would have been as displeased with an African American as they would have been with a White American daughter-in-law. This point underscores the differences in experiences and problems faced by Black men in intimate interracial relationships. Not surprisingly, whether their partner was foreign born or was born in the U.S., and whether she was White or a member of a minority group in the United States clearly influenced the experiences the men reported having, as well as the reactions of others to them.

In the final chapter of the text, chapter 10, I have presented a discussion about the future of race relations within the United States. This is a discussion that necessarily involves the men's perceptions about what the future holds as well as their ideas about their own children and the offspring of other interracial couples. Also in this section I refer briefly to an informative text recently published that extols the potential virtues and decries the likely perils of interracial adoption and parenting.[10]

In this project, twenty-five Black men voluntarily agreed to talk at length about their experiences and involvement in intimate interracial relationships. The reasons for their participation varied, and while some explicitly offered reasons for why they had agreed to participate, others did not. When they did not, I gathered that their participation resulted from either their own curiosity with the study or a sense of obligation they felt to the contact person who arranged our introduction. In this regard, at least two of the men participated at their mothers' requests. I was aware of this and remain indebted to their mothers for introducing me to their sons, and of course, to the men for participating. They agreed to speak with me about their intimate interracial relationships "sight unseen." Before the interview, they knew very little about the scope of the project or my intentions. In contrast, when I was able to interview men with whom I was personally acquainted, I was able to tell them upfront about what the interview would entail and what kinds of questions I would ask them.

Overall, a number of different reasons propelled the twenty-five men presented here to disclose details of their intimate social lives to me. GARY, who came to me by way of a mutual friend who was a

Black woman, spoke at length at the end of the interview about the reasons for his participation. He said that some time ago he had been talking with one of his buddies, and they both "kicked around the idea" of writing a book on interracial relationships. When he heard of my interests he couldn't help but participate. He hoped to be able to help me, and at the same time gain some valuable direction for his own project.

The interview responses have only been altered so that they appear within a reasonably coherent format. This required me to select certain passages, delete others, and put the remaining ones together in ways that illustrated best the themes that I identified. At the outset, I considered paraphrasing the responses but subsequently realized that this would result in a disservice to the reader as well as to the men interviewed. Consequently, I elected to include verbatim accounts. It is useful to keep this in mind while reading the responses. Excerpts from the actual interviews are included. In some cases, when I was unable to remember a potentially important detail, I had to contact the men well after the interview had been conducted. I did so by telephone and by email.

As anyone who has ever relied upon self-report and interview data knows, this kind of material is notoriously susceptible to errors in recollection, as well as deliberate misrepresentation.[11] Only the person being interviewed can distinguish between these two potential liabilities in their responses, and in some cases the actual truth may even prove elusive for the men. They may be unable to recall events as they actually occurred, and even when they are able to remember particular events, their recollections may be tinged by their own biases, preconceptions and stereotypes. That said, it is instructive to note that to the extent that the men to whom I spoke saw their stories as real and representative of reality, then it was—at least for them. Sociologist W.I. Thomas wrote almost a century ago, "if men define situations as real, they are real in their consequences... ."[12] This view is especially appropriate in considering the veracity of the men's comments. The point here is that no one knows better the reality of a situation than the individual who is interacting in that situation. Although social scientists and authors may speculate about the forces, psychological and structural, influencing Black men's involvement in intimate interracial intimate relationships, only Black men in these relationships can provide firsthand accounts of those experiences.

Notes

1. Black women of all ages referred me to a large portion of the men. However, in at least a few cases, either a Black man or a White woman referred me to someone.

2. See *The Decline in Marriage Among African-Americans* by M. Belinda Tucker & Claudia Mitchell-Kernan (Eds.) which discusses, among other things, the lower rates of marriage and higher rates of divorce for Black women (New York: Russell Sage Foundation, 1995).

3. For an interesting discussion about how friendships between Black and White women are influenced by race, see Kathy Russell and Midge Wilson's, *Divided Sisters. Bridging the Gap Between Black Women and White Women.* (New York: Anchor Books, 1996).

4. See the article appearing in the *New York Times* by Bebe Campbell Moore. *"Hers: Brothers and Sisters."*

5. See note 1. above.

6. The U.S. Bureau of the Census shows rates of interracial marriage as greatest in the Western region of the U.S. Additional research reveals that these trends are explained by a complex interaction of factors such as region of birth, the nature of race relationships in that region, and knowledge about race relations. Although forecasting changes to occur within the past decade, the article "New trends in Black American marriage: The social structural context," by M. Belinda Tucker and Claudia Mitchell-Kernan effectively describes these trends (*Journal of Marriage and the Family 52* (1990): 209-218).

7. Admittedly, theories such as these often pathologize Black men in interracial relationships. This type of an approach is premature in the absence of empirical data and represents only one way of viewing Black men in interracial relationships. For extensive discussion about the tendencies to pathologize interracial relationships in general see the article "Theories about Black-White Interracial Marriages: A Clinical Perspective," by Jeanette R. Davidson in the *Journal of Multicultural Counseling and Development 20* (1992): 150-157.

8. For reference to the distinctive way that gender and racial stereotypes influence perceptions of Black males and Black females see the following three materials: Patricia Bell Scott's chapter, "Debunking Sapphire: Toward a Non-Racist and Non-Sexist Social Science" In the early feminist text *All the Women Are White, All the Blacks Are Men, But Some of Us are Brave* edited by Gloria T. Hull, Patricia Bell Scott, & Barbara Smith (Old Westbury, NY: Feminist Press, 1982); the article by Althea Smith and Abigail Stewart, "Approaches to Studying Racism and Sexism in Black Women's Lives," *Journal of Social Issues 39* (1991): 1-15; and the article by Sandra I. Ross and Jeffrey Jackson, "Teachers' Expectations for Black Males' and Black Females' Academic Achievement," *Personality and Social Psychology Bulletin 17* (1991): 78-82.

9. To be sure, the image of the Black female as loose and Sapphiric has always existed within American Society. This hypersexualized image, however, tends to be inconsistent with the more frequently sought virtues of femininity or beauty. I am grateful to the scholar Cornel West who addresses this point in detail in his text *Race Matters* (Boston, M.A.: Beacon, 1993).

10. See *Interracial Intimacies. Sex, Marriage, Identity and Adoption* by Randall Kennedy (New York: Pantheon Books, 2003).

11. John and Lyn Lofland's *Analyzing Social Settings: A Guide to Qualitative Observation and Analysis* , now in its third edition, provides useful information about how to conduct qualitative research involving interviews (Belmont, CA: Wadsworth, 1996).

12. This quote appears in William Isaac Thomas and Dorothy Swain Thomas', *The Child in America: Behavior Problems and Programs*, 571-572 (New York: Alfred A. Knopf, 1928).

4

Theories of Interracial Intimate Relationships

Perhaps the best way of thinking about theories explaining interracial relationships is to think of a continuum. At one end are the kinds of explanations that focus on the internal attributes of a person.[1] This would involve a focus on such things as motives, preferences, and beliefs. At the other end of the continuum are explanations focusing on external factors such as desegregation and legislation. When the interracial relationship is believed to result primarily from large-scale changes in patterns of interaction between people from different racial groups, external factors are said to have played a role. When barriers to integration are eliminated, and policies ensuring interracial interaction and assimilation of minorities are implemented, relationships that were previously prohibited or circumscribed now become possible.[2] Because this type of explanation focuses on the changes that have occurred in institutional accessibility, public policy and legislation, it is referred to here as a "structural" explanation.

There are a number of versions of the structural explanation for interracial relationships.[3] For example, in some cases, researchers and theorists have focused on the absolute size of the minority group in a given location. These experts believe that the smaller the size of a minority group, the more likely intermarriage is to occur between members of the minority group and the majority group. Another variation of this explanation involves consideration of the sex ratio of minority group members and suggests that unbalanced sex ratios lead to greater rates of "outmarriage" for minority members who cannot find mates among members of their own group. When a minority group has a relatively greater number of members of one sex, then, according to this perspective, those minority group members are most likely to venture out and establish interracial relationships. Yet, this particular version of the structural explanation would seem

to be least appropriate as an explanation for Black men's involvement in interracial relationships. Why? Because although there is
clearly an unbalanced sex ratio among African Americans, it is a
ratio that is generally in favor of African American men. That is,
more Black women are available as potential mates for Black men
than Black men who are available as mates for Black women.

Indeed, this very point seems to instigate and account for many
Black women's reactions to Black men in interracial relationships.
All too often, Black women are inundated with statistics reporting
the extent to which their representation far outweighs that of Black
men. Having to experience the reality of these numbers can be unsettling enough, but when the popular press and other media outlets
weigh in on the subject, the likelihood of finding a potential mate
seems to be next to impossible. This is the case for Back women at
every age, from the very young to the postmenopausal. In recent
years, my experience in teaching at a historically Black university
where young Black women are present in significantly greater numbers than their male counterparts reveals that the very issues my
thirty-something and forty-something year-old single Black women
friends are confronting are all too familiar to these eighteen and nine-
teen year old college students.

A structural explanation suggests that as Black men (and other
previously disenfranchised members of racial minority groups)
achieve parity with Whites on important social indicators of progress,
intimate interracial relationships with women from other races should
become increasingly likely. In this context, interracial intimacy is
regarded as the "last frontier" towards the complete assimilation and
acceptance of minorities in a multiracial and multicultural society.[4]
Presumably, according to this perspective, when African Americans
as a group have achieved sufficient parity with Whites in society,
interracial relationships between African Americans and others will
occur with as much frequency as interracial relationships now occur
between members of other races, and as frequently as same-race
relationships occur within groups. Furthermore, with a sufficient
passage of time, we would expect that Black men and women would
be involved in interracial relationships at comparable rates.

Clearly, it is reasonable to question whether any form of the structural explanation for interracial relationships can be useful as the
sole explanation for understanding Black men's experiences. What,
if anything, can this perspective contribute to understanding Black

men's involvement in interracial relationships? Can it explain at least some aspect of the experiences of Black men in interracial relationships?

In its extreme form, this explanation for interracial relationships has typically been viewed as a "solution" to the inherent problems associated with a racially and ethnically diverse society. It forebodes what its proponents desire: a "melting pot" in which African Americans as a visually distinctive racial minority group would eventually disappear. The noted anthropologist Franz Boas articulated this point and went so far as to employ complex mathematical computations in an effort to predict (based on population figures) the precise number of years necessary to "pale out" African Americans. According to Boas and others who held this view, this would be in the best interest of the greater society. Boas wrote in 1921,

> The greatest hope for the immediate future lies in a lessening of the contrast between Negroes and Whites.... . Intermixture will decrease the contrast between extreme racial forms.... . In a race of octoroons, living among Whites, the color question would probably disappear.... . It would seem, therefore, to be in the interest of society to permit rather than to restrain marriages between White men and Negro women. It would be futile to expect that our people would tolerate intermarriages in the opposite direction. [5]

One of the men with whom I spoke was explicit in his beliefs about the way that a decline in segregationist policies had contributed to an increase in the numbers of Black men in interracial relationships. At the time of the interview, CARLTON was a forty-two-year-old, independently employed attorney working out of a small office in Southern California. He was involved in a long-term relationship with a thirty-six-year old White woman who, according to him, was "on the fast track to success." Carlton talked at length about the consequences of the civil rights movement. As he saw it, foremost among those accomplishments was an increased acceptance in interracial relationships.

> Interracial relationships can be cool, and sometimes they're not. I mean take the 1960s for example. That was the period that most effectively brought young Blacks and Whites together. They were together in so many ways and that included interracial relationships. This was clearly different from the past, like in my parents' generation when they just didn't occur like that.

I spoke with Carlton on several different occasions on the phone as well as face to face. He was always engaging and happy to talk with me. I had met him previously through a family member in Chicago. Carlton grew up in and around the relatively diverse Hyde

Park section of Chicago. That area, which surrounds the University of Chicago, occupies a unique position in history as it was among one of the first residential areas in the city to witness the changes (and strife) brought about by desegregation.

More than once during our conversations, Carlton attributed his experiences and ideas about interracial relationships to the fact that his mother was, as he called her, "a dysfunctional Jewish woman," and his father, about whom he said little, was Black. Carlton's complexion was dark brown and most resembled my idea of a dark-skinned East Indian. When asked about the way he most often identified himself, he said "Black...and sometimes, though rarely, Jewish." At various points during our conversation, he spoke enthusiastically about what he thought of as some of the most interesting changes that had occurred during and after the Civil Rights movement. At one point he said,

> Well, looking at the last 40 years there have been some real changes in the way that people interact with each other and get together ....and, I have no doubt that many of these changes are a direct result of legislative changes and changes in policies that occurred in the post-Civil rights era. Am I willing to say that the interracial relationships out there today, including my own, wouldn't have occurred without those legislative changes? No...I couldn't say that because it's impossible to answer that question, but I have to say that they are certainly more likely because of these changes.

At a later point in the conversation, Carlton discussed the difficulties he had as a teenager when he first dated a girl who was White. He characterized his girlfriend's parents' reactions as "stereotypical." He said it was what he would have expected from them, given that particular time period and generation. He spent some time discussing her parents' reactions and went on to recount an exchange he recalled having had with a coworker back in 1975. According to Carlton, that conversation also reflected the time period —a time period when Black men just did not date White women openly.

> Back then during the movement, I'm talking about the mid-1970s, there were different reactions to interracial relationships across the board. What I found to be most striking in people's reactions, and here I'm referring to Black folks I knew, what was most striking was not their opposition, but their curiosity. I remember there was this one Black guy I worked with for a while in San Francisco in 1975, and he was originally from somewhere in Florida. He was about nineteen, and this guy marveled at how I interacted with White women. I mean one time he said to me, "you act like they are anybody else." He thought it was amazing that I had relationships with White women and that I thought of them and treated them like they were "normal." But you have to remember that at that point we hadn't made many of the gains that have since been made....

Times have clearly changed for Carlton and many others, and he remains aware of this incident even now, more than twenty years later.

Sometime after I interviewed Carlton, I learned that he had moved with his girlfriend to Sacramento. The move was prompted by her acceptance of an appointed position in California's state government. For her, the move was accompanied by a substantial increase in income and influence. According to Carlton, she had given him an ultimatum—either he came with her or they would permanently separate. The two have since married and started a family. Although I have not spoken with him in quite a bit of time, I learned that Carlton no longer works outside of the home and is enjoying being a "stay-at-home" father.

If progress towards social equality influences actual patterns of interracial intimacy, and if there are more interracial relationships now than ever before, then relevant social indices should reveal equality between racial groups and the absence of widespread anti-Black prejudice. Many theorists see the increased educational and occupational opportunity that became available to African Americans within the latter part of the twentieth century as having caused the increased availability of potential White mates.[6] These theorists also suggest that decreasing residential and occupational segregation has created increased interracial social contact such as the kind that occurs in dating.[7] Proponents of this type of perspective tend to suggest that in addition to large-scale structural changes, there are related demographic factors like residential location and increases in socioeconomic status which are also responsible for the increase in the numbers of interracial relationships. They also note that these types of changes are initially more evident in the behavior of males because parents traditionally keep a tighter rein on female children than they do on male children. Consequently, boys and young males are permitted to venture out into a wider geographical area, which provides them with a greater likelihood of experiences with people from other racial and ethnic backgrounds.

Another Type of Explanation for Interracial Intimacy

The other type of explanation for interracial relationships that focuses on the internal characteristics of the individual sees individual motives and personal preferences as most influential in precipitating these relationships. As was the case with the structural explanation for interracial intimacy, there are several variations to this type of an explanation. When viewed collectively, they suggest that a person's preferences for a particular phenotype,[8] or their specific attitudes about a racial group are likely to cause that person to establish (or at least pursue) an interracial relationship. That is, a person's belief about the merits of one race relative to another is considered to be the driving force behind their decision to seek out individuals of one race rather than another. Taken together, theories like these emphasize characteristics that are internal to the individual (e.g., their preferences and beliefs) and are, therefore, considered to be more "psychological."

In comparison to a structural explanation for interracial relationships, a psychologically based theory about these types of relationships focuses on an individual's conscious consideration of racial differences. One of the underlying assumptions of this type of theory is that people in interracial relationships have different motives than do those who are in relationships with people of the same race.[9] To the degree that this explanation accounts for Black men's involvement in intimate interracial relationships, the responses of men in these relationships to questions about the circumstances leading up to their involvement should reflect this.

In all but one case, the men that I spoke with denied having had any preferences for a particular look or appearance. In the case of the one exception, BRIAN was quite explicit about his preference for women who appeared to be of one racial status rather than another. He said,

> Well, I don't quite know why it is, but to be honest with you I have to admit that I have a real preference for aquiline features. You do know what aquiline means, right? What I mean is that I just don't like women who have Negroid features...

In Brian's case, a variation of the psychological reasoning for interracial relationships that explains that Black men's involvement in these relationships is the result of a preference for women who do not look Black would seem to be accurate.[10] Explanations like this vary in terms of whether they regard this preference as stemming from a person's disavowal or denigration of that which is associated with "Blackness" or as being a result of their concerns about affiliating with women who are most consistent with societal images of womanhood.

One longstanding theory in social psychology, the Resource Exchange theory, can shed light on the way that a person's decision to affiliate with someone who is not Black can be taken as evidence of their endorsement of mainstream norms that generally dictate White superiority. The Resource Exchange theory (which sometimes appears as the Social Exchange theory) contends that people in intimate relationships behave in ways that are similar to the forces at work within the economic marketplace.[11] This theory assumes that people are motivated by the rewards they receive from their partners. These rewards can be tangible, as when one person in the relationship receives jewelry or money from their mate; or intangible, as when one partner gets a boost in self-esteem because they believe their mate to be very attractive. In the United States standards of physical attractiveness and beauty are derived from European ideals. Beliefs about superior physical attractiveness continue to be more frequently associated with White people in such a way that lighter skin color accrues a greater racial (i.e., social) status.[12]

Although he did not say anything about skin complexion, Brian's expressed preference for a woman with non-Negroid features illustrates well the way that a preference for certain racially linked traits (e.g., aquiline facial features) influences the decisions to become involved with someone from one rather than another racial group. Some have gone so far as to suggest that for Black men, like Brian, who prefer mates who do not resemble a majority of Black women, an even deeper desire, conscious or not, is to be White.

Do Black Men in Interracial Relationships Want to Be White or Is It More a Matter of Wanting to Be with Women Who Look White?

As a group many African Americans, men and women alike, continue to be plagued by an obsession with artifacts of "Whiteness." Most African Americans recognize that the desire for light skin color, although rarely voiced, remains prevalent within the Black community.[13] This desire is apparent in the tendency to equate what is good and desirable with what is White. Some of the African American community's most insightful writers have addressed this point, and it is raised periodically in a number of popular Black magazines and movies.[14] As evidence, recall popular filmmaker Spike Lee's movie *School Daze* that showed the nearly pathological obsession of African Americans with skin color. This fascination with what is White has even garnered a few minutes of attention on the often tawdry talk show circuit.

Because racism works in conjunction with sexism in American society, the effects of racism and sexism have necessarily impacted Black men and women quite differently. For some Black women, an obsession with Whiteness is most apparent in the quest for light eye color, long straight hair, and skin bleaching efforts.[15] But for some Black men, regardless of their own physical appearance, this obsession is apparent in their almost exclusive pursuit of women who (when judged according to mainstream America's racial categories) most resemble White women.

Interestingly, Martinique-born psychiatrist and activist Frantz Fanon effectively linked a desire to be White and to be partnered with a White person to the pernicious effects of European colonialization in his book *Black Skins, White Masks*.[16] Fanon wrote extensively about the negative effects of European colonialization on his countrymen in Martinique as well as its effects on the people of Algeria, another colony of France. Drawing from his own experiences as well as from his extensive mental health training, he believed that Black men had an obsessive desire for and pursuit of White women. The following provocative excerpt from a section in the book reflects a degree of self-criticism, given that he saw himself as a culprit of this type of an obsession:

> Out of the Blackest part of my soul, across the zebra striping of my
> mind, surges this desire to be suddenly White.
> I wish to be acknowledged not as *Black* but as *White*.
> Now (and this is a form of recognition that Hegel had not envisaged)
> who but a White woman can do this for me? By loving me she proves
> that I am worthy of White love.
> I am loved like a White man.
> Her love takes me onto the noble road that leads to total realization...
> I marry White culture, White beauty, White Whiteness...

Fanon explicitly links colonial domination and imitation. For him, France's domination over Martinique (as well as Algeria where he later wrote) created a pathological obsession within their inhabitants to emulate their oppressors. What better way to do this, he reasoned, than to have relations with a White woman?

As for the men I interviewed, only two expressed motives of the kind described by Fanon. In one unusual case, the young man DER-

RICK acknowledged that his notion of female beauty was most consistent with the image of the comic book character Wonder Woman. For him, she most effectively epitomized womanhood and, consequently, guided his quest for the perfect mate. In the second case, KEITH, who at the time of the interview was employed as a janitor but who was later to become incarcerated, was explicit about his desire to have a relationship with a White woman because she was White. He said,

> In the beginning for me it was all about sex. I wasn't interested in White people at all. Being with a White woman was something you couldn't do, or you weren't supposed to have. So, of course, that's what I went for. Shoot, those were the days.....I even had two White wives.

I spoke with Keith over the course of two telephone conversations. A friend of mine, who also lives in Chicago, introduced him to me. In contrast to his previous relationships, the thirty-nine-year-old was married to a Black woman at the time of the interview. He summed up his experiences with his interracial marriages as being "all about sex."

Importantly, most of the men I spoke with expressed views that were at odds with the idea that Black men in interracial relationships want to "be White" by being with someone who was not Black. Although this explanation may help in understanding the motives of a small number of the men, it was inconsistent with what most of the men with whom I spoke described. Indeed, some of the men were quite emphatic in pointing to and claiming their "Blackness."

These men, as well as many well-known public figures, had an explicit and conscious appreciation for "Blackness." Events such as the Million-Man march that took place in Washington, D.C. in 1995 and the widespread adoption of items marketed because of their links to Africa provide examples of the current popularity of certain aspects of "Blackness." Today, many different forces influence what it means to be Black, as well as American. In this context, being Black is truly a state of mind that is apparent in the people, events, places, and things with which one affiliates. It is not any one thing, and it eludes attempts at classification. In this post-1990s era of ethnic appeal, sexual permissiveness and imagery, one can "be Black" and "sleep White" without compunction.

Ironically, at least three of the men I spoke with explicitly stated that they were "not trying to be White." In each of these cases, these men specifically asked that they not be identified by name in the text. These men seemed to be especially concerned with what others who were close to them would think of them if they learned of their interracial relationship. Although they spoke of a preternatural love for their "Nubian sisters," they acknowledged "chasing White girls" for a variety of reasons. These reasons ranged from rebellion, to rage, to lust, and love.

O.S., who seemed to be driven by at least three of these reasons, spoke to me from the offices of his California-based company. He was quite clear about the reasons why he was with his current girl-friend of two years who was White. He generally referred to White women as "Europeans."

> It's not that complicated…there are less headaches with a European woman. I mean it…European women give me less headaches than African American women…No kid-ding, after a 30 minute conversation with a "sister," I know her financial situation inside and out. Black women have this attitude that's like "if you can't help me, then don't fuck with me."

I spoke with the forty-six-year-old entrepreneur over the course of several telephone conversations. I had met him previously through a mutual acquaintance in Los Angeles. He agreed to the interview, but because we were repeatedly interrupted (he was at work at the time), it was necessary to talk with him on several different occa-sions. O.S. was divorced from his wife of seventeen years who was Black.

But Unlike O.S., who explained his interracial relationship as re-sulting from his quest for peace and fewer headaches, GARY was quite clear about having married his wife because he loved her and not because she was White. Gary, who was forty-years old, had re-cently divorced from his wife. The two had been married for eleven years.

> I married her because she was the person I loved, I was not trying to make some kind of political statement…it was not because of some outsider's perceptions. I mean if you really want to put it in those terms, you could say that I married her in spite of the fact that she was White.

Gary had recently decided to remarry shortly before the interview. He described the woman who was to become his second wife as "not looking Black." She was Mulatto, the product of a relationship between a foreign born Black man and an American White woman. He said,

> "People don't really know what she is…a lot of times I think they think she's Hispanic."

As I suggested earlier in this chapter, a number of writers across a variety of disciplines have suggested that when a substantial number of people from one racial group begin to have intimate relationships with people from another racial group, it signals a shift in the larger society's treatment of that racial group.[17] Indeed, according to some of the theorists in this area, when racial minorities begin to marry and interact with members of the majority group, assimilation of the minority group has occurred. Presumably, restrictions on interracial unions no longer exist and are no longer enforced. These writers believe that someone from a minority group, in this case an African American, could become a part of the dominant group by way of association with a mate from that group, and that this association has been a primary indication of improvement in the quality of interracial relations. Whether this theory accounts for the involvement of African American men in intimate interracial relationships remains to be seen.

On the one hand, some very specific examples of a reduction in racial discrimination against Blacks has occurred within the last thirty years. Though not of the kind that Irish, German, and Jewish immigrants may have experienced, some assimilation of Blacks into society has certainly occurred. One need only think about the number of middle-class Blacks to be convinced of this change. At no other time in this nation's history has the Black middle class boasted such numbers. America's economic prosperity (though still elusive for a majority of the African American population that still occupies the ranks of the poor and the working poor) has trickled down to benefit nearly one-third of all African Americans.

Also more Blacks are being elected to city, state, and federal positions than ever before. For example, the Congressional Black Caucus, formed in 1970, now includes nearly forty members of the House of Representatives. Although this number has varied over the years, when viewed across time periods, the current figure suggests that progress—economic and political—has occurred for at least some African Americans.[18]

Yet race continues to matter, and for every step forward, every gain achieved, African Americans symbolically (and sometimes literally) must often take two steps back.[19] As a group, African Americans continue to wind up with the proverbial "short end of the stick." For example, assaults on affirmative action polices during the 1990s attest to the continuing significance of race. What is perhaps most notable and contradictory about the majority of White America's (and the current Bush administration's) desire to dismantle this particular protective armor against racial discrimination is the accompanying rhetoric affirming racial equality.

Opponents of affirmative action policies contend that because no American should be given preferential treatment, policies that seek to ensure a level playing field for African Americans must be eliminated. The rationale is that civil rights legislation initiated during the 1950s and 1960s, and subscribed to throughout the 1970s, effectively eliminated what 350 years of history had ensured. Therefore, as some of these people suggest,[20]racism and bigotry have disappeared. Black people no longer encounter discrimination in the labor market, in the educational system, in the political arena, and in their day-to-day lives.[21]

Importantly, however, a thorough review of the contemporary state of affairs for Black America reveals that those who contend that racial discrimination no longer exists are largely engaged in an exercise of polemics rather than informed analysis or critical discourse. Seven years ago, the brutal slaying of an African American man in Jasper, Texas, brought to the forefront of the nation's collective consciousness the fact that race can and still does matter. When William Byrd, Jr. was savagely beaten and dragged to his death, Americans were reminded that not only does race continue to matter, but in some places in this country you may be killed simply because you are Black.[22] News coverage of this tragedy focused on the psychopathology of Byrd's murderers. Most of the news stories highlighted their depravity and distinguished them from the majority of White Americans. While it is true that members of organized hate groups such as the kind in which Byrd's murderers boasted affiliation represent less than 10 percent of all of the people who commit hate crimes,[23] this incident, perhaps more than any other in recent history, makes clear the fact that deep-seated racial bigotry still exists. The men who murdered Byrd may have been unique in their affiliation with an organized hate group, but the racial bigotry that fueled their actions is probably much more common than many Americans would care to admit.

As evidence of this prevalence, current social science research reveals the continuing existence of racial bigotry, and in particular anti-Black sentiment. Although most researchers note that blatant expressions of racial bigotry have declined within the last forty years (e.g., It is no longer socially acceptable for Whites to address Blacks as 'nigger'), many White Americans still privately express racial ambivalence, and in some cases downright hostility, towards Black Americans.[24]

From the beginning of this project, I was curious about whether and to what extent Black men in intimate interracial relationships were conscious of the continuing existence of racial discrimination. Choosing to be intimately involved with a non-Black mate would seem to bring this point home, at least on some occasions. One of my interests in carrying out this study was to determine the extent to which Black men in these types of relationships see their relationships as in some way connected to the broader social processes influencing race relations in contemporary America. That is, do they see their relationship as an indication of racial progress? Do they attribute the challenges they experience in their interracial relationship to the continuing presence of anti-Black sentiment? These sorts of questions provided a framework for the comments that follow.

Several of the men interviewed acknowledged that although progress has occurred, racial discrimination is still evident and that race relations have a long way to go. For example, according to J.J., the ex-all American and professional football player:

> There are still some problems with race relations. I think there will always be problems. In this country, yeah, there are always going to be problems. It is getting better though…But, it depends on where you're at. I mean I would not be comfortable in Mississippi or Alabama. Man, you take your life into your own hands sometimes. You gotta' know who your opponent is, you know its like football. And, you may be walking down the street sometime, and all of a sudden you might be at some KKK headquarters. 'Cause you never know. There's a lot of hatred, there is still hatred (he emphatically shakes his head at this point), there is too much hatred, and down South there is some deep-rooted hatred with interracial stuff. You gotta' be careful…

Another man I spoke with, E.M., employed in the health insurance industry expressed ideas similar to J.J.'s. He said,

> "It seems like it is getting progressively worse. We're not making any effort to get to know people beyond the color of their skin… "

E.M. talked at length about the way that he believes racism and anti-Black sentiment in particular had impacted on his marriage as well as the development of his three-year-old's ethnic identity. For him, being involved in an interracial marriage was a constant reminder of the problems he attributed to the state of race relations in the United States.

"We (me and my wife) don't deal with outside forces much.... A lot of what we have to put up with has to do with where we live. My youngest daughter who is bi-racial may have more of a barrier....Yeah, she goes through what most young Black children go through."

E.M. identified his age as being in the "twenty-five to thirty year range" and his wife, who was from El Salvador, as being in the "thirty to thirty-five year range." He was unwilling to be more specific about either of their ages. The two have a daughter together and are raising his wife's El Salvadorean daughter from a previous relationship. E.M. told me that his wife was studying and working in a dental office. He stated that the couple's collective income was in the "$70,000 range."

When asked, E.M. did not see any particular problems or challenges with interracial relationships. At the same time, however, he expressed concerns about the effect of his daughter's bi-racial status on her identity development. On the surface, these two impressions appear to be inconsistent with one another. But upon closer inspection and considering all of E.M.'s other comments, these two seemingly disparate impressions—that he saw no particular problems with interracial relationships and yet was worried about his biracial child—actually do fit together. The concerns E.M. expressed were associated with the lower status African Americans generally have in our society. For him, any and all of the problems he experienced in his marriage, as well as the problems he feared for his daughter, were because of anti-Black sentiment, and because he was Black. There were no problems with interracial relationships per se. The problem, as E.M. saw it, was in society's treatment and depiction of Blacks.

One of significant ways in which the men differed from one another was in the extent to which they regarded racial discrimination as an enduring feature throughout society. Another man I spoke with, A.D., was the son of Haitian immigrants. He had been married to his wife, who is White and was born in France, for twelve years. For him, the significance of race and its impact differs according to where you live and where you are in the United States.

It depends on what part of the country you're in. Once when we were in Atlanta, and that was supposed to be a progressive place...but race relations are backwards in most of the country. California is the best state for interracial relationships, though I think that there is a lot of room for improvement. People just don't understand one another and create divisions along racial lines.

And while A.D. touted California, his home state, as being the "the best for interracial relationships," he also spoke of less than hospitable reactions from his wife's coworkers. A.D.'s wife recently returned to the workforce on a part-time basis only. He said,

> She's never brought pictures of our home life into the office…like most people do. And, she probably never will. I know that she's just not comfortable doing so. Of course, I can't say what would happen if she did, but I just know that she wouldn't be comfortable doing so.

I was curious about this latter point, and so I asked him whether his wife's reluctance to take photographs from home into work resulted from a heightened degree of self-consciousness on her part or whether it truly was a matter of adverse reactions to her interracial marriage by her coworkers. It was clear that he did not know, but what he was certain of was that her decision not to take any pictures of her family into work was, in some way, related to the continuing significance of race and the existence of racial bigotry.

He spoke at length about the problems he had experienced that he attributed to his interracial marriage. A.D. blamed these problems on a distinctively American quality of racism. At the end of the interview he offered the following:

> Interracial relationships are very difficult if you are an American. So much has to do with how you understand "the other." The traditional Black-White relationship in America is full of stuff… The economic problem is exacerbated with the race thing. Why they feel hostility is never really examined. The race difference is just an excuse for every group going out and getting their own…

In this section, I have tried to describe the different theories that have been used to explain interracial relationships in general, as well as Black men's involvement in these relationships. These explanations range from having a strictly psychological focus—where the relationship is believed to result from the person's motives and preferences—to those explanations focusing on structural factors—where large-scale social forces are seen as most influential in precipitating these relationships. Although three of the men interviewed did express responses that revealed their own idiosyncrasies and, for example, their preferences for "Whiteness" as being influential in their involvement in the interracial relationship, an even greater number of the men acknowledged the importance of the widespread decline in barriers to interracial social interaction. These men tended to see the Civil Rights Movement as not only pivotal in history, but they also saw it as important for race relations in general and interracial relationships in particular. Where previously African Americans would not have been permitted to venture, they could now do so, and consequently, they could interact with and meet women they previously would not have.

At this point, it should now be clear that a complete understanding of the factors responsible for the involvement of Black men in interracial relationships requires an awareness of the complex interaction between the various intrapsychic variables and the societal level forces that make any form of interracial interaction possible. The following model illustrates one way of visualizing this interaction. It represents an amalgamation of several other theorists' models.

Intrapsychic factors   **Sustaining Behavior**

{e.g., acceptance of ethnic stereotypes,   active pursuit of interracial friendships
preferences for certain phenotypes,   and intimate relations
self-esteem issues, past
experiences, & curiosity}

- -

   INTERRACIAL   INTIMACY

Societal Level factors   **Sustaining behavior**
{e.g., decline in overt racism &   conscious colorblind ethos
discrimination, changes in social mobility
& isolation, popular appeal of Black male
sexuality & continuing Zeitgeist of a colorblind society}

This model includes factors that, according to a purely psychological explanation for interracial intimacy, are proposed to make the formation of an interracial relationship more likely. These factors are collectively referred to as "intrapsychic" factors and include such things as an endorsement and belief in ethnic stereotypes, a conscious preference for a particular phenotype, problems with self-esteem, a long-standing history of such relationships, and curiosity. The model also includes the "societal level" factors that a purely structural explanation regards as causal determinants to interracial intimacy. These factors include a decline in overt discrimination and barriers to opportunity, changes in social mobility and social isolation, changes in geographic diversity, popular appeal of Black male sexuality as well as an esprit de corps touting the benefits of a colorblind society.

The presence of any one of the intrapsychic or societal level factors alone is not a sufficient condition for an interracial relationship to occur. Moreover, in addition to the intrapsychic and societal level factors, there must also be what I have referred to in the model as a "sustaining behavior" in which this type of a relationship is actively pursued. In the case of the purely structural explanation, the societal factors are proposed to precipitate an interracial relationship only when the individual adopts and maintains a colorblind ethos. When these factors occur and are accompanied by the requisite sustaining behaviors, an interracial relationship is especially likely to occur.

Based on what each of the men said up to this point, clearly neither type of explanation alone fully accounts for all instances of interracial intimacy. Indeed, it is safe to say that the more accurate approach to understanding interracial intimacy is one that borrows from both the psychological and structural types of explanations. Because of this, and as I proposed at the outset of this chapter, explanations for interracial relationships should be viewed along a continuum. The explanations that are most helpful in explaining these types of relationships are located somewhere near the middle of that continuum.

Notes

1. I have elected to propose a continuum rather than an either/or framework because the latter is too simplistic and artificial to reflect the factors that influence the actual formation of an intimate interracial relationship.

2. For examples of theories such as this see Robert Merton, "Intermarriage and Social Structure: Fact and Theory," *Psychiatry 4* (1941): 361-374; and Gunnar Myrdal's *An American Dilemma: The Negro Problem and American Democracy* (New York: Harper & Brothers, 1944).

3. See Paul Spickard's *Intermarriage and Ethnic Identity in Twentieth Century America* (Madison, Wisc.: Wisconsin University Press, 1989). A more recent discussion is found in Maria Root's *Love's Revolution: Interracial Marriage* (Philadelphia, Pa.: Temple University Press, 2001).

4. The reader is referred to Milton Gordon's *Assimilation in American life* (New York: Oxford University Press, 1964); and Robert Merton's article "Intermarriage and the Social Structure: Fact and Theory," *Psychiatry 4* (1941): 361-374.

5. This quote by Franz Boas appeared on page 104 in Roger Sanjek's chapter "Intermarriage and the Future of Races in the U.S.," in *Race,* edited by Steven Gregory and Roger Sanjek (New Brunswick, N.J.: Rutgers University Press, 1994), 103-130.

6.   See the article "Negro-White Marriages in the United States" by D.M. Herr in *Journal of Marriage and the Family 27* (1966): 262-275.
7.   It should be noted, however, that an explanation that attributes rates of interracial intimacy entirely to increasing economic opportunity fails to account for the fact that interracial marriages make up only a relatively small portion of the marriages that actually take place. If increasing economic opportunity were solely responsible for rates of interracial intimacy, there would be many more interracial unions than currently exist. Moreover, an explanation based solely on increased opportunity fails to explain why interracial marriages between Blacks and Whites more frequently assume the form of Black men/White women.
8.   "Phenotype" is a term borrowed from biology and refers to the appearance of an individual that results from the interaction of his/her genetic composition with their environment. A Black phenotype would include features most frequently associated with Black people, including darker skin and curly or kinky hair textures.
9.   See, for example, the article by Ernest Porterfield "Black-American Intermarriage in the United States," in *Marriage and Family Review 5* (1982): 17-34.
10. For further discussion of this point, see the chapter by William Grier and Price Cobbs, "Marriage and Love as Components to Black Rage," in *Black Male/White Female: Perspectives on Interracial Marriage and Courtship*, edited by Doris Y. Wilkerson (Cambridge, Mass.: Schenkman Publishing Co., 1975); the book by Frantz Fanon, *Black Skins, White Masks* (New York, NY: Grove Press, 1967); and the article by T. Joel Wade, "The Relationships between Skin Color and Self-Perceived Global, Physical, and Sexual Attractiveness and Self-Esteem for African Americans," *Journal of Black Psychology 22* (1991): 358-373.
11. For a test of the applicability of this theory for interracial couples, see the article by Stanley Gaines & Diana Rios, "Romanticism and Interpersonal Resource Exchange between African American-Anglo and Other Interracial Couples," *Journal of Black Psychology 25* (1999): 461-490.
12. The following chapter discusses the way that beauty, as the American media conceptualizes it, tends to be restricted to Whites or to those who look most like people of European descent.
13. According to some authors, the desire for lighter skin color is nearly universal. See chapter 3 of *The Color Complex* by Kathy Russell, Midge Wilson, and Ronald Hall (New York: Anchor Books, 1992). The privilege afforded lighter-colored complexions is evident in Asian, African, and Central and South American societies and reflects European patterns of colonialization.
14. See Itabari Njeri "Sushi and Grits: Ethnic Identity and Conflict in a Newly Multicultural America," in *Lure and Loathing*, edited by Gerald Early New York: Penguin Books, 1993).
15. The reader is referred to *The Color Complex* by Russell, Wilson, and Hall.
16. From Frantz Fanon's *Black Skin, White Masks* (New York, NY: Grove Press, Inc., 1967, p. 63).
17. For important examples of this perspective, see the following selections referenced earlier this chapter: D.M Herr (1966), Milton Gordon (1964), Robert Merton (1941), as well as the more recent publication by Paul Spickard, *Mixed Blood: Intermarriage and Ethnic Identity in 20th Century America*. (Madison, Wisc.: University of Wisconsin Press, 1989).
18. See Andrew Hacker's *Two Nations: Black and White, Separate, Hostile, Unequal* (New York: Simon & Schuster, Inc., 1995.)

19. Several scholars and writers have written about the continuing effects of racism in contemporary America. Two examples include Cornell West's *Race Matters* (Boston, Mass.: Beacon Press, 1993); and 2. Micheal E. Dyson's *Race Rules. Navigating the Color Line* (New York: Vintage Books, 1997). Also for engaging first-hand interview reports of its significance, see Studs Terkel's *Race. How Blacks and Whites Think about the American Obsession* (New York: Anchor Books, 1992).

20. One example of this position was heard in a speech delivered by past California governor Pete Wilson, "Securing our Nation's Borders" at a Los Angeles Town Hall meeting (April 1994).

21. As a result of the efforts of like-minded individuals, the representation of Blacks and Hispanics in the 1996 freshmen class for most campuses of the University of California system resembled their numbers in the days before the landmark Civil Rights legislation of 1964.

22. The journalist Joyce King published a book focusing on what happened to Mr. Byrd and what has subsequently happened to his convicted perpetrators. See the book *Hate Crime. The Story of a Dragging in Jasper, Texas* (New York: Pantheon, 2002).

23. For extensive discussion of hate crime activity, see Jack Levin and Jack McDevitt's *Hate Crimes. The Rising Tide of Bigotry and Bloodshed* (New York: Plenum Press, 1993).

24. See Feagin's "The Continuing Significance of Race: Anti-Black Discrimination in Public Places," *American Sociological Review 56* (1991): 101-116.

5

Beauty in the Eye of the Beholder and According to the Media

Most people in the United States are exposed to popular cultural images of our society on a daily basis. As evidence of the pervasiveness of these images, among people in other countries who have never even visited the United States there is some familiarity with the images we consider to be attractive and desirable. Popular cultural images are distributed by way of television and music video shows, billboard and magazine advertisements, and even children's fairy tales. These outlets and the images they depict reflect the American media's strength and power as a socializing agent. Much of what we "learn" or come to believe about men and women—what makes them tick and what they are like—is communicated by some source of the media.

This chapter includes a discussion of the extent to which the men interviewed were aware of the way that cultural images depicted in television, video, and film affect people's ideas about beauty and influence sexual attraction. In this section, I have provided a discussion of each of the men's ideas about physical attractiveness as well as their confessed ideals for beauty. I was especially interested in whether, and to what degree, Black women were regarded as potentially desirable mates by each of the men. Asking such questions as "What attracts you to a woman?" and "What does a beautiful woman look like to you?" prompted this discussion.

In movies and films, we learn that good triumphs over evil and that goodness is associated with beauty and evil is associated with homeliness.[1] In popular music, the current trend is one of blatant sexuality, and ironically the most successful entertainers in today's music industry, who also tend to be sexually explicit, serve as role models for impressionable adolescents.

Television is perhaps the most potentially powerful segment of the media, and it provides viewers with implicit as well as explicit exemplars of interpersonal and intimate relations. As evidence of this, some research on the effects of television has shown that more Americans' beliefs about the world come from television than from any other medium. An estimated 98 million homes in the United States have from one to three televisions, and these TVs are in use! American adults watch an average of seven hours of television each day, and for children—whose television viewing rates have increased steadily within the decade of the last century—the number of hours spent watching television is even greater.[2]

Today there are more interracial couples shown on television, in film, and more generally, within art forms than was the case as recently as fifteen years ago. Yet, these depictions of interracial liaisons continue to be relatively rare. A number of writers have speculated about the reasons why so few interracial couples are shown on TV and why there are even fewer such couples with Black men. Some writers in this area have blamed the lack of images of interracial couples on the provincial values and attitudes of Middle America. They point to specific occasions when angry viewers have written producers to threaten withdrawal of their viewership following the depiction of a nontraditional (i.e., interracial) relationship. Alternatively, others have suggested that relatively few interracial couples are shown because representatives of the Hollywood television and film industries do not really think of these types of relationships as viable ones. Whatever the reason, television and movie producers, photographers, and casting agents have generally shied away from frequent portrayals of interracial relationships.

Of course some exceptions do exist, and their notoriety stems from their status as exceptions. One exception, which also happens to be one of the earliest Hollywood depictions of an intimate interracial relationship, occurred in a 1967 film starring Sidney Poitier. The film "*Guess Who's Coming to Dinner?*" involved the story of a successful, young Black man and his well-to-do girlfriend who was White. The plot of the film revolved around the events of one particular night when the two decided to break the news of their relationship to both sets of parents. The movie was both radical and controversial, a fact not surprising given that laws prohibiting interracial marriage were still in existence in at least fifteen states at the time of the movie's release.

Today, a cursory review of the contemporary images in film and television reveals that the depiction of heterosexual interracial relationships continues to be rare. Consider the term "jungle fever." Many Black and White Americans are familiar with it and generally recognize it as a colloquial term for interracial relationships. This term, and all that it connotes, suggests not only the rarity of interracial relationships but also something less than positive about them.

My search for the actual roots of this term failed to yield little more than speculation. At least three possible explanations for this term are worth noting. The first is perhaps the most benign. The term "jungle fever" may be based on the notion that relations among inhabitants of the jungle are primitive and, therefore, based on biology and species similarity rather than something as superficial as race or ethnicity. A second explanation for the term "jungle fever" has to do with its typical association with interracial relationships involving an African American. Because of the pervasiveness of stereotypes about Blacks as animalistic and less human than Whites, this term may be an especially effective way of derogating African Americans and those who associate with them. When applied to interracial relationships with Blacks, it has the effect of questioning, however subtly, the humanity of Black people by equating them with jungle inhabitants.

The third explanation for this term is equally as problematic, and it is based on erroneous beliefs that most Westerners share about the contemporary patterns of living among inhabitants of the African continent. Most Westerners fail to perceive the size and diversity of Africa's populations. They erroneously believe that Africans, with few exceptions, live in conditions comparable to those they see in the popular classic movie *Tarzan*. Hence, the term "jungle fever" when applied to relationships involving Black people may have its roots in the belief that Black people around the world are only a few generations removed (if at all) from the jungle.

In a relatively recent movie which was called "Jungle Fever," a professionally employed and married Black man had an affair with a White woman who worked with him. The movie, which appeared in 1991, was especially provocative because of its frank portrayal of the covert nature of their relationship. In the movie, the couple candidly discussed the implications of their liaison. For the White woman, there was the problem that her working class Italian family had with Black people because of their racism, and for the Black man, there was the problem of infidelity that resulted from the extramarital affair as well as the problem of his involvement with a White woman. Perhaps most compelling was the scene in which the male character's wife, who was Black, discussed the implications of her husband's infidelity in a down-to-earth consciousness-raising session with her girlfriends. The movie depicted each of the characters in ways that corresponded with audience expectations and stereotypes about Blacks and Whites, and about men and women.

Further insights about interracial intimate portrayals on television and in films can be gleamed from an informative research paper that examined the way that interracial relationships are shown on daytime soap operas. According to researchers Bramlett-Solomon and Farwell, the very first mixed couple to appear on a soap opera did so in 1968 on the show *One Life to Live*.[3] The woman in the relationship was a Black person with an extremely light complexion who "passed" as a White person.[4] To the shock of viewers, the character had an intimate relationship with a popular male character that was very clearly White. As the researchers noted in their paper, it was not until the late 1980s that interracial intimacy occurred with less surprise. In a study of interracial portrayals on daytime television, the researchers examined the top three soap operas during an eight-week period in 1995 for a comparison of the portrayal of Black, White, and interracial intimacy between Blacks and Whites. During that time period, they found that of the 421 depictions of romantic intimacy, 372 involved White characters, 49 involved Black characters, and none depicted interracial intimacy. Consequently, these researchers concluded that "Intimacy was depicted as something that White couples do, while Black couples occasionally partake in intimacy. The fact that no scenes depicted interracial couples suggests that such portrayals on the soaps are miniscule and limited."[5]

Quite a few of the men I spoke to indicated that they believed that the media had played a significant role in influencing the way that they came to view themselves, as well as the way they viewed members of the opposite sex and members of different racial groups. These men believed that the media had played a role in influencing their ideas about beauty, physical attractiveness, and the reality of interracial relationships. According to E.M., who was introduced in the previous chapter,

> As for movies, I know for a fact that there were very few interracial relationships shown in movies. There was this one movie, I forget what it was called, and I remember

it because it was so unusual. The movie showed a Black guy, it was the actor Larry Fishburne, and he was in an interracial relationship with a White woman. It was surprising to me, but I remember the Black male star had a physical relationship with the female star, and they showed it in detail...

The movie, called *Bad Company*, was released in 1995. It included a scene in which Lawrence Fishburne was shown performing cunnilingus on a White woman played by the actress Ellen Barkin. Of course the movie was provocative because it depicted sexual behavior and did so with a Black man and a White woman. It is not surprising that E.M. was able to recall it vividly. The scene was quite graphic. It is worth noting that the sexual act shown—the Black man "going down" on the White woman—is one that is not widely (or at least publicly) endorsed by people outside of the sex industry. At least publicly, many people profess feeling somewhat squeamish about it. Therefore, it could be argued that its portrayal between a Black man and a White woman in that movie was *especially* intended to influence audience perceptions of the characters. The White female character was taken down a notch because of her "contemptible" behavior (she was, after all, having sex with a Black man) and preexisting suspicions about the oversexed nature of the Black male character and Black men in general (they all lust after White women) were confirmed. The latter outcome is particularly problematic in light of the dearth of positive images of Black men and women in mainstream Hollywood films.

E.M. was well aware of this portrayal, and said that his problems with the media had to do with the lack of images, particularly positive ones, of Black people and of interracial relationships. In a similar vein, A.D. who was also introduced in the previous chapter, was especially critical of the media's tendency to limit the portrayal of interracial relationships on television and in film. According to him, when they were shown, there was something unnatural and negative about them. He said,

> When I was about 16 and interracial relationships were aired, it was telling. I really would have thought that the subject would have been dealt with more openly. First of all, they're rarely shown. I noticed early on the absence of interracial relationships. When they actually did portray interracial lovemaking, it was portrayed as dysfunctional with an absence of love...a totally inaccurate portrayal. Lovemaking was portrayed negatively...it looked like gymnastics to me!

For A.D., the negative images associated with the interracial relationships he observed in his youth have gradually given way to more positive ones.

"Today interracial relationships are more acceptable than what they used to be. Now you can even see it on television and in the movies. There are even celebrities involved in it."

Today, most marketing and advertising executives agree that the television networks' recent decisions to offer Black-oriented shows as a staple of their regular line-up is as much a matter of good business acumen as it is a matter of reality. These new shows are more realistic in that the largely Black casts on these shows deflect the invisibility that has, up until this period, cloaked the African American experience on television. For Whites who have never interacted with Blacks before, they now come face- to-face with them during prime-time lineups. Of course, these shows are no panacea for the problem of negative stereotyping, as they tend to present only a limited number of images of African Americans, which are typically comedic, but they do represent a necessary first step.

There is yet another way in which the decision to offer shows featuring Black casts is practical. According to most studies, African Americans watch more television than any other group in the United States.[6] One researcher in this area has noted that because Black and White Americans have different viewing preferences and habits, it makes sense to provide Blacks with television shows reflecting their unique cultural basis.[7] The bottom line here is that Blacks represent a significant potential market for advertisers. Furthermore, Black viewers, like E.M., feel better represented when they see shows with Black characters. According to E.M.,

"Even though everything on television is geared towards Whites, at least now there is the WB network, and you can at least see more TV shows that are Black-oriented...."

Aside from Black cable stations, the WB network offers the largest share of primetime TV shows in which African Americans are depicted in starring roles. Like E.M., other African Americans have expressed dissatisfaction with the actual numbers of Black characters appearing during prime time. Moreover, a majority of African Americans surveyed have also expressed disdain for the way that Blacks are portrayed on television.[8]

Several of the men I spoke to expressed particular concerns about the role of the media in shaping their ideas about interracial intimacy, standards of beauty, and physical attractiveness. Yet very few suggested its potential in influencing their children's beliefs and ideas. E.M. was one of the few exceptions. He described the problems he had with the lack of Black images on television as well as the potential problems this posed for his biracial daughter's identity. He said,

> "The problem has to do with her growing up as a young Black person and constantly being bombarded with ads containing White people…This is obvious when she begs me to buy her a White doll instead of a Black doll, and I had to explain to her that both dolls were pretty and that she could play with either of them."

In comparison to E.M., most of the men interviewed did not regard the media as a potentially problematic influence upon their children's development. They typically denied any such concerns and, when probed for additional comments, tended to state that they were not aware of any particular issues or problems concerning the media as far as their children's development was concerned. Most suggested that they had effectively shielded their children from its effects. However, as is apparent from the comments of A.D. and E.M., when asked about its impact upon <u>themselves,</u> at least seven of the men explicitly noted the impact of the media in shaping their own views about interracial relationships.

This was certainly the case for one man, C.R., who was referred to me by his mother. Upon hearing about the project, she mentioned that her son would make a "good participant." She contacted him, and he agreed to participate. Following our initial telephone contact, I spoke with C.R. during two subsequent conversations. C.R. was a thirty-eight-year-old computer program analyst living in the Belmont Shore area of Southern California. He indicated that although he had previously dated women from a variety of racial groups, he was currently involved with a woman who was White. She was twenty-seven years old, employed as a sales clerk in a wedding store, and had been dating him for the past two years.

C.R. was conscious of the media's influence on his own ideas about interracial relationships and the extent to which it had contributed to his "negative views" about them.

> Well, I think that the media may have reinforced some negative views for me…negative only insofar as seeing and thinking about those situations where there were differences for men who were Black versus those who weren't when they were in an interracial relationship. Men who weren't Black did not get so much flack for dating women of other races as Black men did…I was aware of this in the media…It was seen as so much more of a problem for Black men than for other men.

For the most part, when I asked the men to think about whether and to what extent they believed that the media had influenced them, they raised two issues. First, they criticized the lack of images of

Blacks on television and in films. And, at least some of the men noted that the images that did appear tended to be negative. According to DAVID who had married a young White woman,

> It seems that the media sensationalizes differences or situations…its always one race versus another. For example, if there is a fight in school between a Latino and a Black person, it turns into a race riot. It's easy for the media to hype things up with respect to race. They really focus on those things…The American public believes what they see and hear from the media. They form their opinions from that…I think that that really sets relations back between people. For me, I try to base my opinions without the media….

The second issue raised by at least five of the men specifically had to do with the representation of Black interracial intimacy in TV and film. These men were most disturbed by what they regarded as either the underrepresentation or marginalization of interracial relationships with Blacks. For them, real portrayals of such relationships occurred far too infrequently.

Most of the men who thought that there were problems with portrayals of interracial relationships were particularly distressed over the lack of portrayals of mixed couples with Black men. More than anything else, it was the lack of these sorts of interracial heterosexual relationships that bothered them. What is ironic about their impressions is that at the same time that only a limited number of interracial couples with Black men appear on television and in the movies, there seems to be an increasing number of recent mainstream films starring Black actresses in interracial relationships.

Consider the movie, *Monster's Ball*, which starred Halle Berry. In the movie, she appeared in a graphic sex scene with a White male character.[9] Her on-screen appearances and the circumstances that have characterized her rise to stardom speak volumes to the media's representation of Blacks in general and to interracial relationships with Blacks in particular. For Ms. Berry (who became the first Black woman to win an Academy Award for Best Actress for her role in the movie) as well as a number of Black actresses, reality has been the exact opposite of the observations made by several of the men, including A.D. and E.M.

Consider the fact that rarely does Ms. Berry appear in intimate liaisons with male characters who are Black. In fact, her biggest popular film roles have called for her character to have intimate/romantic relationships with White men. Apparently, it was this tendency for Ms. Berry to repeatedly play characters who had romantic relationships with White men which prompted one outraged Black man to post the following critique on an internet web site. Titled "At What Price Oscar," he wrote,

As an African American man, I find nothing to be proud of in actress Halle Berry's recent Academy Award nomination...With its profanely incongruous and utterly implausible scenario, the plot of this film is a sneering, in-your-face taunt to all Black men...Monster's Ball is unfortunately just the latest screening, at least since 1992's "Boomerang" in which we must endure seeing her in the throes of passion with White men. Her character boldly exposed her breasts to a White man in the movie "Swordfish," another 'got down' with an old White senator in "Bullworth," and had two White men, husband and lover/co-conspirator, in playing "The Rich Man's Wife." Of course portraying Dorothy Dandridge required Berry's character, as Dandridge once described her own romantic/marital relationships, to 'throw herself at White men.' It seems that that's all Hollywood will throw at Ms. Berry... Angela Bassett, a critically acclaimed and enchantingly beautiful actress, was Robert DeNiro's character's girlfriend in "The Score." Thandie Newton's character in the second "Mission Impossible" movie was shared between two White characters. Even the original super-sister Pam Grier had a White lover in "Jackie Brown....

Hollywood continues to be dominated by White men who create films that appeal to their own psyches. As such, it is generally the character that is White and male who gets "the prize" in the end and "lives happily ever after." In an industry dominated by men where women are more often viewed as sexual conquests, "the prize" is the beautiful woman. For the few Black actresses who have the opportunity to star in mainstream, well-financed movies, being the star often means being intimately involved with a White male character. For Black men, who are disproportionately represented in movie roles as undesirable characters (e.g., as thieves, gangsters, and homosexuals), starring in such roles often precludes appearing in intimate relationships with the female character depicted as "the prize." One study that provides some support for this observation employed a content analysis of television commercials during a two-year period. It concluded that 1990s television commercials depicted White men as powerful, White women as sex objects, African American men as aggressive, and African American women as inconsequential.[10]

But How Do Mainstream American Beauty Standards Affect Black Men's Pursuit of Women?

"Too many Black men rank their preferences for beauty on how close a woman is to looking White...."[11]

Standards of beauty in the United States are consistent with both the preferences and appearances of White Americans. In general, beauty standards for women have varied more than men's over the years and have included, among other things, narrow waists, big breasts, flared hips, and boyish figures. But what has remained constant is the extent to which the criteria for beauty have been systematically associated with White Americans.

Paradoxically, what is regarded as a beauty feature at any one time by Whites may actually be a common physical feature that members of a racial minority group routinely possess. A particular physical feature or attribute may be regarded as valuable when it is associated with Whites, but when it is viewed in conjunction with Blacks or other members of racial minority groups it loses its aesthetic value. This has clearly been the case for at least one facial feature characteristic of African Americans—full lips. Stereotypic caricatures of African Americans in the seventeenth and eighteenth century consistently accentuated this feature resulting in portrayals of African American characters with lips that were grossly exaggerated. Indeed, in most of these portrayals, the lips represented the most defining feature of the faces. Today, full lips on Whites have suddenly become fashionable. White supermodels and Hollywood starlets who are judged as beautiful, more often than not, possess this feature. Even though many African Americans have full lips, they are not regarded as uniquely beautiful, nor are their lips perceived to be a beauty asset.

As evidence of this, recall that during the media's earliest fascination with White film actress Julia Roberts, beginning in 1990, she was repeatedly described as being the distinctively "full lipped" beauty. Since that time, this feature appears more commonly among White actresses and supermodels. Not surprisingly, there has also been a corresponding increase in the number of advertisements and reports describing the various techniques available for lip enhancement. The recent rise in popularity of collagen lip implants reflects not only the current widely accepted beauty feature of full lips but also mainstream America's tendency to regard certain features as beautiful only when they are associated with Whites. As A.D. noted,

"The American media has spent a lot of time conveying its cannons of beauty that are not necessarily consistent with most men's cannons of beauty. If you listen to the media, the most beautiful woman is the tall, buxom blonde with flared hips... ."

For researchers Yang and Ragaza who have studied the effects of the media's obsession with certain physical features, the "White beauty yardstick" that defines beauty in the United States operates oblivious to people of color.[12] According to this yardstick, tall, thin,

White people epitomize beauty. Men and women of color who do not conform to these standards are excluded from portrayals that require or advertise beauty. These researchers write, "In Western society, beauty is tall. Beauty is thin. Above all, beauty is White." They note that only with the gradual increase in the numbers of advertisers, directors, and actors of color can we expect to see a more inclusive definition of beauty.

For GARY, first introduced in Chapter 3, it was the tendency not to revere those characteristics deemed attractive in mainstream America that he believed distinguished him from other Blacks. He said,

> "I'm attracted, actually, to a lot more of the traits that are attributed to Black women…of course, that's more from a superficial standpoint, but that's my perspective. I mean I like women who have large thighs, and…hmmm…you could say generous rear ends. These are things that I'm sure are more often seen on Black women than say White women."

Gary regarded these body features as more typical of Black women, and for him they contributed to his perception of a woman's physical attractiveness. His expressed preference for large derrieres and thighs also appears to contribute to his beliefs about himself as, in some way, progressive or distinctive.

So, while Gary may be different from the other men in expressing a preference for body features typically not revered by mainstream America, he is quite consistent with media portrayals in his apparent preference for women with lighter skin colors. Gary's first and second wives do not (with the exception of those particular characteristics below the waist) look like a majority of Black women. His first wife of eleven years was White, and the mulatto woman he was engaged to at the time of the interview looks, according to him, "Hispanic or Italian."

There are a number of writers who have described the inflexibility of Western beauty standards when it comes to the inclusion of "non-Western" people. Some writers have even focused on the extent to which African Americans who, when reacting to these standards, have sought to Whiten their own skin pigmentation and straighten their hair.[13] At the outset of one chapter that describes this reaction, writers Russell, Wilson, and Hall attribute it to the hegemony of Western cultural images and values. According to them,

> "Countless Black girls in the United States share the fantasy of being White. How could it be otherwise in a society whose ideal beauty –blond, pale-skinned, with blue or green eyes—embodies everything the average Black female isn't?"[14]

Slowly, the tendency to exclude people of color from mainstream depictions of beauty is changing. For example, today in most contemporary polls of the "100 most beautiful people" at least one person who is included is of African descent, and in some cases there may be a person who is Asian or who hails from a Spanish-speaking country whose inhabitants are mostly "Brown."

Of course, these "exceptional" people of color included in popular polls of the most beautiful people also tend to look a lot like Whites. In other words, the solo Black or Asian included looks less like typical members of the ethnic minority group in which they boast membership. It is no coincidence that those women of African descent with celebrity status who the American media currently tout as beautiful do not resemble most Black women. What celebrities such as former Miss America turned pop star and actress Vanessa Williams and super model Tyra Banks have in common are their aquiline features, straight (and in some cases long) hair, light complexions, and light eye color. Most African American women do not look like these women or like actresses Jasmine Guy and Halle Berry.

Concerns about skin color and hair texture continue to plague Blacks in the United States, and although they probably operate most strongly for women, they also have implications for Black men. Not surprisingly, there are Black men with dark colored complexions who are sensitive to the pervasive preference for light skin color as well as the facial features typically associated with Whites rather than Blacks. In the most obvious cases, this sensitivity results in their pursuit of women with light or White- colored complexions who possess such facial features. This preference was probably the case for BRIAN, the attorney introduced in the preceding chapter. In other cases, concerns about skin color and corresponding physical features result in a degree of self-consciousness and dissatisfaction with their own appearance.

One well-known actor publicly disclosed his own struggle in reconciling society's preference for light skin with his own dark-skinned complexion. Screen actor Yaphet Kotto, a large Black man who is very dark skinned and whose facial features are most often associated with people of African descent, described his own experiences. In an interview for the online magazine *Salon* he spoke openly about the way that he believed his physical appearance restricted his opportunities with Black women.[15] In the *Salon* interview he said,

I was not able to attract a light-skinned Black woman to my life, or even a Black woman throughout the 1970s. They perceived me to be too ethnic looking and not Caucasian looking enough. My entire experience in my 20s was with Caucasian women. I never knew what it was to be dated by a Black women. I don't think Caucasian women care what race you are or how light you are. Black women do and they let you know it….[16]

Kotto's remarks highlight the pervasiveness of the desire for light skin color. Not only does this criterion define physical attractiveness for women, but it may also affect perceptions of the relative attractiveness of Black men. In reacting to Black women's rejection of him, Kotto concludes (and I would argue incorrectly) that White women do not care about skin color or race and consequently, have embraced him. According to him, Black women, the group that is most denigrated by Western standards of beauty, are the real culprits. Mr. Kotto's wife of a number of years who is the mother of his children is White.

Clearly, individual mate preferences differ from person to person, and this was the case among the men I spoke with. In reviewing their responses, it was also apparent that they differed according to the extent to which they explicitly noted a preference for features more often associated with White rather than Black people. Of the men with whom I spoke, only a small number explicitly noted a preference for women who possess physical attributes that are not typically associated with Black people. PEYTON was thirty-four years old and worked as a security guard in Chicago. At the time of the interview, he had recently fathered a child with a Mexican American woman. He noted several of the physical features shared by all of the women he thinks of as beautiful. First among them was long, straight hair. He said,

I love women with some long, loose hair. I flip over that. I prefer a woman to have long pretty, straight hair. That's what I first notice. The mind is fine, if a woman has a brain that's cool too. But it's the physical aspect that attracts me, especially her hair…And I like a woman that keeps herself together…has her nails done…I mean if she is going to wear sandals, then she should make sure her toe-nails are done. And, please don't wear curlers outside…As long as she looks good, I'm attracted to her.

Another man I spoke with, B.H., also noted that a certain hair type or style was important in his perception of a physically attractive woman. I met the twenty-three-year-old college student through a relative of his best friend. He had been dating a twenty-two-year-old Puerto Rican woman for the past three years. Previously, he had been involved with another woman who was also from Puerto Rico. Since the interview, I learned that he was well on the way to completing medical school at a premiere historically Black university and had made plans to wed his Puerto Rican girlfriend. In answering my question about what attracts him to a woman, he said: "First, it's looks of course....Girls I'm attracted to look kind of like my sister. They tend to have light skin, and nice hair. I don't like baldies. I really don't like it when a woman has less hair than me... ."

Long, loose hair was a preferred feature for Peyton. Presumably, the Mexican American woman with whom he was currently involved possessed such tresses. For B.H. it's fair skin and "nice" hair. In contrast, whether a woman had a specific hair length or style was not important to C.R., introduced in an earlier section of this chapter, and who compared media depictions of Black men in interracial relationships to depictions of men of other races. About a preference for a certain hair type or length he said,

> "The length of a woman's hair doesn't much matter to me…it could be long or short…it really doesn't make a difference…"

According to a number of writers who have considered the value of hair and its relation to perceptions of physical attractiveness, C.R. is not typical. Writers Russell, Wilson, and Hall note in another chapter of *The Color Complex* that in addition to skin color, hair operates to delineate status within the African American community. Long or straight hair has always been valued among African Americans. It has long served as a clue to one's ancestry. When it is straight or especially long, it betrays its non-African ancestral contributions. For a race of people who have historically been devalued, features associated with other racial groups (e.g., long straight hair, thin lips and noses, and light eye color) are considered valued commodities.

> "The politics of hair parallels the politics of skin color. Among Black women, straight hair and European hairstyles not only have been considered more feminine, but have sent a message about one's standing in the social hierarchy. 'Good hair' has long been associated with the light-skinned middle class, 'bad hair' with Blacks who are less fortunate."[17]

It is probably safe to say that most Black men who express a preference for long, straight, or "loose" hair, as in Peyton's case, have not seriously considered the politics of hair. Although it is unlikely that many Black women have done so either, when Black women yearn for long, straight hair, the meaning of hair length and texture is very real.[18]

According to one feminist scholar writing at length about the social meaning of straightened hair for Black women,

"Within White supremacist capitalist patriarchy, the social and political context in which the custom of Black folks straightening our hair emerges, it represents an imitation of the dominant White group's appearance and often indicates internalized racism, self hatred and low self esteem."[19]

In a later section of this article, she notes that although social progress in the elimination of overt forms of racism has occurred, the politics of hair continue to affect Black women. "Despite many changes in racial politics, Black women continue to obsess about their hair, and straightening hair continues to be a serious business. It continues to tap into the insecurity Black women feel about our value in this White supremacist society."[20]

Whether in possession of light skin and long straight hair or not, Black women are typically aware of the way that American beauty standards affect judgments of their physical attractiveness. Although most Black women acknowledge that the women they see on television, in magazines, and in movies are women that mainstream (i.e., White) Americans deem beautiful, most are unable or perhaps reluctant to articulate the way these standards of beauty have influenced their own behaviors, affected their self-esteem, and encouraged feelings of insecurity.

I'm Also Attracted to Women Who Are...

It is important to note that a number of the men in this study mentioned preferences for physical characteristics other than skin color, hair, and eye color when asked to describe what most attracted them to women. Some examples follow.

According to M.B., who described himself as "liking all types of women,"

Its hard to say because its not just one thing. The face and eyes because the eyes tell a lot. She can be a little thick, but not too big. Its really everything about her...there is no one feature...

CHESTER in Indiana, who was twenty-nine years old, had been married to his wife, who was White, for ten years. He preferred a woman:

...with a big butt, and big long legs...with enough chest to fit into one hand....

BRIAN, introduced in chapter 4, was pretty upfront about the features of a woman's body that weigh most heavily in his perceptions of a woman's physical attractiveness. He said,

In an intimate relationship, physical appearance matters…I'm not drawn to any particular body shape or design. I tend to lean towards, in laymen's terms, I am a leg man. I am not a boob man…

In contrast, C.R. introduced earlier in this chapter said,

I prefer athletic looking women… I like women with nice legs…I don't care if she wears glasses or not. I don't know…just as long as she's not ugly. I've never dated anyone who was excessively skinny or heavy.

DAMON, the psychotherapist from St. Louis, had something similar to say. He expressed a preference for

…A more athletically built woman with broad shoulders and big legs…

Most distinctive was KEITH'S preferred physical feature. Keith, who was previously married on two occasions to White women, began by acknowledging that looks matter less than what is inside. And, somewhat surprisingly, he went on to say,

I like a woman with big ankles, yeah, big ankles turn me on…

There were also two men who explicitly expressed a preference for women with particular hygiene standards. These men noted that cleanliness was as important as any one of the physical qualities they preferred in the women with whom they were intimate.

In some cases, the men's answers to the question "What makes a woman beautiful to you?" yielded a discussion about the merits of inner qualities over and beyond physical attributes. For these men, a compatible personality was key. They said that only after they determined that a woman had a good personality did they find her to be physically attractive. Not surprisingly, what constitutes a good personality was different for each of the men. For example, according to K.F. the musician from Southern California:

Ummm…her personality and her mannerisms. The feeling that she gives you when you're talking to her, or are with her at dinner, or when you spend time together. It's like being at ease, being comfortable. Feeling like, you're glad to be yourself… I guess ummm, interests, having interests that are compatible with one another. Physical appeal comes later, I think…I think it is all a part of what attracts me to woman.

D.M., a fire captain recently divorced from his wife of seventeen years who was White, expressed a similar response. I contacted D.M. by telephone on the basis of a referral from a mutual friend. At first guarded in his responses, he later warmed up and described the characteristics that most attracted him to a woman.

"Well believe it or not it is not color. Physical appearance is important…but its also personality… how she carries herself, her self esteem…beauty is in the eye of the beholder…"

Following this pronouncement, the forty-four-year-old firefighter later acknowledged that what had most attracted him to his wife was the way she looked. According to him, she was very, very pretty. She was a petite brunette. The two had met years before in high school.

It is worth noting that only a minority of the men I spoke with specifically stated a preference for particular physical features. What's more, an even smaller number of these men noted a preference for women who "looked White." Most of the men steered clear of doing so. Did the men purposefully avoid saying more about physical features in order to avoid discussion of what continues to be a provocative issue—that of a preference for features characteristic of a White phenotype? I can only speculate about this. However, several of the men talked about the conflicts they had had with other Blacks who accused them of either "selling out" or "wanting to be White."

Notes

1.   This belief is so pervasive that social psychologists have devoted significant effort to explicating its components. Within social psychology, the implicit association people make between beauty and goodness is called the "beauty is good" stereotype or "the beauty bias." Those who study it conclude that it is primarily comprised of people's ideas about the superior sociability of attractive people.

2.   See *The 1998 Report on Television* (New York: Nielsen Media Research, 1998).

3.   See the chapter by Sharon Bramlett-Solomon and Tricia Farwell, "Sex on soaps: An analysis of Black, White and Interracial Couple Intimacy," in *Facing Difference. Race, Gender and Mass Media,* ed. Shirley Biagi & Marilyn Kern-Foxworth (Thousand Oaks, Calif.: Pine Forge Press, 1997), 3-10.

4.   "Passing" refers to the process by which a minority group person (e.g., an African American) uses the fact of their resemblance to a majority group person (e.g., a White American) as a way of verifying their humanity, ensuring their dignity, and legitimizing their quest for prosperity. According to Harvard Law School Professor Randall Kennedy, "The classic racial passer in the United States has long been the 'White Negro,' an individual whose physical appearance allows him to present himself as 'White' but whose 'Black' lineage (typically only a very partial Black ancestry) makes him a Negro according to dominant racial rules." See pg. 283 in his book *Interracial Intimacies* (New York: Pantheon Books, 2003).

5.   See note 3. above, p. 9.

6.   Nielsen Media Research, 1998.

7.   See the chapter by Paul Farhi, "A Television Trend: Audiences in Black and White" In *Facing Difference. Race, Gender and Mass Media,* ed. S. Biagi & M. Kern-Foxworth (Thousand Oaks, Calif.: Pine Forge Press, 1994), 202-204.

8.   From *The State of Black America 2001.* Washington, DC: The National Urban League, 2001, p. 34.

9.   Halle Berry, whose mother is White, and whose father is presumably Black, is of mixed racial background. In the movie, she plays the wife of an African American man who is put to death. Ms. Berry's character then falls in love with the White prison guard who physically led her husband to his execution and then later carries out a graphic lovemaking scene with the actor Billy Bob Thornton who plays the guard.

10.   For a report of this research, see the article by Scott Coltraine and Melinda Messineo, "The Perpetuation of Subtle Prejudice: Race and Gender Imagery in 1990s Television Advertising," *Sex Roles 42* (2000): 363-389.

11.   From the book by July Williams, *Brothers, Lust and Love* (Houston, Tex.: Khufu Books, 1996), 51.

12.   See the provocative chapter by Jeffrey Yang and Angelo Ragaza, "The Beauty Machine," in *Facing Difference. Race, Gender and Mass Media,* ed. S. Biagi & M. Kern-Foxworth (Thousand Oaks, Calif.: Pine Forge Press, 1994), 11-15.

13.   This point was advanced more than 3 decades earlier by William Grier and Price Cobbs in *Black Rage* (New York: Basic Books, 1968).

14.   The chapter "Embracing Whiteness" in *The Color Complex* by Kathy Russell, Midge Wilson and Ronald Hall provides a thought-provoking discussion of this very issue. (New York: Anchor Books, 1996) 41.

15.   Interview with Yaphet Kotto by Amanda Spake appearing in *Salon* magazine (www.salon.com/12nov1995/feature/kotto.html), November 11, 1995.

16.   Ibid.

17.   See note 15. above, page 82.

18.   For an engaging discussion about the continuing politics of hair for Black women, see *Hair Story. Untangling the Roots of Black Hair in America*, by Ayanna Byrd and Lori Tharps (New York: St. Martin's Press, 2000).

19.   See pg. 34 of Bell Hooks' article "Straightening Our Hair," from *Sisters of the Yam*.

20.   Ibid, 35.

6

The Different Types of Interracial Relationships with Black Men

Relationships differ just as people do. No two relationships will function identically, though upon close inspection, similar patterns may be evident. This chapter examines the different types of interracial relationships involving Black men by considering the responses of the men I interviewed, and to a lesser degree, by considering some of the ways that these relationships have been represented in popular culture. A typology consisting of five types of interracial relationships involving Black men is proposed here. What follows is a detailed discussion of the factors that are associated with each of these types of relationships. Throughout this section, the candid responses of the men who were most representative of each type of relationship are highlighted.

Importantly, this typology does not speak to the experiences of every single Black man who is now or has been involved in an interracial relationship. It is limited to the experiences described by the men with whom I spoke for this project. There are some who might argue that the distinctions I have drawn among the men are too finite, and there are probably others who may see them as being too broad. But what most people will agree on is the fact that there are a variety of ways of representing these relationships. Consider an alternate typology presented by one writer who addressed the subject of Black men in interracial relationships in one chapter of his book called "Brothers, Lust and Love." According to Texas-based writer July Williams, there were three types of Black men who can be found in interracial relationships: the "revenge Rambo," the "status seeker," and the "circumstantial martyr."[1]

The most popular characterization of any type of interracial relationship involving Black men involves a description of the man as a rebel. Having been popularized in novels, film and television it attributes the interracial relationship to the Black man's rebellious motives. This characterization is similar to Williams' description of the "revenge Rambo." In actuality, it can be useful in understanding the motives of not just one person in the interracial relationship but both people. When the interracial relationship stems from its participants' desire to shock and rebel, the focus is on the stigma associated with them. Because these relationships are not regarded as "normal" and, consequently, likely to be beset with unique problems, people tend to believe that individuals who participate in them do so because of the social taboo associated with them.[2] For some couples, the desire to rebel stimulates their attraction.

Of course, this characterization of the interracial relationship as rebellious is not specific to the experiences of Black men. To the extent that there are well-known taboos operating against the formation of a particular type of interracial relationship, it is possible that its participants are motivated by the desire to rebel. However, given the unique hostility directed at interracial relationships between Blacks and Whites (particularly those between a Black man and a White woman), this aspect of rebellion may be most salient for Black/White interracial relationships. Furthermore, when the Black man himself views his interracial dating as a conquest or as a means of political expression, the "rebel" takes on a distinctively African American quality of experience. This may be the "ultimate way for some Black men as rebels to reclaim their status as men."[3] According to writer Williams, the Black man in such a relationship, the "revenge Rambo," exploits existing sexual myths about Black men's prowess, and as such, endorses the mantra "once you go Black, you'll never go back."

Alternatively, some writers have concluded that forces similar to those apparent within an economic marketplace regulate the formation and maintenance of interracial relationships. Consequently, they argue that individuals who participate in them do so in exchange for the rewards they receive.[4] Black men in interracial relationships, who actively seek out such relationships because of their beliefs about the rewards they receive as a result of their affiliation with a woman who is not Black, form the type of relationship referred to here as an "obsession." Any interracial relationship in which the participants describe their relationship in terms of the "souvenir" status of their mate or in terms of their beliefs about their mate's greater race-based social status, I refer to as an "obsession."[5] In Williams' tripartite typology, Black men in interracial relationships like this are called "status seekers." Williams sees these motives as resulting from their lowered self-esteem as well as concerns about inferiority that are elicited when in the presence of a Black woman. He suggests that in cases like this, Black women unwittingly remind Black men of what it is they most wish to forget about themselves.

What was most apparent in the descriptions provided by several of the men I spoke with was their devout (and often repeated) descriptions of themselves as "non-racist." I referred to the interracial relationship in which the man, as a way of explaining his involvement in an interracial relationship, suggested that first and foremost he was not racist as a "color-blind" relationship. In each of these cases, there was evidence of a certain degree of pride in what they regarded as their socialization to appreciate "all of humanity." For them, love was indeed "colorblind," and they consciously saw themselves as having evolved sufficiently enough to fall in love with someone from any race, creed, and culture. I think it can be argued that this type of individual is most consistent with Williams' "circumstantial martyr"—the Black man who sincerely just happened to fall in love with a woman of another race. On the other hand, the following characterization might correspond better to Williams' circumstantial martyr. The reader can decide.

For at least three of the men I interviewed, there appeared to be a note of apology in their recollections about how they came to be involved in an intimate interracial relationship. According to these men, they found themselves in relatively mainstream, homogenous environments, and had little choice in the matter of mate selection. Because of these circumstances, the label "lonely hearts" seemed applicable to their relationships. These men described the fact of their interracial relationship as being merely a matter of happenstance or fate.

Finally, in a small number of cases, some of the men indicated that they sought out their relationship and pursued their partners *because* of their different racial status. In each of these cases, the interracial relationship was described as having been sought after the demise of a particularly painful relationship with a Black woman. For these men, the circumstances of their involvement with a particular Black woman had come to symbolize their expectations about involvement with any Black woman. They consciously and explicitly made the choice to avoid romantic entanglements with all Black women. For this reason, the interracial relationship with this type of man is characterized here as a "retreat."

Admittedly, in a few of the cases, the decision to characterize a relationship in one way rather than another was difficult. Consider the case of L.G. who regarded himself as a "multiracial lover," and whose relationship I initially characterized as "color blind." Later, after reviewing the tape-recording of the interview a few times, I decided that the characterization of "retreat" best described his relationship. I also changed the characterization for the relationship described by the respondent DERRICK. Initially, characterized as "color blind," I subsequently came to view Derrick's relationship as being more representative of an "obsession."

One additional characterization of the Black man in an intimate interracial relationship is important to note. Though it does not appear to be applicable to any of the men I interviewed, it deserves to be mentioned here because of its notoriety and almost mythical status. It involves the description of the Black man as a "predator," the relationship as "predatory," and is most frequently applied when an interracial relationship involves a Black man and a White woman.

The depiction of the Black man as a predator has a long history. The roots of this characterization are located in the antebellum South, and it has been associated with Black men subsequently. In its most egregious form, the depiction of Black men as predators has been used as an excuse for White violence against Black men and women. This characterization, however inaccurate, says that Black men perpetually lust after White women and girls, and only with well-enforced laws coupled with threat of severe harm are they (Black men) able to refrain from their natural urges.

In general, the depiction of Black men as predators of White womanhood has justified the unmitigated abuse of African Americans, including both men and women. When Black men have been accused of transgressions against White womanhood, ranging from "illicit" intimate relations to physical assault and rape, retribution that was swift and merciless usually followed. This occurred even when the White woman in question was known to have initiated the relationship, or when the Black man who was accused provided indisputable evidence of his innocence of assault or involvement.

The characterization of the Black man as a predator has been so persistent a blemish upon the American psyche that a literary tradition popular during the earlier part of the twentieth-century century has evolved out of it. Borrowing from this characterization, writers of that period weaved the theme of the Black man as a predator into a variety of literary productions including novels, short stories and plays. In many of these vessels, Black men were characterized as depraved creatures that might at any time fall back into their natural ways and compromise the well-being and virtue of a White woman.[6] In other literary productions when the authors were genuine sympathizers of the plight of African Americans, or when they themselves were Black writers, the protagonist accused of predatory motives had some redeeming quality and either acted in self-defense, or was a noble, innocent victim of White racism.[7]

Today, Blacks and Whites are still familiar with the characterization of the Black man as a predator. This image persists because of the relative appeal of this negative stereotype that continues to be trotted out periodically when White womanhood is perceived to have been victimized by Black male sexuality. However, the characterization of the Black man as a predator now competes with other popular images of Black men in interracial relationships. Furthermore, because interracial relationships are no longer illegal, proportionally less publicity surrounds charges about a Black man having compromised the virtue of an innocent White woman. As a result, the notion of the Black man as a predator, though still well known, has become less popular a weapon against Blacks.[8]

Given this, it should not be surprising that none of the men I spoke with described themselves as predators; nor did any of the men make reference to this type of characterization.[9] The only reason I opted to discuss this depiction of the Black man in an interracial relationship at some length here was because of its notoriety as well as its prominent role in regulating certain forms of interactions between Blacks and Whites. As bizarre as it may be, one Black author and activist chose this characterization in describing his own motivation before his self-described intellectual transformation. In what is one of the most provocative descriptions of the notion of the Black man as predator, former Black Panther and political activist Eldridge Cleaver wrote about the evolution of his thinking and self-admitted decision to become a rapist following his initial release from prison. He said,

Somehow I had come to the conclusion that, as a matter of principle, it was of para-mount importance for me to have an antagonistic, ruthless attitude towards White women. The term rebel appealed to me, and at the time my parole date was drawing near, I considered myself to be mentally free –I was a "rebel." At the moment I walked out of the prison gate, my feelings toward White women in general could be summed up in the following lines:

'TO A WHITE GIRL'
I love you
Because you're White,
Not because you're charming
Or bright.
Your Whiteness
Is a silky thread
Snaking through my thoughts
In red hot patterns
Of lust and desire.
I hate you
Because you're White.
Your White meat
Is nightmare food.
White is
The skin of evil.
You're my Moby Dick,
White witch,
Symbol of the rope and hanging tree,
Of the burning cross.
Loving you thus
And hating you so,
My heart is torn in two
Crucified.[10]

For the former Black Panther, "rape was an insurrectionary act." And though he "delighted in defying and trampling upon the White man's law…and defiling his women," he admits to starting out "by practicing on Black girls in the ghetto." Cleaver's characterization of himself in this way is as provocative as it is rare. Few people in interracial relationships actually see themselves in this way, and even fewer freely admit to having motives as sinister as those that he ex-pressed. Though he saw himself as a rebel, he also freely admitted his desire to become a rapist, and as such was a predator.

The Rebellion

The characterization of the intimate interracial relationship as re-bellious, or as including a rebel, is well known and has not only appeared in books but, as noted earlier, it has also appeared in television and in movies. Presumably, African American men in interracial relationships who are characterized in this way, or who in some cases identify themselves as rebels, see their involvement in an intimate interracial relationship as one way of striking out at a social system from which they have been largely excluded. Here, it is the "forbidden" nature of the relationship that enhances its desirability. This type of a reaction is common when people perceive a threat to their freedom, and psychologists refer to it as a state of "psychological reactance."

When the interracial relationship was described by the individual as resulting from either his or his partner's efforts to rebel, I characterized it as a "rebellion." Because of the angst historically associated in America with Black men in interracial relationships with White women, the characterization of relationships such as this as rebellious has remained popular.

Within the sample of men I interviewed, only one of them explicitly disclosed this type of a sentiment. Because the depiction of the interracial relationship involving the Black man as a "rebellion" has "fed the dangerous myth that Black men would abandon their wives, lovers, children, relatives, and their community in a shameless and never-ending carnal hunt for White flesh,"[11] I have elected to describe this man carefully, and his remarks taken from my interview with him.

I met KEITH, a thirty-nine-year-old-year-old janitor, through a mutual acquaintance some years ago in Chicago. I knew that he had been married to two different White women over the years and had had a child with one of them. I contacted him and asked him whether he would be willing to talk about his involvement in interracial relationships. He was enthusiastic and the interview was subsequently conducted over the telephone. Keith spoke at length about his past, and the relationships he had had with White women.

> I guess when I was younger I wanted to be with a White girl because that was just what I wasn't supposed to do. I mean I went after them, and I always had a White girl back in the day. I was living the life. I was into all sorts of things. Being with White girls was just another thing I was into. Because I couldn't have it, or I mean I wasn't supposed to have them…because of that I went after it.

The ultimate relationship taboo in Keith's eyes was for him to marry a White woman. Even now many years later and after having married a Black woman with whom he now lived, he seemed to enjoy the fact that he had married two different White women on two different occasions. He said,

> You know I was married a couple of times to a White woman. Yeah, that was me...But that didn't last...I was doing all kinds of things. When we would go out and if there was a lot of Blacks, we always got stares. It was a trip. I would get a lot more attention from Black women when I was with her. From Black men too...If we went somewhere with a lot of Whites, you could just feel it. You could feel it in how they would treat you...I got the sense that they were not really supporting it...

Keith felt that his wives were also aware of the sometimes subtle and not so subtle reactions of others. But neither of them ever made an issue of it or made race an issue in their relationship. At least 2 times in the course of the interview, Keith informed me that "even in arguments they [his White wives] never once called me a 'nigger.'" It was clear that he was pleased about this and took it as evidence of his wives' non-prejudicial dispositions.

Although Keith may have waxed nostalgic when recalling his past, he was also clear about his feelings for his current wife, as well as one of the "perks" he attributed to being with a Black woman.

> "Its real hard being a Black man, especially with a White woman. You know, if you have been with a Black woman before you realize certain things...and it's just not the same."

Among other issues, Keith talked a great deal about his involvement in the "underworld." He was extremely matter-of-fact about his experiences in illicit activities. At times, he almost seemed to miss his past lifestyle that, on more than one occasion, resulted in brushes with the law. Ironically, several months after the telephone interview with KEITH, I learned from our mutual acquaintance that he had once again found himself behind bars.

The Obsession

For the relationship characterized as an "obsession," a preoccupation or fascination with specific attributes that are associated with the racial status of the partner exists. More often than not, these attributes are physical (e.g., skin color and facial features). The Black man in an interracial relationship who is an "obsessor" pursues women who are not Black because of his beliefs about the meaning of observed differences. More often than not, the differences that these men perceive to exist usually include beliefs about the relative superiority of women who are not Black. Of course, what is considered superior varies from person to person. For some it is skin color while for others it may be hair texture. But the point here is that the obsessor in an interracial relationship *especially* values his partner's different racial status, and he believes that it provides him with something greater than could be achieved with a Black woman. Whether it be a fascination with thin noses and lips or the sense of satisfaction he experiences by just being with women of other racial groups, the Black man who is an obsessor represents yet another type of individual involved in an interracial relationship.

What kind of person best typifies this characterization? According to the writer Michael Dyson who characterized O.J. Simpson's affection for the late Nicole Brown Simpson as a sexual obsession, "The obsessor fixes on the object of desire as a way of realizing his own desire. Hence, sexual obsession is a disguised form of narcissism. It ultimately refers back to itself. Such self-reference contains the seeds of the obsessor's dissatisfaction."[12] Although the author was specifically referring to O.J. Simpson, his point is relevant here because it makes clear that for obsessors, the quest for a mate of a different race is not only linked to a preoccupation with phenotypic features, like fair skin complexions and long straight hair, but it is also associated with concerns about self-identity and self-presentation.

As for the men interviewed, BRIAN the attorney who disclosed his preference for women "with non-Negroid features" represents this type of characterization well. Recall that when asked to provide a description of "an attractive woman," Brian noted his aversion to those features most often associated with women of African descent. Brian's preference for a woman who "doesn't look Black" is characteristic of an obsessor. What does this type of characterization suggest about Brian's own identity? Can we, as the author Dyson has done with respect to O.J. Simpson, infer something about his views of himself?

Perhaps one way of better understanding Brian's pronouncement is to provide a more detailed description of him. Brian is a fifty-one-year-old successful attorney who is divorced from his wife of seventeen years who is Black. His daughter, who currently attends a college in the area, often stays at his condominium. Brian, who stands about six feet, is a heavyset man and one who enjoys wearing stylish and even trendy clothes. He has a brown complexion, and his hair is lightly sprinkled with grey. He drives a luxury sedan and describes himself as "the quintessential bachelor."

My first impression of him was that of a man who was as pleased with himself as he was with his material possessions. Brian exudes a certain kind of confidence that borders on conceit. When asked to describe his current partner and intimate relationship, he indicated that he was currently intimately involved with seven different women! He counted off each of the women for me while providing information about each of their racial backgrounds. They included a Japanese woman, a Thai woman, two White women and three African American women. He went on to say that by mutual choice he was not currently in a "one-on-one" relationship with any one of those women.

Given that Brian had explicitly articulated a preference for women whose features did not "look Black," I was somewhat surprised that he counted three Black women within the ranks of his partners. I asked him to explain why that was so, given his expressed preference for women who did not look Black. He told me "I don't know...I am simply attracted to women who look a certain way." Apparently, the Black women with whom he was involved had relatively fair complexions with features most frequently associated with Whites, the kind of features he explicitly noted preferring.

Although Brian may be something of an enigma, it is likely that his stated preference for a particular phenotype is linked in some way to his vision of himself. Whether this type of stance results from a grandiose view of self or whether, as some have suggested, it results from low self-esteem, it is difficult to determine conclusively. What is clear is that Brian seeks women who least resemble women of African descent. Whether they were of European or Asian ancestry or were "Black" but fair with narrow noses, lips, and hips, his stated preference was for women who looked this way.

In some cases, the obsessors, who only pursue and have relationships with women from other races, have never dated or ever been involved with a Black woman. This was the case for another man I interviewed whose relationship I have characterized as an obsession. At the time of the interview, DERRICK, who was twenty-three years old had been married to his wife who was Mexican American for a little over a year. Halfway into the interview, he mentioned that when he was eighteen years old, he had fathered a son with another woman who was Cuban. He sees his son from time to time and provides the mother with financial support for him. At the time of the interview, he had no children with his wife.

I met Derrick during his lunch break in the cafeteria of the building where he was employed as an insurance enrollment representative. I contacted him after a friend who works with him obtained his permission to do so. When she heard about my interests, she immediately thought of Derrick and told me about a conversation the two of them had had. According to her, the two were discussing their opinions about beauty, when Derrick told her that until he was about seventeen years old, his idea of the most beautiful woman in the world was that of Wonder Woman.[13] Because Wonder Woman represented everything that was beautiful she was the protagonist of his day and night fantasies. Derrick also told his coworker that he believed that there was no such thing as an "unattractive White woman."

Derrick was not only enthusiastic about participating, but he seemed to be flattered at the invitation to be interviewed. He was an articulate young man who was slight in stature, somewhat nondescript, with a brown complexion. We talked during a tape-recorded interview for a little over an hour. At the outset, Derrick told me that he had had little experience in relationships and never gave much thought to the idea of interracial relationships.

> Actually I didn't think of interracial relationships until I got married…well, then again I guess I have to say a little bit before that. When I was in high school all my friends, who were, all my boys, that's what I call them…they were Black and everything. And, they dated a lot of women who weren't Black. But when it came to the point of asking who would they marry, they said in terms of "well you know I have to stay true to my Black princess." Which was kind of odd because I said "what woman would want you after your resume?" But I think that's the first time I actually thought of it…yeah, it was in high school.

When I asked Derrick whether his thinking about interracial relationships had changed since he had married, he said,

> "When I was younger, race didn't mean anything to me. Now that I'm married it means a lot….as far as culture goes, I mean. You're not only dealing with you and your partner, but you've got to deal with your families too… "

Derrick described the circumstances under which he first became involved in an interracial relationship. In a very self-deprecating manner, he said he knew that he was "always considered strange." When I asked him what he meant, he simply shrugged and was nonresponsive. He then went on to tell me about how he became involved with his wife. Apparently, because of his completely platonic relationship with her, he was invited to move in with her family when he began having problems with his own mother because of the birth of the child he had fathered with the Cuban woman. Though that move ultimately resulted in an intimate relationship with the woman who later became his wife, it also seemed to have triggered a perpetual state of anxiety in Derrick because of her family's reactions to him. He said, "Her mom, back in the past didn't like me because of my skin color...So, the relationship was so innocent as far as us being just friends. We had proved to everybody that we were strictly brothers and sisters. But, in a time of need, when I needed a place to take care of my son, their family let me move in with them."

Derrick spoke of having had a number of problems with his in-laws because he was Black. Being with his wife's family often required him to "tough it out." His wife's relatives frequently made racial slurs, and emphasized the fact of his Blackness. Not surprisingly, this tension clearly bothered Derrick.

> On her side of the family, they,um...it's funny, because when we're all around they say, you know, racial slurs. But some things that would offend my friends, they don't offend me.... They laugh, and they kid about it, and they think I'm oh so cool about it...But I told my wife that I don't like going around her family. And she says, "why?" And I said, "because if I want to be with a comedian then I can go around with Eddie Murphy...you know what I mean?

Derrick also talked about the extent to which he and his wife interacted socially with their peers and the extent to which they shared friends who were Mexican American and African American. He expressed regret about the fact that his wife did not feel comfortable around other Black people, including his friends and family. He elaborated with the following:

> "We don't have any friends together only because like I said, because of the culture thing, it would clash for the simple fact that I really couldn't go out with a whole bunch of Black people. I mean I could, but I'd probably end up alone by myself, instead of having my wife there. Even if she was there, you could tell that she would feel uncomfortable...."

Derrick said that when he mentioned this observation to his wife, that she did not appear to like being around his friends, her response was that it was not "a racial thing," but instead it was because she was not a sociable person. Derrick also said that he had had a number of problems with his own mother over the years. His mother raised him alone, and it was clear that the two had had a close, if sometime difficult, relationship. He saw a lot of the problems that he and his mother now had as directly related to the fact that his wife was Hispanic and, he added, "because she is not especially religious."

Clearly, there were problems that Derrick was aware of experiencing not just because he was in an interracial relationship but also because his wife and her family had real problems with him being Black. Yet, it was also clear that being her husband was an important aspect of his identity. These two thoughts were at odds for Derrick, and I suspect caused a significant strain for him.[14] About being Black, he said

> I know for a fact that when I was growing up I was always thinking I was just human, and purposefully not saying that I was Black. A lot of times a lot of Blacks that I run into want to say "yeah, I'm Black but I'm mixed." But I am Black, I can't do that, I mean can't or I guess I don't say that I'm mixed.... It's funny, I only became comfortable with being Black, and not like those other people who want to be mixed, when I got married.

One might expect that the latter comment by Derrick would be followed up with some reference to a particular moment of enlightenment or event. But with the exception of his hostile encounters with his in-laws, this epiphany does not seem to have occurred. For the time being, Derrick has decided to endure the repeated racial slurs. As a result, and admittedly because of my awareness of his ideal of female beauty, I elected to characterize his relationship as an obsession.

One other man's relationship, that of A.D. who was mentioned in an earlier section, can also be characterized as an obsession. Recall that A.D., the son of Haitian immigrants, had been married to his wife, who was born in France, for twelve years. According to A.D., who was born in the United States, although the racial status of his wife mattered little to him, the fact that she was foreign featured prominently in his attraction to her. Given France's past colonial domination of Haiti, many Haitians today see their first allegiance to France and elect to identify with White French people rather than other Black people from the Caribbean, Americas, or Africa. Presumably, this case was true for A.D. and his parents. The fact of his wife's Whiteness was secondary to her French status. For A.D., it was all about culture:

> "The color never really has been an issue. It was more about upbringing and culture. In my relationships there were always two issues to deal with when it came to dating: there was my family's immigrant perspective, and there was also the Black/White difference that was more a matter of class."

Importantly, A.D. acknowledged never having had a relationship with a Black (American or Haitian) woman. Because of his professed concerns about culture, he seems to have consciously and purposefully avoided any relationships with African American women. He attributed his exclusive involvement with women who

were not Black to concerns about culture that he, in turn, attributed
to parental influence:

> My folks would have been most pleased and accepting of a Haitian woman. They
> would have preferred for me to have been with a Haitian woman first and foremost. But
> that wasn't happening. They were least excited with the idea of me being with an
> American woman, Black or White. They've got this thing about American values....But
> the fact that my wife comes from France, they saw this as a good thing. It's sort of like
> a compromise for them.

For A.D., culture rather than race was more influential in his selection of mate. His story is instructive in that it underscores the
unique way that race has been constructed in American society. My
decision to cast his relationship as an obsession reflects the fact that
A.D. described his preference for women who are not African American in terms of an immigrant's ubiquitous concerns about the "cultural divide." He had never before dated a Black woman, largely
because, like his parents, he was concerned about the potential for
cultural differences to emerge in a relationship with an American
woman, Black or White.

> "My parents were never really accepting of a woman who was an American. They were
> like...it was a cultural thing, a class thing about upbringing. They never felt that the
> American society gave enough of that upbringing to its people."

Thus, culture not race was what A.D. believed to be the defining
feature in his selection of a mate. Importantly however, although
A.D. sees race as separate and unrelated to culture, the two are inex-
tricably intertwined. For a Black man (in this case, a first generation
American) to express a preference for a person who is not American, effectively eliminates all African American women as potential
mates. For this reason, A.D. is best characterized here as an obsessor.

The Color Blind Relationship

Among the men interviewed, at least two were quite explicit about
their lack of racial prejudice, and they attributed their repeated involvement in intimate interracial relationships to this particular virtue. These men conceptualized their beliefs about interracial intimacy in terms of their non-prejudicial self-image. According to them,
because they were socialized to appreciate everyone, they were ca-
pable of loving anyone, regardless of that person's racial status. Although all of the men in the study may have thought of themselves
this way, only the men whose relationships I've characterized as
"color blind" were emphatic about this point.

This was certainly the case for WARREN, a forty-seven-year old African American man who grew up in Southern California, who was living and working in the Long Beach section of Los Angeles county at the time of the interview. Warren was an impressive figure. He stood well over six feet and was physically fit. The latter was one of the unanticipated rewards that came from his extensive bike-riding activities, which also served as his primary way of getting around.

Warren was dark brown, fashionably bald, and a pleasant, affable man. At the time that I met him (we both patronized the same local bike shop), he was employed as a gardener at a local nursery and was renting a small room in an apartment building in the beachside community of Long Beach, California. On a table in his room was a picture of his teenage daughter. At first glance, she looked like an attractive teenager who happened to be White. Warren's contribution to her genetic make-up was only apparent upon very close inspection. Warren had been estranged from her mother, who was White, for many years. He expressed regret when he noted that he only saw his daughter "from time to time."

At the time of the interview, Warren was not involved with anyone, but he had recently come out of an eight-year relationship with another woman who was also White. Warren began our conversation by telling me his thoughts about interracial relationships in general.

> "I think interracial relationships are fine. As far as I'm concerned, I have no real problems with them. I think that all relationships should be based on individuality...."

Warren saw nothing particularly remarkable about his involvement in an interracial relationship because he was "raised to appreciate all people." As he explained it,

> My family is real open-minded about things like that. There's no color lines in my family at all...None of my friends have had any problems either because in the neighborhood I grew up in, everything was pretty interracial. My parents always... I mean I was raised up in interracial relationships all the way through. The neighborhood I grew up in was that way. If there were any problems, I wasn't aware of it......

Without prompting from me, Warren spent a fair amount of time describing certain economic realities that he believed often posed problems for interracial relationships. Based on his description of his ex-partner's employment ("she worked in an office in the telecommunications field") and his efforts at that time to enroll in a national culinary institute, his point seemed to be particularly self-descriptive. Ironically, though, he made a point of saying that this was not the case for him personally.

> I see problems that I haven't personally had to deal with myself, but I do see problems with an interracial relationship where for example uh, either or, mostly if the female is working in a corporate environment and the spouse or mate is invited or involved in any type of function with her job, I see where there would be a problem…where pressure would be put on her at her job because of that type of situation. I do see that….You know it may prevent her from a promotion or something like that…social gatherings with her co-workers, I see that. Mostly from the males.

Warren noted that when he was out with his partner, there were often uncomfortable reactions from others. He recalled that if he pointed it out to her she was "usually totally oblivious to their reactions and could have cared less." I asked him why he thought it was that he was aware of other people's reactions and his partner was not. He said,

> Well because, umm…my being Black and I have to deal with this. I have to be aware, and them not, you know I don't think that they are…as a matter of fact with her, I didn't know her parents for a long time, and we were adults at that time. I would notice it because it, the racial tension, just because I know it exists. I know how people observe it in a negative way.

He went on to describe how this situation was inconsistent with the circumstances under which he was raised:

> It just so happens, where I was raised, I was never raised in an all Black community or anything, so I didn't have to deal with experiences other people I know have been in…and that barrier is more or less instilled in them from childhood. I wasn't exposed to this, as much. I was raised to appreciate all human beings.

At the end of the interview, Warren had some additional thoughts. As an afterthought, I kept the tape running. Ironically, at this point, he became most animated about what it was he was saying:

> What is this [being with someone of another race] detrimental to? It's just too small for them to magnify so much. And if people would at least take the time to understand different cultures, you'd get around a lot better….
>
> I like meeting other cultures…see that's why I, I get along with the Mexican culture real well because where I grew up is one of the very few places in Southern California where Blacks and Browns get along. This town? No way! And, as a whole? Nope. That's why when I moved here I was shocked, you know, yeah, because where I grew up, I mean that's why I get along with a lot of different people because they're amazed that I know as much about their culture as I do. Well I was raised around them, that's why. And, I think if you have an understanding of a culture… See the media, like for example, the media they feed a lot of negative ideas about our culture…it feeds these ignorant people that have no clue. They think we're all criminals. They think we're all…and they are like so afraid, they're afraid to talk to us…

As a result of my conversation with Warren, I came to see his periodic involvement in interracial relationships as a reflection of his color-blind approach to seeing the world. Though he was aware of the problems in society that result from anti-Black racism, he continued to advocate an appreciation for all. In short, apart from the problems other people pose, interracial relationships are "just like any kind of relationship if you appreciate people based on individuality," according to Warren.

In addition to Warren, I characterized another man's relationship as color-blind. I met M.B., the thirty-one-year old personal trainer through an acquaintance of mine who happened to be related to him. After obtaining a Bachelor's degree from a historically Black university located on the East Coast, M.B. moved across the country to California and settled in Los Angeles. He was originally from the same small town where I lived in Central Illinois before I moved west. M.B. was an attractive man with a caramel-brown complexion who was just short of six feet. After contacting him at the suggestion of his cousin, he agreed to meet with me at a coffee shop in his neighborhood. We met first at the apartment he shares with a roommate, and I followed him to the coffee shop from there.

At the time of the interview, M.B. had been dating a twenty-eight-year-old woman he described as "Jewish and White" for about a year and a half. M.B. told me that he had had a number of dating experiences and had previously dated women from a variety of racial groups. As for his current girlfriend, he met her at work, and noted that their relationship "just sort of happened." And as luck would have, according to M.B., both of their families were "cool with it."

> Because my family is all mixed up anyway, they really wouldn't have a problem. My mother has White blood in her and she looks Spanish, so me being with a White woman is not really a problem. Besides they taught me to appreciate everyone. We're not prejudiced people, you know.

I asked him to elaborate on this point, and he explained that,

> We view people as people. For us, color just doesn't matter.... Sometimes when my girlfriend and I hang out, I'm the only Black person around, and sometimes she's the only White person. And that's just fine. It's no big problem…being with someone from another race provides you with an education of another culture.

I characterized M.B.'s relationship as color blind because according to him neither he nor his girlfriend think much about their race and because both have previously dated people from other racial groups. M.B. noted having had relationships with Black, White, and Hispanic women. As it happens, prior to meeting M.B., his cousin disclosed that although he referred to his relationship with the White woman as being monogamous, he maintained a covert intimate relationship with another woman who was Black and with whom his cousin was personally acquainted. At one time, he and the Black woman had openly dated, but they had since broken up. Not surprisingly, M.B. did not discuss this arrangement with me, nor did I bring it up. M.B. epitomizes the image of the "multiracial lover" and prides himself on having no racial prejudices.

The Retreat

I interviewed another man at the home of an African American man I was dating at the time. The latter introduced me to him because he knew of my interests in this project and his friend's serial involvement in interracial relationships. L.G. was thirty-four-years-old, and single at the time of the interview. He was employed in the finance industry and resided in the Philadelphia area. L.G. was of a medium brown complexion and wore a short curly Afro hairstyle. He was about 5'6," and had a well-developed physique. He had recently had a relationship with a woman who he described as being "Mexican."

L.G. began the interview by describing his own racial status as "multiracial." Later during the course of the interview he spoke at length about being "Native American mixed with Black" and pointed to his facial features and his hair emphasizing its curly texture. He told me that his ex-girlfriend once told him that she had initially approached him because she thought he was "Black Puerto Rican." L.G. also said that he was proficient in Spanish.

Like M.B., the color blind lover, L.G. graduated from a historically Black college and indicated having had previous relationships with American women who were Black, Mexican, and on one occasion, Vietnamese. In the case of his most recent relationship, he said his parents were not only accepting of the woman but also happy for him.

> "Although they never met her, they used to talk to her over the telephone...so they were always very receptive. They were just like, well, don't really look at the color of her skin, look at the content of her character. I know that sounds like an offshoot of Martin Luther King, but that's the way they have always been."

Later in the interview, L.G. talked about his appreciation for all cultures, which he attributed to his "multiracial heritage."

"I love all cultures. I think that each culture has something that we can teach each other... And, it makes sense because of my own multiracial heritage."

Ironically, however, although L.G. expressed an appreciation for all cultures, he was not as open-minded about the prospect of intimacy with an African American woman. L.G. spent a fair amount of time describing some of his friends'—in particular Black female friends'—reactions to his interracial relationships. He said:

One person was almost to the point of saying "Well, you're offending me," And I was just like, "Oh, I'm offending you, huh? How am I offending you?" And they said, "Well, aren't there any quality Black females out there?" And I said, "Well, at this point in my life one thing I don't like to fool around with is a lot of bull. I don't like to fool around with a lot of games and a lot of nonsense. I'm very much into my career, and I have my master's degree. I have a strong sense of who I am and where I want to go, and so far the Black females that I've come into contact with haven't had their act together... financially, emotionally...and spiritually, or any of those types of things. So... I guess I tend to back it up with that statement every time, and then people would kind of back off from me."

By his own admission, L.G. has "backed off" from relationships with Black women. Although he could recount having had relationships with them previously, he no longer regarded them as potentially viable partners. About a year after the interview took place, I learned from our mutual friend that L.G. was overseas where he was meeting his fiancée face-to-face for the first time. Apparently, after a lengthy correspondence in cyberspace with an Indian woman, he "popped the question." The two had decided to marry, and he made the journey to the far East to see her in person and to meet her family. Several months later, she joined him, and the two were married in a ceremony in his hometown. Three months after their wedding, the couple proudly announced the upcoming arrival of their first child.

I characterized L.G. was as a "retreatist" because of his explicit disavowal of Black women. According to him, they failed to measure up and were generally "economically, emotionally, or spiritually" lacking. As for economic viability, it is interesting to note that his new wife rarely works outside of the home. Apparently, his requirements for a relationship with an African American woman were not the same for a relationship with a foreign born Indian woman.

The second individual whose interracial relationship I characterized as a "retreat" was the first person I formally interviewed for this project. One of my relatives introduced K.F. to me. He was a very tall, solidly-built man with a very fair complexion who was always casually dressed. He had freckles, and each time that I saw him, he wore his "uniform" of baggy shorts and a tee shirt. At the time of the interview, he lived in a suburb of Los Angeles and was dating a young woman who had recently emigrated from the Philippines.

K.F. was a musician who earned his principal income performing musical accompaniment for commercial jingles and occasionally playing back up for live entertainers. Since the interview, I learned that K.F. married his girlfriend and the two moved to Las Vegas where they currently reside. He is now a permanent back-up musician for a well-know country music vocalist. K.F. had been divorced for several years from his ex-wife, a Black woman.

K.F. told me that his family was "very open to interracial relationships," and he said that both of his older brothers were in interracial marriages. At the outset of the interview, K.F. said that he "did not have any particular thoughts about interracial relationships and no strong thoughts about them." Although what K.F. said during the interview was illuminating, I actually chose to interview him because of what his friend told me *before* introducing me to him. According to his friend, K.F. had stated on a number of occasions that he would "never become involved with a sister again." Because his relationship with his ex-wife had been so combative and the circumstances surrounding the dissolution of his marriage were so painful, he consciously chose to avoid relationships with any Black woman.

Both of the men that I have characterized as "retreatists" had had previous relationships with Black women. But following the end of these relationships, these men decided to avoid any subsequent relationships with Black women. Their aversion results from specific events that took place in the relationship as well as the antagonism that occurred with its end.

Interestingly, a review of the autobiography of the pioneering Black boxer Jack Johnson reveals similar motives for becoming involved with non-Black women. In 1908, he became the first African American to obtain the world's heavyweight title. During his late teenage years, Johnson was seriously involved with a young, light-skinned Black woman, Mary Austin. Shortly after, he was linked with a Black prostitute whose name was Clara Kerr. Apparently, Johnson regarded these two relationships as pivotal to his later exclusive pursuit of White women. On one occasion, he publicly stated that "The heartaches Mary Austin and Clara Kerr had caused me, led me to forswear colored women and to determine that my lot henceforth would be cast only with White women."[15] True to his word, Johnson, who lived a public life long after his reign as heavyweight champion, was not seen again in the company of a Black woman.

The Lonely Hearts

Among the men interviewed, there were two who, unlike the others, regarded their involvement in an intimate interracial relationship as a result of serendipitous circumstances. These men neither professed a preference for women of another race, nor, as was the case with the "retreatists," did they express an aversion to Black women. Although these two men differed with respect to the specific circumstances surrounding the initiation of their interracial relationship, the men were similar in that they both acknowledged no one could possibly have been more surprised about them being in an interracial relationship than they themselves. In both cases, they noted that at the time they met their future wives, they were open to having an intimate relationship. But both men also said that they never imagined that the woman with whom they would eventually become involved and marry would be White. The situation, that is the interracial nature of the relationship, prompted considerable introspection for the two men I have described here as "lonely hearts."

The label "lonely heart" was appropriate for W.G. who, at the outset of the interview, was explicit about his initial opposition to interracial relationships. For him, being in this type of relationship was inconsistent with the way he saw himself and what he envisioned for his future. But today, interracial relationships, particularly those with Black men and White women, no longer elicited distinctive reactions from W.G. At the time of the interview, he said he had finally become comfortable with the fact that his wife was White, and as evidence of this he no longer noticed the reactions of others. He also said that although he had experienced doubt early on in the relationship because of her racial status, this was no longer the case. Enough time had passed, and the two had been together for longer than he had ever dreamed. He stated somewhat emphatically that the two were very happily married.

Another person with whom I spoke and who was first introduced in chapter 3 was particularly expressive. Although my communication with DAMON was limited to telephone conversations and email correspondence, his responses and his description about the circumstances, which initiated his sixteen-year marriage, were particularly insightful. At the time of the interview, Damon was a forty-eight-year old psychotherapist. I contacted him at the suggestion of a family friend who works with his wife who is White. The couple lives in St. Louis, Missouri, where they are raising their two children.

At the outset of the first telephone conversation, Damon described how he met his wife.

> "We were both in the St. Louis Symphony chorus. We both sing and still do. When I saw her I was immediately attracted to her. It was her overall immediate physical appearance, and she had some great legs… "

The fact that she was White caused him a fair amount of consternation. He had some serious reservations about their relationship. He said,

> "I prayed for my wife, and I got what I needed. But it was like, 'Wait a minute, she is White!' and God said, 'you didn't say anything about race.' So when you pray you had better be specific… "

At a later point in the interview, Damon described what he believed were the many other reasons interracial couples could have for being together.

> "There is a run of the gamut from where you have Black males with White females because he is looking to boost his ego. Or, in some cases because she is trying to rebel against her parents. And there are those who just simply avoid talking about race… "

Damon was also aware that some people believe that Black men's self hate propels them to seek out interracial relationships. He was adamant that this was not the case for himself. He was also curious about the other explanations some of the other men I interviewed had given for their own involvement in interracial relationships. In an email message he sent me after our initial telephone conversations, he asked,

> But I am curious, in that regard, as to what else you've heard. The reason being that I have been accused of that very thing [self hate], and I didn't like it. It is almost impossible to explain to some Black women and here I was doing the same thing. So what else did you hear?

I wrote back the following,:

> When I said that the explanation of self-hate for some Black men's involvement with women who aren't Black is too neat, and that there is more to it than that, I was referring to the responses of men who are vehemently opposed to that type of characterization of

themselves, and yet who are simultaneously hung up on Western standards of beauty. These are men who are aware of the notion of self-hate, deny it, appear to love and even cultivate the traits in themselves that identify them as "Black," but who can't (or won't) accept such characteristic features in the women they are involved with (e.g., kinky hair, full lips, broad noses, etc.)....

As luck would have, my response to Damon was based on having already interviewed all but two of the men in the study. Damon was the twenty-third of the twenty-five men with whom I spoke, and, consequently, as is apparent from my response, I was able to draw from the preceding men's comments in formulating my response for him.

Notes

1. The writer July Williams discusses, among other things, Black men in interracial relationships in his book *Brothers, Lust & Love.* (Houston, Tex.: Khufu Books, 1996). Although his characterizations are consistent with those included in the typology that I have derived, the types of interracial relationships described by the men in this study suggested at least two additional characterizations.

2. No doubt, social taboos exist to sanction all forms that interracial relationships assume. However, the taboo is particularly extreme for those relationships involving Blacks and Whites. For further discussion of this taboo see the article by Ernest Spaights and Harold Dixon, "Socio-Psychological Dynamics in Pathological Black-White Romantic Alliances," *Journal of Instructional Psychology 11* (1984): 132-138.

3. From Devon Cardabo's chapter "The Construction of O.J. Simpson as a Racial Victim," in the book *Black Men on Race, Gender, and Sexuality: A Critical Reader* also edited by him, p. 174 (New York: New York University Press, 1999).

4. These rewards can be monetary but can just as likely be intangible, as in the case of individuals who receive enhanced social status and privileges, as well as greater social mobility and access.

5. One popular criticism of many of today's most successful Black professional athletes and entertainers is based on this particular characterization of interracial relationships. The critique is directed at those African American men who, after having reached a pinnacle of success, appear to seek out interracial relationships. According to critics, these men regard their affiliation and public display of affection with women who are not Black as, in some way, symbolic of their achievement and success. A number of these men were previously married to Black women long before they achieved their greatest successes.

6. The celebrated 20th century American writer William Faulkner's *Light in August* illustrates well this literary style (New York: Cape & Smith, 1931). The protagonist of this intense dramatic tale who is bi-racial transgresses Southern social norms by co-habitating with a White woman, and then brutally murdering her.

7. See Richard Wright's *Native Son* and 2. Harper Lee's *To Kill a Mockingbird* as literary examples in which the African American male "predator" acts in self-defense, or is completely innocent, respectively.

8. It is important to note however that this characterization continues to linger in Americans' consciousness. It represents a fundamental component of White racism in the United States, and as such it still musters power to mobilize White antipathies towards African Americans as a group.

9.   This is not particularly surprising given that such an admission or self-description is completely negative. The person who is a predator is dangerous and immoral. Consequently, it is safe to assume that because of common concerns about self-presentation any reasonable (i.e., mentally normal) person would avoid this type of characterization of themselves.

10.   Excerpt from Eldridge Cleaver's book *Soul on Ice* (New York: Dell Publishing, 1968).

11.   From p. 18 in *Beyond O.J.* by Earl O. Hutchinson (Los Angeles, Calif.: Middle Passage Press, 1996).

12.   From p. 29 in *Race Rules* by Micheal E. Dyson (New York: Vintage Books).

13.   The Marvel Comics action figure Wonder Woman appeared in a cartoon and television series. In the latter, she was played by the actress Lynda Carter, an attractive, buxom blue-eyed White woman.

14.   The experience of cognitive dissonance is well established in the social psychological literature. The theory describing it suggests that having two apparently inconsistent cognitions is uncomfortable and prompts a person to find ways to resolve the dissonance psychologically. This can include a tendency to elevate one's thoughts over the other, or by consciously denigrating one rather than the other cognition. In Derrick's case, this involves the dissonance he experiences in knowing that he has married into a Mexican American family, coupled with the knowledge that because he is Black he is not fully accepted. He appears to have resolved at least some of the angst that comes from this state of affairs by downplaying the impact that their racism has had upon him. How long this will continue to be an effective strategy for Derrick remains to be seen.

15.   From pg. 37 in *Jack Johnson. Heavyweight Champion* by Robert Jakoubek (New York: Chelsea House Publisher, 1990).

7

Challenges in Dealing with
Other People's Reactions

In an earlier section of this book, I noted that although the number of interracial relationships has steadily increased since the 1960s Civil Rights Movement, they occur with much less frequency than do relationships involving individuals of the same race.[1] I also pointed out that interracial relationships in which the man is Black occur even less frequently than do interracial relationships with men of other races. Given that these types of relationships are rare, and given that many people still think of interracial marriages as a violation of some sort of taboo, reactions to interracial couples are often quite unique.[2] Whereas couples with the same racial status can take certain attitudes and reactions for granted, this is certainly not the case for the interracial couple. Furthermore, the race and gender of the perceiver (the person the couple is interacting with) and the perceiver's own experiences in relationships also influence their reactions to the interracial couple.[3] In addition to these influences, there is the added detail concerning the fact that people's reactions to the couple are also affected by the race, gender, and economic status of both members of the couple.[4]

All of the men with whom I spoke had something to say about the various ways that others have reacted to their relationship. In some cases, they spoke at length about the reactions of members of their own families, and in cases they discussed the reactions of their partners' families. Some of the men also talked about the different ways that their friends, acquaintances, and coworkers had responded to their relationship. In addition to their answers to my questions about the reactions of family and friends, the men also described reactions of strangers to them and to their mates. These reactions ranged from verbal threats to actual rejection from business establishments. I also asked the men whether there were certain people who were more likely to react negatively (or positively) to the inter-racial couple. They noted the people who were most likely to react negatively to them when they were out in public with their partner. Oftentimes this entailed a discussion of the reactions of White men and Black women.

All in the Family

Among the married men interviewed, family reactions were par-ticularly revealing. It is worth noting that the way that a person re-acts to news of a son's (or daughter's) involvement in an interracial relationship says a lot about that individual's own experiences, be-liefs, and biases. Regardless of their age, all of the married men in the sample discussed reactions of their relatives and in-laws that they specifically attributed to the interracial nature of the marriage. It may come as somewhat of a surprise to note that not all of the reactions were negative. Quite a few of the men, even those who hadn't mar-ried, said that their families had no problems with their relationships and had accepted their partners completely from the beginning.

This was clearly the case for BARRY, a forty-seven-year-old jazz musician. I interviewed Barry at his home in St. Albans, New York. where he lived with his mother, his sister, and niece. He was an attractive, youthful man with a fair complexion. At the time of the interview, he had recently returned from an extended stay in Japan where he had been involved in a serious relationship with a thirty-three-year old Japanese woman. In the months immediately follow-ing his return from Japan, there had been talk about his girlfriend visiting him in the United States. At the time of the interview, that had not happened, and seemed increasingly unlikely. I spoke with him shortly after he had officially ended the long distance relation-ship with the Japanese woman.

When I asked Barry about his family's reaction to news of his involvement with his Japanese girlfriend he said,

"There were no problems whatsoever. My family has always been completely open-minded when it comes to interracial relationships...I mean, I've brought White women over here for dinner, and the whole nine...and they always treated her like they would treat anybody else."

Barry spoke similarly of his partner's family, which he had met while he was in Japan. He said that they were extremely fond of him, and not surprisingly, thought of him first and foremost as an American. Although this reaction is common for Americans abroad, African Americans often find it surprising when traveling to foreign countries. For Barry, family reactions, whether those of his own family or those of his partners,' were very positive, and they posed no real problems for him.

Barry's description of his and his girlfriend's family's reactions to the interracial (and international) relationship was ideal. Rarely, did most of the men speak of both sets of families having such positive reactions. In many ways, Barry's description of his situation was quite similar to that which one well-known interracial couple wrote about in a book about the evolution of their relationship. In that book, *Love in Black and White*, Black South African Mark Mathabane and his wife Gail, a White American, describe their families' reactions to their relationship.[5] Most notable were Mark's recollections of his mother's reaction to Gail. He wrote,

> My mother knew from previous conversations that Gail was White, but not once did she make her color an issue. This hardly surprised me. Her judgment has always been based on one criterion: their character. As long as Gail was a good human being, was not lazy, did not smoke or drink, was respectful and compassionate, and loved me as much as I loved her, my mother unreservedly approved of our relationship.

Gail's parents, on the other hand, appeared to be more concerned with the challenges the couple would face than they were about Mark's race. In another section of the book, Gail described an exchange she had with her father concerning her relationship with Mark. She wrote that her father had said,

> It's the first time that you've gone out with someone who's a real class act—who's on your intellectual and creative level. He's a real prince. And one assumes that princes and princesses belong together. But that's not always true. There are other issues to consider and, oh "—he sobbed again—"it's so tragic."[6]

Although her parents were taken aback and somewhat alarmed by her decision to marry a Black South African man, they gradually came to realize that she was in love and would suffer more without Mark in her life. Their book about their relationship includes photographs of the happy family including Mark and Gail, their new-born babies, and in-laws.

Unfortunately, not all of the men described family reactions as positively as either Barry's, or the Mathabanes'. A fair number of the men with whom I spoke mentioned having had specific problems with family members because of the interracial nature of their relationship. CHESTER, who was introduced first in chapter 5, had to deal with the extremely negative reactions of his partner's family.

I interviewed Chester during the course of a long distance telephone call while he was at work. He specifically asked that I contact him at work because he could talk at length and do so uninterrupted. A mutual friend of ours, an African American woman with whom he'd had a professional relationship, had arranged the introduction. Chester was articulate and very cooperative. He was happy to talk about his marriage and himself. On the demographic questionnaire completed for each of the men interviewed, Chester indicated that his wife's educational background included "some high school" and that she was employed part-time by a moving company. Chester, whose wife was White, had a college degree and was employed as a financial analyst for a large company in Fort Wayne, Indiana.

Only after we had talked for some time did Chester reveal that he was the offspring of an interracial marriage between his mother who was White and his father who was Black. He considered himself to be "Black," although he noted that he had suggested to his children that they "might have a better break if they classified themselves as White."

Even though it happened well over ten years ago, he clearly remembered how upset his wife's father had been when the two first began dating. According to Chester, his wife's father was extremely angry about their relationship. As luck would have, his future father in law not only had to contend with his daughter's involvement with a Black man, but because the couple had unexpectedly become pregnant, he was forced to face the reality of having grandchildren of mixed races. Not surprisingly, this did not go over very well. As Chester said,

> "Yeah, he was real upset about it in the beginning. He had a problem when he found out that she was pregnant by me... It was difficult at first, but it's been so long now, he's gotten over it...Our relationship is a lot different now, its ok now, so much time has passed and so much other stuff has happened."

Chester and his wife were born and raised in Indiana. His father-in-law's initial reaction to the relationship reflected his own staunch, Midwestern upbringing—an upbringing that Chester believed had discouraged intimate interracial interactions. Although Chester's own parents also lived in Indiana, they had had different experiences that precipitated their own involvement in an interracial relationship. Not surprisingly, their reactions to his relationship were quite different. Chester talked about this, and acknowledged that this "open-mindedness" was limited to members of his immediate family only, which, he was quick to point out, consisted of his mother and father only. The same could not be said for his half brothers and half sisters who were his mother's children from an earlier marriage to a White man.

> "There weren't any negative reactions to my relationship in my immediate family. They were okay with it because my dad's Black and my mom's White. My mom and dad are interracial... Maybe, yeah there is some negative stuff with my stepbrothers and stepsisters...but not with my mom and dad."

Another man to whom I spoke also described negative reactions from his girlfriend's family. Although the relationship that J.H. described had ended many years before, he talked about his experience as though it were yesterday, and he still seemed bitter. Time had not dimmed his recollections of his ex-girlfriend's family's reactions. His girlfriend was White, and the two had met while he was working on a fine arts degree at New York University. The relationship lasted for a number of years, and since that time, he had lived and worked as an actor in the New York City area. At the time of the interview, J.H. was fifty-eight years old, and worked regularly as a theater and television actor. I'd met J.H. many years earlier through a member of my own family and contacted him by telephone. The interview was conducted over the course of two telephone conversations. J.H. spoke eloquently (his voice training was apparent), and he was charming.[7]

J.H. had little to say about his own family's reactions because, as he put it, "I don't deal with my family...haven't for years... ." According to him, the worst of the reactions came from his girlfriend's family, which responded strongly and abusively even when they were just friends and had not yet become romantically or sexually involved with one another.

> In the beginning we became like brother and sister. We were very close, and she was always with me. There was no romance. During this time, one of her father's friends saw us out somewhere, I forget where exactly, and he told her father something. The next time she saw her father, he pulled a gun on her and threw her out of the house. She came to my apartment, and from then on we just started living together.

He went on to say,

> Let me tell you, her family was not with it. They had to keep it from the old grandmother.

They didn't want to tell her for fear that the news was so bad, that it would harm her. Her whole family was against us being together. Once I remember, her cousin who was a cop insulted her. He went off on her, and actually threatened her. He wanted her to terminate the relationship. They were really quite prejudiced. But then of course some of that had to do with the period of time because we began dating in the seventies...

D.M., the firefighter introduced in chapter 5, also described hostile reactions from his partner's family. In his case, his in-laws reacted most negatively to his marriage to their daughter, which was in direct contrast to his family's reactions. He described his parents as being "pretty open." And, he said, "as long as they are not stealing or doing drugs, they're okay with me being with them." But as for his wife's parents, he said:

They were definitely against it. Her father was especially against it. Her mother was a little better. Things eventually loosened up after our first daughter was born, but that was five years into our marriage! I'll never forget it, one Thanksgiving Day he called me up and invited me over to dinner. After that things changed.

According to the men described here, there are many different ways that family members expressed their opposition to the interracial relationship. Some did so by talking or arguing, and others resorted to other tactics. For GARY, who was introduced in an earlier section, dealing with the in-laws was one of the biggest challenges early on his marriage. His in-laws, who were White, were very unhappy about their daughter's marriage to a Black man. After the initial confrontation in which they vocally protested the marriage, their opposition was expressed in other more subtle ways.

Any problems that occurred between my wife, that is my ex-wife, and my family had to do with personality differences. They were just different people. But that was not so with her family. Personality had nothing to do with it. Eventually her father got over it, but her mother never did. Subtle things were done. Things like never having our pictures up on the wall where all the other siblings' ones were. All of their pictures were there where they appeared with their spouses, they would all be up on the wall, but ours never was.

Although the reactions of their partners' families were problematic for each of the men discussed up to this point, some of the other men noted the less than enthusiastic reactions of their own families. For example, C.R. talked about his mother's reactions to his twenty-seven-year-old White girlfriend. Interestingly, his mother actually referred me to him, so when I asked him whether his family had reacted differently to his girlfriend because she was White, I was not at all surprised that he said,

Yes, I definitely think so…they have a different sort of reaction. It's mostly my mom….I couldn't tell you about how my sister feels. It's with moms…you know how it is, they have different ideas about who you should date. But it's never to the point where we get upset. As far as Dad goes, he didn't have a problem one way or another….

Sometimes because of the intensity of their family members' negative reactions, individuals in interracial relationships find themselves faced with a painful dilemma. They can decide to continue seeing their partner at the expense of any contact with their own families, or they can terminate their relationship with the person they love or are attracted to in order to satisfy their families. Given that I was interviewing each of the men precisely because of their involvement in the interracial relationship, few of them, with the possible exception of those who had recently ended their relationships, fell into the latter camp. None of the men had terminated their relationship with their partners in order to satisfy their own or their partner's family. Moreover, even when family reactions were negative, none of the men reported permanent dissolution of the ties to their own family or of their partner's ties to her family.

Recall the comments of DAMON who spoke at length about his mother's reactions to his impending marriage a number of years ago. At that time, his rapport with his mother suffered as a result of his interracial relationship with the White woman who was to become his wife. According to Damon, his mother had a very hard time accepting his relationship. Although his wife's family took about four to five months "to come around," it took his mother close to a year. Eventually, she did, and Damon, his wife, and mother currently enjoy a rewarding and mutually appreciative relationship.

In cases where no resolution is possible with parents or in-laws, individuals who marry interracially may be forced to sever their relationship altogether with their families of origin. This decision is obviously painful and is made only when all else fails. In another autobiographical text, writer James McBride describes what he learned about the choices his own mother, who was White, was forced to make.[8] Having married a Black man, the writer's father, his mother was shunned by her own family. The writer, McBride, regards this as the ultimate testament of her love for her husband and her children. With the exception of J.H., who had already severed all ties with his family, none of the men with whom I spoke reported having to do this. Although they described having had difficult periods of time with their families and in-laws, they had not been forced to sever those ties completely and permanently.

This latter point brings to mind yet another observation. Within the sample of twenty-five men, all but three reported having their own families' complete support and encouragement.[9] Obviously, for the majority of these families, having an interracial relationship in the family and a daughter-in-law who was not Black was not a problem. Recall the interview with A.D. who was first introduced in chapter 3. The son of Haitian immigrants, A.D. noted his parents' opposition to American women. For them, their son's marriage to a White woman who was French represented something of a compromise. Yet, there were still problems. Though he professed love for his wife and expressed no real regrets about the choices he had made, at a point well into the interview, he acknowledged the following:

> "Sometimes I would say that if I could do it over…life would be so much easier if I had just married a woman of the same color… ."

Friends and Allies

During the course of the interviews, I also asked the men whether their friends had reacted to their interracial relationships in ways that they directly attributed to the interracial nature of the relationship. For most of the men, their friends' reactions were dependent upon whether the friends had personally had their own experiences in interracial relationships. Friends who were in complete acceptance and generally supportive of these relationships, were usually also in, or had previously been in, interracial relationships. This was especially the case for the men's male friends.

Another observation about the men is relevant to this latter point. Within the sample, there was quite a bit of variability regarding the racial diversity of the men's closest friends, and the racial status of their best friends was uniquely associated with the friends' reactions to the interracial relationship. When the men's best friends were something other than African American, they tended to have more favorable reactions to the relationship. For example, DAVID said that his best friend who was "Latino" was not only comfortable with the interracial nature of his relationship, but he, too, was involved in an interracial relationship. David said,

> On my side, I pretty much just have a small group of friends. Two males, one is White and the other is Latino. On my wife's side, I would say that in her close-knit group of friends there are a few White, Black, and maybe a Latino. My best friend is Latino, and he is in an interracial relationship with a White woman.

David described the absence of any animosity from his or his wife's friends.

> "I think that as far as my friends go, they're a pretty diverse group of people, so to answer your question, no, there wasn't any type of backlash or negative feelings because I married my wife. On her side, they're diverse, and they had no problems that were race-based...."

In contrast, for W.G., it took his closest friends, who were Black, quite a bit of time in adjusting to his relationship and subsequent marriage to a White woman. Though he attributed this reaction to the fact that they had a hard time no longer coming first in his life, he believed it was also a matter of her not being Black. In the end, however, he felt that things had worked out for the best.

> They don't actually have interracial relationships, and in the beginning there were real problems between us. But it wasn't only a matter of race, it was also because they were used to always coming first.... .Since that time they have both married, and I'd say our relationship is about 3/4 of the way back to where it was before...

The men generally reported having had satisfactory reactions from their friends following a sufficient period of time during which the friends adjusted to their new relationship, and this adjustment occurred regardless of whether their closest friends were Black or of another racial status. For at least one of the men, navigating friendship networks seemed to require some degree of strategizing, or conscientious planning. CHESTER, the twenty-nine-year-old financial analyst in Indiana, indicated that he deliberately refrained from visiting certain types of social settings because his wife was White. Though he noted that among their "true friends" there were no problems, he said,

> "We have a mixed group of friends. But we usually go to predominantly White bars and clubs. I would never take her to a bar near where I grew up. You know the kind of place where its mostly Blacks and the friends that I'd have there would be Black...."

When I asked him about this he said,

> "Because it would be a Black bar, and that could be trouble. Even if there was not trouble, it would just make her uncomfortable I think."

Chester felt that his wife would feel uncomfortable in a predominantly Black establishment because of the possibility that something unpleasant would happen. What that something was he could not say with any certainty, but he was certain that something *might* happen. During the course of the interview, Chester also mentioned the fact that he generally avoided seeing certain "Black" movies with his wife. When I asked for an example he noted the movie "Waiting to Exhale" in which the Black male character leaves his wife who is also Black for his young White secretary. Chester suggested that that kind of movie would have made her, his wife, uncomfortable. Chester's comments reveal that for some men, being in an interracial relationship involves consciously considering the situations and the friends with whom one socializes in order to avoid experiences that either partner might find unpleasant.

As for the reactions of the men's female friends, three men specifically noted having experienced problems in their friendships with Black women. In these cases, their friends either explicitly told them of their opposition to the relationship or behaved in ways that made the men aware of their opposition. When asked whether his friends had had problems with his interracial relationship, BARRY said,

> "Yes, as a matter of fact some of them have. It has been almost exclusively my Black female friends...I've only met one guy who ever thought there was a problem."

PEYTON, first introduced in chapter 5, noted similar reactions.

> "Yeah, I got a lot of feedback from Black women friends. They had problems with it. When the relationship broke up they threw it up in my face. They were talking all this stuff about how I shouldn't have been with her to begin with...you know things like that."

And, according to L.G., first discussed in chapter 6, one of his Black female friends pointedly asked him "aren't there any quality Black women out there?" [10]

The fact that some of the men indicated that they had experienced problems in their friendships with Black women is not especially surprising. In an earlier section of this book (chapter 3), I described an exchange published in a magazine that took place between a White woman and a Black woman. For that Black woman, there was a clear degree of disdain expressed for Black men involved in interracial relationships. In that section, I also described the enthusiasm Black women expressed in learning about this project. I believe that, taken together, these occurrences reflect many Black women's dissatisfaction with interracial couples involving Black men. These women sense that Black men have purposefully passed them over for women of other races.[11] Consequently, it is no wonder that some number of the men found their friendships with their Black women friends to be strained or tested.

"You Don't Know Me": Reactions From Strangers

In general, reactions to interracial couples run the gamut, ranging from surprise and shock to anger and, in some cases, aggression. Whether most people realize it or not, their personal beliefs about different racial groups are often strong predictors of their reactions to interracial couples.[12]

Without doubt, the greatest amount of scientific research and theory in this area has focused on the negative reactions to interracial couples that involve anger, fear, or disgust. Historically during the American slave period and for some time thereafter, a person's social mobility and very existence was tied to other people's perceptions of that person's racial status. Consequently, the racial status of the person selected as a mate was necessarily of great social importance. This was particularly the case for those who were castigated to the bottom rungs of the social hierarchy, i.e., African slaves and their descendents.

An artifact of this state of affairs is that today when people see interracial couples, it calls into question their ideas about who should be with whom. When faced with an interracial couple, individuals are forced to confront the possibility that their own personal beliefs might be flawed or in some way inaccurate. For someone who is unwilling or unable to alter their ideas, the reaction is often one of anger and disgust. These are the people who are rude, hostile, and in some cases physically abusive to interracial couples.

Such was the case for another man with whom I spoke, W.A., who at the time of the interview lived in a small town in central Illinois with his wife, who was White and their two children. I spoke with W.A. in person on two occasions. W.A. was employed as an attorney (his wife was a secretary), and he was referred to me by one of his colleagues who knew of my research interests.

Although W.A. was happily married to his wife of ten years, neither he nor his wife was particularly happy about their current housing situation. For most of the time that the couple has been married, they have lived in a moderately sized house in a quiet, residential neighborhood of a small town. Within weeks of moving in, the couple was besieged by threats, verbal insults, and angry reactions from the people who lived in the house next door to them. The family living in that house made it clear from the outset that they were deeply opposed to the fact that W.A., a Black man, was living next door to them. They also made it clear that they were vehemently opposed to his interracial marriage to a White woman.

What began as verbal harassment, in which these neighbors routinely shouted racial epithets at W.A., gradually escalated such that, at one point, W.A. and his neighbor were actually physically fighting each other. The end result was at least two opposing lawsuits, which were pending during the time that I spoke with W.A. He said:

> This guy, he was the "neighbor from hell." Really, if there was a dictionary entry for the most-disagreeable-neighbor-possible, you could open the book, and there would be this guy's picture... . From the very beginning he has insulted me and my family. He is an out and out racist. For more than a year I ignored him, not giving him the satisfaction of a response, but on the day that he approached me, got into my face when I was with my son, and then shoved me, I couldn't take anymore of it.

It was at that point, according to W.A., that he punched the man.

As discussed in an earlier section of the text, most social scientists and writers have suggested that anti-Black prejudice throughout the eighteenth, nineteenth, and twentieth centuries has its roots in White fears about the consequences of interracial sex and mulatto offspring.[13] Consequently, reactions to interracial couples involving a Black man can be extreme because the couple has "violated" the perceivers' ideas about who should be with whom, but perhaps more importantly, because the interracial couple brings to mind deep-seated beliefs and fears about interracial sex involving African Americans.[14] This obviously represents another aspect of people's reactions to interracial relationships involving Black men.

A number of the men in this study described incidents in which people whom they did not know reacted angrily to them. J.H., the actor, whose White female partner was shunned by members of her family, mentioned several occasions when he was on the receiving end of a stranger's hostility. The experiences he recounted were among the more extreme ways that service personnel can express their opposition to the interracial relationship.

> We ran into things like going to an upscale restaurant on Park Avenue. It was a very nice restaurant, and they would have specials from time to time. I remember one night we went there for one of the specials, and they wouldn't let me in supposedly because I didn't have a jacket on. But that wasn't really the issue because I looked inside and I could see that there were many men in there without jackets on... .Another time, I recall that we went to a Thai restaurant in the Park Slope area of Brooklyn. Now this was sometime in the 80s, and they wouldn't even wait on us there... Sometimes it was just the attitudes of the waiters that would let us know that they didn't approve and didn't want us there.

When describing the specific incident when he was refused service, he said,

> "Oh, they admitted us, and allowed us to be seated. But then they ignored us, and never once came to take our order. So, basically they refused to serve us… We left."

PEYTON also noted similar problems in restaurants when he was with his girlfriend who was a Mexican-American woman.

> Hmm…let's see, like if I took her to a Mexican restaurant, there would always be tension there. The Mexican men would say stuff to her in Spanish. And I don't speak Spanish but I could tell they had no business saying stuff to her about her being with me. Once we were at an Italian restaurant, and they were polite, but still there was definitely some tension there too…

Although CHESTER from Indiana and his wife were seated in one particular Midwestern restaurant and later served, it was only after he had successfully convinced the restaurant staff that they were, in fact, together. The confusion and misperception was quickly resolved, but the episode had clearly been unsettling for Chester.

> "Yeah, things like that happen. There was this one incident when we, my wife and me, went out to a restaurant. We get there and they admit her, but separately from me. They didn't believe I was with her…It was crazy. It was like I had to prove to them that she was my wife or something."

GARY also mentioned experiences like this, but he was quick to add that with the exception of one or two extremely overt reactions from strangers:

> "It was mostly a matter of perception…for example, if we get a bad table in a restaurant, or very slow service…you're never really certain…"

Twelve of the men explicitly identified more benign (though negative) reactions from strangers. The most frequent reactions that the men described involved stares, comments, or whispers. Taken together, they said the following:

> People are always looking, though it's more acceptable now than it was before of course. But still people do stare….—D.M.

> A lot of times when we're out and I'm paying attention to them, I notice that strangers will whisper…—Chester

> Well, even though I'm not really looking for other people's reactions, sometimes I can't help but notice that we do get looks….—M.B.

> When we're out we still get stares. And, sometimes people will say something in a way that they know we can hear it like "Oh, no!" ….—David

> Even if they didn't say anything, people would stare at us, and she would get upset. That happened a few times when we were on the subway… —J.H.

> It's hard to say. There is nothing outright. But sometimes you just get a feeling. Like with the neighbors, I can't really put my finger on anything specific, and they've never actually said anything to me, but it's just that feeling … —C.R.

> Occasionally when we're out people will stop what they are doing and just stare. I'm like "can I help you with something?" It used to really annoy me, but I guess you just get used to it.…—Derrick

Among those interviewed, several men could not recount having had any negative experiences as a result of strangers' responses that they attributed to their interracial relationships. This is particularly noteworthy. Their inability to describe any such negative experiences may signal a shift, however gradual, in the way that people generally react to interracial relationships. If such a shift is underway, it could reasonably be taken as evidence of a decline in anti-Black sentiment. The testimonies of at least three of the men suggest that this may indeed be happening.

Consider E.M., the respondent in his mid twenties, I first introduced in chapter 4. He suggested that the absence of negative reactions was as much a matter of the era in which we are living as it was a matter of the diversity of the neighborhood where he lives. His wife, who is "30ish," is from El Salvador. The couple is raising their three-year-old, and a daughter from his wife's previous relationship with a Hispanic. When asked whether there were negative reactions from others that he attributed to the interracial nature of his relationship he said,

> Not at all. Where we live its pretty well integrated, so we don't encounter any negativity because of our relationship. But, my first girlfriend she looked a little more Anglo. When we would go out we'd get looks.… .It's probably a matter of the passage of time or the time period we're in now...

In addition to the passage of time and the diversity of the neighborhood, the fact that his current wife "looks less Anglo" may also account for the decrease in the number of negative reactions from others that he can recall having had. Presumably, her skin complexion is dark rather than fair. Curiously, E.M. does not attribute any importance to this factor. Instead, he prefers to see the absence of negative reactions from others as a result of "the passage of time" and the relative diversity of the neighborhood.

The musician Barry was also fortunate in that he could recall having had no negative experiences with strangers because of his interracial relationships.

"For the most part, because of my experiences, I'd have to say no. And as far as strangers go, I can't say that I've ever noticed any antagonism."

B.H., the medical school student involved with a Puerto Rican woman, echoed a similar response.

"No, there hasn't been any problems like that....At least, I'm not aware of any of it... "

Who Reacts Most Negatively?

In addition to understanding the general reactions of family, friends, and strangers to Black men in intimate interracial relationships, I was also interested in finding out whether specific types of people, among strangers, reacted more strongly than others to the couples. Because of the popularity of those theories which suggest that hostility towards interracial couples stems from people's perceptions about the pool of available mates, I was curious about whether people who were from their partner's racial groups reacted uniquely negatively to the couples.[15] I was also interested in knowing whether Black women, who might be most apt to perceive a decline in the pool of available mates, would be likely to top the men's list of those most likely to respond negatively to the couple. I asked each of the men whether there was a category or group of individuals who were most likely to react negatively to them when they were out with their partners.

The men disclosed a variety of experiences in dealing with the responses of Black and White men and women, as well as in a few cases, those of Hispanics and Asians. The latter responses were limited to seven of the eight men who were in relationships with women originally from Spanish speaking countries or the Asian continent and surrounding areas. When the men's partners were Hispanic, the most common experiences noted involved negative or hostile reactions from Hispanic men. Sometimes, as noted by PEYTON, this involved strangers actually speaking in Spanish to their partners, and at other times it simply involved prolonged stares.

Only one of the men that I spoke with, L.G. who at the time of the interview was involved with a Puerto Rican woman but who later married an Indian woman born in Asia, disclosed having experienced negative reactions from a *variety* of different groups of people. He acknowledged that he most frequently received stares from Asian and Black women, as well as Hispanic women, though responses from the latter would seem to have been most common when he was involved with the Puerto Rican woman.

Almost half of the men (i.e., eleven) specifically noted having had negative experiences in dealing with Black women when their partners accompanied them. And of these men, nine stated that the group of people most opposed to their relationship with their partner was that of Black women. For the most part, the men spoke of overtly hostile stares and unsolicited, impolite comments. DAMON, the psychotherapist from St. Louis, was particularly expressive:

> Well, we've noticed that people's reactions to us have changed since we have had children. There are the "before children" reactions and "after children" reactions which we get from folks. But, if looks could kill, and I mean Black women's looks, we'd be dead all over the place. It's not so bad when the kids are with us…

Chester in Indiana made a similar observation:

> "When strangers whisper and they stare, it's usually Black women. I figure that they think that I got a Black woman at home waiting for me, like I'm fooling around on them or something…"

The next most frequently mentioned category of people who the men indicated having negative reactions included White men. In at least five cases, the men spoke of negative reactions from White men, and three of them indicated that they believed White men to have been the most opposed to their relationship. Not surprising, each of those men was also in a relationship with a White woman. According to M.B. the thirty-one-year-old trainer who was dating a twenty-eight-year-old Jewish woman at the time of the interview,

> "Those people who were most prone to give the looks, or stares were Black women, and White men. Black women think 'there goes another one,' and White men stare because they think that all White women belong to them."

O.S., the recently divorced entrepreneur who was currently dating a White European-born woman, felt similarly. He said,

> "Black females and White males are usually the ones being the most negative. Probably because it's a taboo, and they're both coming from the same place…"

DAMON speculated about the reasons for the reactions of Black women and Black and White men to interracial relationships involving Black men. He spoke at length.

> White males' reactions are not nearly so overt, but I wouldn't want to be in a situation with them. There is a certain degree of coolness from them…With White females there isn't very much there. With Black males, there is sometimes hostility. It seems to be along the lines of 'if she's with you, then she could be with me.

Although Black women demonstrated the most overtly negative reactions to his interracial relationship, both the responses of Black and White men are also problematic for Damon, though for very different reasons. He continued by saying,

> Really, with Black women it's about sleeping with the enemy. With White men, it's that I'm with one of their women as well as that 'other issue.' And, I think that that other issue is also a serious impediment in corporate America. It is extremely primitive. Folks probably don't even know that that is what they're reacting to....[16]

Reactions of family, friends and strangers not only reveal the personal beliefs of individuals, but as was suggested in the introductory chapter, they can also tell us something about the nature of contemporary race relations. That many of the men could not acknowledge being on the receiving end of White men's hostility in response to their interracial relationship may signal significant changes in the U.S. treatment of African Americans overall, even though, according to DAMON, their reactions are still cool. Where previously African American men involved with White women could expect a quick and violent response from White men, this is no longer the case. While it is true that today laws are more likely to be enforced to ensure certain protections for African Americans than was the case previously, the fact that Whites, in particular White men, do not overwhelmingly react with overt hostility suggests that interracial relations today are quite different from those as recently as thirty years ago. The following chapter explores whether and to what degree each of the men in this study actually believed that changes in race relations were occurring, and if so, whether they saw them as in some way connected to their own personal experiences in interracial relationships.

Notes

1.   For detailed discussion about the patterns of ethnic group assimilation and interaction, see Stanley Lieberson and Mary Waters', *From Many Strands: Ethnic and Racial Groups in Contemporary America* (New York: Russell Sage Foundation, 1988).

2.   A number of writers and researchers have discussed the changes that have taken place in taboos against interracial unions. See, for example, *Race Mixing. Black-White Marriage in Post-War America* by historian Renee Romano (Cambridge, Mass.: Harvard University Press, 2003).

3.   Some experimental research has systematically examined people's reactions to Black-White interracial couples. In one study whose participants were limited to Whites, White men were shown to have reacted most strongly to interracial couples in which

the female was White and the male was Black. See the article by Richard Scott "Interracial Couples: Situational Factors in White Male Reactions," in *Basic and Applied Social Psychology 8* (1987): 125-137.

4.   One study exploring the notion of "hypogamy" for interracial couples makes clear that perceivers' reactions are influenced by their beliefs about the characteristics of the members of the couple. In that study, the author concluded that White volunteer participants perceived the Black male/unattractive White female most favorably. See the article by T. Joel Wade, Marketplace economy: The Evaluation of Interracial Couples, in *Basic and Applied Social Psychology 12* (1991) 405-422.

5.   See Mark Mathabane and Gail Mathabane's, *Love in Black and White* (New York: HarperCollins Publishers, 1992).

6.   Ibid, p. 95.

7.   Not long ago, and well after the interview, I learned that J.H. had married a Black woman. Regrettably, their marriage was short-lived as J.H. recently passed away.

8.   The reader is referred to James McBride's *The Color of Water* for an engaging autobiographical account of growing up "Black" and biracial with a White mother (New York: The Berkley Publishing Group, 1996).

9.   The three exceptions were Damon, C.R., and Derrick. For Derrick, his mother's opposition was related to his wife's Mexican origins, as well as her religious background. As for C.R., although he couldn't articulate just what it was that bothered his mother about his interracial relationship, he correctly sensed her dissatisfaction with it.

10.   He indicated that his response to her was that he could not find a satisfactory Black woman.

11.   I borrow this notion of "being passed over" from best-selling author Bebe Campbell-Moore whose article I referred to in chapter 3, "Hers: Brothers and Sisters," *The New York Times* (August 23, 1992) Section 6, p. 18.

12.   For an explanation of this accompanied by experimental support, see the article by Richard Scott, "Interracial Couples: Situational Factors in White Male Reactions," *Basic and Applied Social Psychology 8* (1987): 125-137.

13.   See Robert Merton, "Intermarriage and Social Structure: Fact and Theory," *Psychiatry 4* (1941): 361-374; and Gunnar Myrdal's *An American Dilemma: The Negro Problem and American Democracy* (New York, NY: Harper & Brothers, 1944).

14.   Earlier writers have long since speculated about the role of Whites' beliefs about sexual threat and their manifestations of racism. For example, see Joel Kovel's *White Racism: A Psychohistory* (New York: Random House, 1971); and the article by G.I. Schulman, "Race, Sex and Violence? A Laboratory Test of the Sexual Threat of the Black Male Hypothesis." *American Journal of Sociology 79* (1974): 1260-1277.

15.   For descriptions of theories such as these, see one of the earliest articles on the subject by Kingsly Davis, "Intermarriage in Caste Societies," *American Anthropologist 43* (1941): 376-395; the article by Ernest Porterfield, "Black-American Intermarriage in the United States," *Marriage and Family Review 5* (1982): 17-34; and the article by Stanley Gaines and Diana Rios, "Romanticism and Interpersonal Resource Exchange among African-American-Anglo and Other Interracial Couples," *Journal of Black Psychology 25* (1999): 461-490.

16.   The "other issue" to which Damon was referring is the stereotype about the difference between Black and White men in the size of their penises. According to that belief, White men "come up short" in comparisons with Black men.

8

Perceptions of Race Relations in Today's Society

Most public opinion polls today reveal promising changes in the ways that Americans think about and react to one another.[1] According to any contemporary poll, Americans interact with people from different racial and ethnic backgrounds more than ever before. These polls, which focus on responses to questions about how frequently Americans work, study, and socialize with people from other races, suggest a more harmonious climate, one in which people from many different racial backgrounds go about their day-to-day routines freely. Unlike what was expressed by most Americans surveyed as recently as twenty or thirty years ago, people today appear to be more accepting of others who are ethnically and racially different.

At the same time, however, a majority of surveys assessing issue-based attitudes about racial and ethnic minorities show Americans becoming increasingly polarized.[2] Though most people who complete these surveys agree that racial progress has occurred since the Civil Rights Movement of the 1950s and throughout the1960s, there continues to be widespread disagreement in attitudes about the actual *quality* of current race relations. Not surprisingly, this difference in opinion is most pronounced in the expressed attitudes of Blacks and Whites about Black/White disparities and interactions. Results of these surveys reveal that Whites are overwhelmingly optimistic about the quality of today's race relations. Blacks, on the other hand, continue to point out the problems that they say result from the continuing existence of anti-Black sentiment and White racial prejudice.[3]

How can this be? Why would Blacks and Whites differ in their attitudes about the quality of race relations? In 2003, forty years after Martin Luther King, Jr. proclaimed his dream of racial equality, results of a Gallup poll revealed important differences in attitudes about the extent to which King's dream had been realized.[4] In that poll, Americans, both Blacks and Whites, were surveyed. Findings revealed that a majority of both groups of respondents believed that the Civil Rights Movement was "mostly successful in achieving its goals." Yet, the respondents differed in ways that were clearly linked to their racial status. Unlike White Americans, African Americans remained convinced of America's "separate and unequal" ethos.

Findings from that poll revealed that Blacks and Whites disagree when it comes to their beliefs about the existence of discrimination. Not only were Whites more likely to discount that discrimination exists, but they were also more likely than Blacks to attribute job, housing, and income inequalities between Blacks and Whites to factors other than discrimination. Results of this particular poll were not unique. These findings are consistent with the study noted earlier in which data gathered in the General Social Survey were analyzed. Clearly, racial differences in perceptions between Blacks and Whites continue.[5]

Mainstream discourse touting the progress of America's racial and ethnic minorities has generally been upbeat and optimistic even though there are significant racial differences in perceptions about whether America really is a society in which people of all races are treated similarly. Public discussions about race relations usually reflect White Americans' views of race relations. Not surprisingly, and as survey results reveal, when these views are compared to those of African Americans (and to a lesser extent other racial minorities), large and meaningful differences surface. That is, in contrast to the attitudes expressed by African Americans and Hispanics (who today represent the third and second largest minority groups, respectively), Whites, as a group, tend to see race relations as relatively conflict free. Even more interesting is the fact that when surveyed, White Americans express confusion and resentment over what they regard as African Americans' collective obsession with race and racial differences. Whites generally see the problems of racism as problems of the distant past having little to do with themselves or their immediate families.[6]

This disparity in perception between Blacks and Whites was recently illustrated in a published account of a "conversation" between a young Black woman living in Washington, D.C. and a similarly aged White woman living in Seattle, Washington. The latter responded in a letter to the editor to an article published by the Black woman in an earlier issue of the *Washington Post* newspaper. The author of the original article, Lonnae Parker, described the experience she had had with her mixed-race cousin who was living downstairs from her. In the article, she wrote about the unique way that race influences racial identity and, ultimately, the way in which she found herself interacting with her extremely fair-skinned cousin. The White woman who responded to the article, Peggy Sakagawa, took issue with Parker's insistence on recognizing the continuing existence of racism, among other things.

Because of Sakagawa's letter, and because of the volume of responses that Parker's initial article generated, the two women were invited to appear on an episode of the ABC network's show *Nightline*. An excerpt from Sakagawa's on-air comments was included in the *Washington Post* article that I happened to read.[7] In the article Ms. Sakagawa said:

> As a woman I'm tired of the race issue. As a White woman I'm tired of being blamed for slavery because—and only because—I am White, when the fact of the matter is I am descended from Irish and German immigrants who didn't arrive on Ellis Island until well after the Civil War. They were so poor they were lucky to own the shirts on their backs, let alone slaves…as a race you want us to continue apologizing and keep us in a perpetual state of guilt, shame and owing. Well I have my own burden of transgressions, and I refuse to carry the guilt and shame of others, especially those who have gone before me…

Before and after the *Nightline* show, the two women wrote letters to each other, and this began what was to become a long-term correspondence between them about the continuing effects of racism upon the lives of African Americans. Though Parker's on-air comments were not included in the *Washington Post* article I read, a sample of excerpts from their letters and emails was published in the article. According to Parker,

> It is not, as you suggest, a lesson of embracing victimization. No. It's merely a concession to the world in which we live. This world has delivered some sort of sucker punch to every single Black person I have ever known, that I have ever loved…. It's not that Black folks are putting their lives on hold to wait for parity or reparation or the cosmic balance of the universe to tilt. We do not think most White folks set out to deny, or discriminate…it doesn't matter if the racism is intentional or not…. The net effect is the same….Income disparity, housing, job, education disparities, infant mortality, disparities in health care delivery and incarceration rates….I don't understand Whites whose default reaction is to deny that race plays any part in anything…

The two women clearly differed in their perceptions of the continuing role of race as a determinant of one's life chances. And not surprisingly, they also had different views about the quality of relations between Blacks and Whites. For Sakagawa, race relations were at their best and would continue to improve if Blacks would just "let go of the hate; stop expecting racism; stop trying to color-code, label and separate... " For Parker, race relations continued to be poor.

Though the opinions expressed by the two women, one White and one Black, represent diametrically opposed positions about the significance of race in today's society, by no means are their different opinions necessarily representative of all Whites and all Blacks, respectively. To be sure, some African Americans see little to no problems with the current state of race relations,[8]and some Whites acknowledge the continuing existence of anti-Black racism throughout society.[9] Yet, the opinions of the majority of Blacks and Whites probably fall somewhere in between these points. For example, results of a recent National Urban League survey of Blacks aged thirty-five and under show that perceptions of racism unify Blacks across job and income status.[10] In that study 63 percent of all respondents indicated that racial discrimination continued to be one of the biggest obstacles to success for African Americans. Ironically, among those reporting higher incomes and levels of education the perception of racial discrimination was even more acute.

Where do the opinions of Black men in interracial relationships lie? Are they more or less likely to see problems with the current state of race relations? Does the interracial nature of their relationship shield them from the problems African Americans like Parker confront daily? Or, does being in an interracial relationship, particularly with a White woman, increase the likelihood that Black men not only perceive that racism still exists but openly acknowledge its effects on their own lives?

I was curious about whether Black men in interracial relationships actually "see" the problems of racism in contemporary America. That is, I wondered whether Black men in relationships with women of other races were aware of the fact that race continues to impact the quality of life negatively for many African Americans? And, even more important, do they see any connections between the choices they have made in their own personal relationships and the problems that plague Black folks today? The importance of being able to see should not be understated. The activist and writer Randall Robinson describes this ability to see as a prerequisite for tackling the problems of America's racist society. Presumably, being able to see that racism breeds problems is a necessary first step in the direction of eliminating racial problems. In his book *The Debt*, he wrote:

> Solving these problems, the first thing is to see them. I mean really see them. That is the hard part....All of us look, few of us see... The blindness is pretty much universal. We've all been acclimated to static expectation and some level of socially acceptable prejudice. [11]

In order to begin to understand how being in an interracial relationship may (or may not) be associated with one's ideas about racism and race relations, I asked the men to provide their thoughts about the current state of race relations. I asked them whether they believed that racism was still a problem for Blacks in the United States and whether they saw it changing for the better or for the worse. This prompted a number of different discussions in which some of the men noted that the quality of race relations was improving, while others indicated that race relations were worse than they had ever been. Whether the men cited specific examples in their own lives also varied.

A common response articulated by at least four of the men was that race relations, though still potentially problematic, were gradually improving. These men regarded the current state of affairs as better than in previous eras, and they were generally optimistic that the problem of racism would eventually be eradicated, perhaps even in their own lifetimes. Such was the case with BARRY, the musician from New York, who spoke at length and had this to say.

> I think that the situation is getting better, I honestly do think it's getting better. I think we have made a lot of strides. I think it's being recognized across the board by private industry as well as the public that with the internet, and the computer age, you have to, you cannot have the boundaries that we used to have. You know...uh...The internet is breaking down so many barriers racially that, you know, its just not coming into play as much. There's so many things that we can do now without necessarily seeing a person, without necessarily coming into contact with them, and it has an effect on whether you're going to be successful in your business or not. You don't have to really take that into account as much as you used to. So I think it's opened a lot of doors, and its making things a lot more free in that respect. And, anyone who can look into the future, with half a brain, can see that... I mean multiculturalism and the mixing of different ethnic or racial groups is the way this country is going....The White people are going to be in the minority, I mean if they aren't already...I mean, whether you like it or not, that's where its going.

For Barry, the influx of immigrant groups and the popularity of the internet were visible precursors to a more diverse society—one in which racism was increasingly less likely to be a problem.[12] From this perspective, with the right amount time, the problems associated with the type of racism that has affected African Americans will eventually disappear.

Two men interviewed, though less expressive, also believed that the current state of race relations represented a great improvement over previous eras. They shared this position with Barry, but these two men also noted that there was still a lot to be done. For example, WARREN in Long Beach, California, said rather succinctly,

> "Well yeah, they've [race relations] come a long way, but they still have a long way to go... I mean I'm willing to admit to the improvements that have happened, but at the same time you've got to see that there is still work to be done."

D.M. the firefighter from Southern California expressed a similar opinion. He said,

> "Race relations are much better than what they used to be, but they have a long way to go...I'm just like anyone else, if I see a Black and a White contestant on TV, I'm going to automatically pull for the Black person..."

Somewhat less optimistic were the responses of C.R., the California-based computer programmer, and DAMON, the psychotherapist from St. Louis. They both blamed contemporary racial problems on the legacy of racism. That is, they saw racism as having been most problematic in earlier years, but they generally attributed the problems of today to that earlier racism. C.R. suggested that his views about race relations were linked to having grown up in a predominantly White area. He also attributed some of the ideas he expressed to his father. He said,

> Well on a scale of one to ten, I'm going to say that race relations are a six. I still feel that there are a lot of people who are working to make things worse than they are. That's just the way I see things. I think I get a lot of this from my dad. I think that my experience as a youth, growing up in an all White area has a lot to do with the way I see racism...

In another part of the interview, C.R. noted a significantly greater potential for race-related problems for Black men in interracial relationships. These problems he saw as being unique to the experience of Black men rather than, for example, Asian or Hispanic men in interracial relationships.

For DAMON, solutions to existing race-related problems and improving race relations had to involve communication. And, given an absence of "real conversation" occurring between people from different racial groups, the quality of race relations was just mediocre.

> I think race relations are fair at best. You will of course see an increase in Black male—White female relationships. But I still think that there is a resistance to really wanting to

talk in earnest about racial problems. My experience and observation is that these matters get interpreted differently…then there is also the problem of presentation. I mean presentation of these issues. Black presentation is often laden with emotion, and White presentation often is not. A lot of the times, presentation of race-related issues is done in such a fashion that Whites have the advantage. In the end, attempts at conversation wind up ending…

DAMON'S comment here is similar to a point made in a book written a little over ten years ago documenting the experiences of upwardly mobile middle-class African Americans. In that book, the author Ellis Cose describes the experiences of professionally employed African Americans who tell their own stories about dealing with prejudice at work, at home, and in general:

"Racial discussions tend to be conducted at one of two levels—either in shouts or in whispers. The shouters are generally so twisted by pain or ignorance that spectators tune them out. The whisperers are so afraid of the sting of truth that they avoid saying much of anything at all."[13]

That Cose's comments mirror those of DAMON the psychotherapist I interviewed is not terribly surprising when one considers that the latter's insight is a prerequisite for at least part of his job description. DAMON routinely speaks publicly in corporate settings about intergroup and interracial problems in communication. During the course of the interview, he spoke at length about his experience in communicating ideas about race relations in these contexts. At one point, he said,

"To come to understand how to make a presentation of this kind so that Whites who are present can hear it is an art form. And, then you have to get them to listen. There is a genuine ignorance that is often translated into indifference…Really there is much that still needs to be done…"

DAMON concluded this part of the interview by waxing nostalgic. He sounded almost sentimental when he suggested that although American President Lyndon B. Johnson may have spearheaded some important changes in the 1960s,[14] more needed to be done.[15]

Up to this point, the men profiled expressed the most favorable perceptions of contemporary race relations, and of those to whom I spoke, these men tended to be the most sanguine about the future. Their responses were clearly more optimistic than many of the other men, and they were also more optimistic than a majority of the respondents in the recent National Urban League survey referred to earlier. Recall that African American respondents in that study felt that although race relations were tolerable, their current state did not portend well for the future. Almost half of the Urban League study's respondents (47 percent) characterized race relations as fair, and more than a third (36 percent) said that they were poor. Only 13 percent of the respondents said that race relations were "good."

It is worth noting that even among the most optimistic of the men I interviewed, there was evidence of their awareness of the continuing reality of racial discrimination. Even though these men believed that race relations were better than they had been in previous eras, they also believed that much still needed to be done. For most of these men, the challenges of being in an interracial relationship loomed large on the horizon of where improvement was most needed.

For example, even Barry, who was one of the most optimistic about where things were heading, said at one point:

> The main problem is the prevailing attitude of racism…I think on both parts. I'm not just attributing that to White people. You know, I think that Black people to a large extent can be equally bigoted and prejudiced against that kind of thing…. And, I think you know you have to weigh the risks…. Your workplace, I think you have to be cognizant of how your interracial relationship might affect your relationships with your superiors. You know you have to be aware of all of that stuff. Of course if you have any children, you've also got to think about how its going to affect them…

This point, perhaps more than any other, makes clear the dual nature of existence for Black men in interracial relationships. For the most part, these men were well aware of the continuing existence of racial bigotry and discrimination (though there was some variance in the degree to which they perceived themselves adversely affected). At the same time, however, they were each involved in relationships that in some sense belie the social reality of racism. This was particularly so for the seventeen men I interviewed who were involved with White women.

The logic of this point becomes clear when one considers the fact that Black men in interracial relationships experience the same day-to-day affronts that African Americans as a group report experiencing. What are some examples of these day-to-day affronts? According to one report prepared by the Urban Institute of the U.S. Department of Housing and Urban Development, African American homebuyers continue to face discrimination from mortgage lending institutions. This report revealed the existence of disparities in rates for obtaining mortgages as well as disparities in the amount and terms under which loans are made.[16] It is also pretty well known that discrimination exists in the rental housing market. Since 1990, more than one undercover news show has provided concrete evidence of prejudice in the refusal of rental agents to rent to Blacks. As a group, African Americans continue to experience discrimination throughout the home-buying and rental process.

Furthermore, most Americans are aware of rising concerns about the role of race in cases of police brutality. Not long ago, this issue received national attention when a California police officer was videotaped slamming a handcuffed youth into a car and punching him in the head.[17] Unfortunately, widespread attention to the problem of police brutality in minority communities is relatively recent, and generally pales in comparison to its actual rates of occurrence.[18] That is, for every videotaped incident documenting police brutality, there are likely scores more who have been victimized by police. Moreover, there is also evidence of discrimination in rates at which police stop and fine minority motorists for alleged infractions. The official term is "racial profiling," but for Black motorists, who disproportionately find themselves under the microscope of police scrutiny, it's called "driving while Black." This last point resonated deeply with the medical school student B.H. He said,

> "The racial profiling thing is really crazy, and it is out of control. Its outrageous…God forbid you're Black and you drive a decent car and have more than two passengers in the car because you're going to get pulled over. Face it, that's a fact…"

CHESTER, married for ten years to his wife, who is White, recalled a similar type of experience in Indiana as evidence that race relations could be a lot better than they are currently. He said,

> I still have incidents with the police. I drive a nice car, it's a Cadillac. When I am in a nice neighborhood, they harass me. So, there are still problems…. Society needs to get over it. Though I know my kids who are mixed will have a better way to go, there are a lot of people who won't…

B.H. and Chester are not alone in their concerns about police practices and what these practices suggest about the quality of race relations. Police practices are a major concern in many African American communities. Findings from the National Urban League Survey revealed that 43 percent of respondents (this included 62 percent of the males surveyed) indicated that the police had stopped them because of their race. As noted by the Urban League, "this percentage was nearly identical to a 1999 Gallup poll in which 42 percent of the Blacks said that they were stopped by the police because of their race."[19]

Other forms of day-to-day discrimination targeting Blacks occur in more subtle ways, and African American reactions, so deeply ingrained, occur almost unconsciously. How is this evident? Consider when Black men deliberately avoid walking too quietly or quickly behind White people on public sidewalks in response to Whites' expressed fears that they will rob them.[20] Or, better still, consider when Black customers at automatic teller machines (ATMs) must provide White customers with a greater than average berth in order to avoid alarming them.[21] These are just two examples of the many types of direct affronts that African Americans risk experiencing on any given day.

Whether most people realize it or not, racism affects everyone living in a society where it is present. In addition to its harmful effects on African Americans, racism contaminates the quality of race relations between Blacks and Whites. Although Black men in interracial relationships experience the same racist indignities that other African Americans routinely experience, they are in relationships, which more than anything else, suggest the absence of racial animus. This state of affairs is paradoxical and one that may be fraught with tension and any number of intrapsychic reactions. As is evident from their responses, the men varied in their conscious awareness of this fact, as well as in the extent to which it had taken its toll on them.

In many ways, this paradox is akin to the well-known and often cited quote of W.E.B. Du Bois in *The Souls of Black Folk*.[22] The passage from which the following quotation is excerpted has been analyzed, criticized, and revised by scholars from a number of disciplines. Du Bois described what he perceived to be a "double-consciousness," which he saw as an inherent part of the African American experience.

> It is a peculiar sensation, this double consciousness, this sense of always looking at one's self through the eyes of others, of measuring one's soul by the tape of a world that looks on in amused contempt and pity. One ever feels his twoness—an American, a Negro, two souls, two thoughts, two unreconciled strivings; two warring ideals in one dark body, whose dogged strength alone keeps it from being torn asunder.

Although the exact meaning of this notion of double-consciousness has been debated extensively,[23] I see it as a useful and straightforward way of interpreting the responses of the men in this study to questions about the continuing existence of racial bigotry and its effects on their own lives.

A number of scholars have questioned the applicability and relevancy of Du Bois' message, conceived of over a century ago, to the life experiences of African Americans today.[24 & 25] While it may be regarded as somewhat passé by these critics, this idea about double consciousness is useful in thinking about the way that Black men navigate the sometimes hostile world of a still racist society and, at the same time, exist in interracial intimate relationships. It is possible that in order to be reasonably satisfied (and what contributes to this is admittedly likely to differ from individual to individual), Black men in interracial relationships must maintain two planes of consciousness: one in which they exist freely, much like their partners, without the constraints inherent to being a Black person in the United States; and the other in which, because of their interracial relationship, they must remain ever vigilant, always aware and mindful of their status as an interloper.

The responses of a number of men to whom I spoke reflected a heightened sensitivity to the continuing existence of racism. These men genuinely believed that anti-Black discrimination was a reality in today's society. Their responses reflected these feelings, and though they differed in their beliefs about its specific effects on their own lives, they shared an acute awareness of its effects on African Americans as a group.

For B.H. not only was discrimination against Blacks in general still a problem, but he considered himself to have been a target of it at various times in his life. These times were not specific to him being involved in a relationship with a Puerto Rican woman, but instead, as he saw it, were part of the experience of being a young Black man. At one point in the interview his anger was palpable as he said,

> Oh, well I am really sensitive to it [racism]. I've actually been pulled over by police and called "Nigger" to my face.[26] There was no reason for that, I didn't do anything. This Black/White thing is a problem.... There are real problems with race today that are out of control. Race relations need a lot of work.

That Blacks more frequently find themselves as targets of police brutality is one way in which the criminal justice system discriminates. Moreover, when that brutality results in the death of a Black person, the discrimination endemic to the criminal justice system is particularly obvious and only serves to hamper harmonious race relations. This point was articulated by M.B., the personal trainer in the Los Angeles area who was characterized as "color blind" because he repeatedly described himself as being "non-racist." When asked about whether racism exists today he cited Black homicide at the hands of the police as one example.

> Hmm…as an example, I'd say that every time a Black person gets killed by the police it doesn't help race relations. Our society needs a lot of work… Just because there are differences, and they can be racial or religious or whatever, it doesn't have to be a bad thing…

GARY, the forty-year old telecommunications manager was similarly pessimistic. Though he recounted no specific instances in which he personally saw himself as the victim of discrimination, he acknowledged continuing racial problems.

> I think race relations are actually going backwards….There are still so many things that people just don't want to talk about. And that includes the prejudices and bigotry that Black folks have amongst themselves. You know how there are problems with skin color within the Black community. And, of course there are still problems existing across racial lines…

Both Gary and B.H. live on the east Coast in the ethnically diverse greater Washington metropolitan area. The two expressed similar sentiments about the way that race continues to operate, but where B.H. cited specific instances of discrimination in his own life, Gary appeared unable or reluctant to do so. Although he talked about being one of fifteen Blacks having attended a predominantly White high school boasting a student population of 1500, he did not recall any personal experiences with discrimination.

The tendency to see discrimination as a problem in society, but less of a problem in one's own life, is not unusual and is referred to in social psychology as the *personal/group discrimination discrepancy*. Social psychologists have conducted numerous studies examining this tendency and concluded that disadvantaged group members typically perceive a higher level of discrimination aimed at their group compared to that which they personally perceive experiencing as individuals.[27] Doing so can be adaptive as it permits people to minimize their perceptions about the likelihood of negative events for themselves. In short, it permits individuals to see themselves as individuals and feel as if they can control their own destinies.

Another respondent, E.M. was similar to B.H. and GARY. E.M. who was married to an El Salvadoran woman somewhat older than he, noted, in an earlier section, that he and his wife generally did not experience discrimination. Yet, at the same time, he acknowledged dissatisfaction with the state of race relations in today's society. He said,

"Its seems like its getting progressively worse. We're not making an effort to get to know people beyond their skin color. And, if you don't fit into the middle class, forget it, you're completely closed off.... I think that racism is still a major problem today."

E.M. was particularly insightful in alluding to the influence of socioeconomic status on minority racial status. Although all inhabitants of a capitalistic society are perceived along class lines, these perceptions are likely to be greatest when an individual is a racial minority person. While there is some debate over whether it is race or economic status that exerts the greatest influence, most contemporary scholars acknowledge that both are instrumental in determining life chances as well as how others will treat an individual. This point was most clearly articulated by the respondent J.H. The fifty-eight-year-old actor from New York said the following:

The race relations that came together in the early 1980s have slowly eroded because of the climate, because of all the talk shows, and the politicians.... And this goes by class. There are conservatives who say forget about race, just be the best you can be. Today it's a matter of race and class. When you are in a lower position they will attack you more.... Politicians need a cause, and it's easy to attack Afro Americans.

According to K.F., the musician who since the interview married a young Phillipino woman, though the effects of racism may appear to have declined, they still operate to keep Blacks, and particularly Black men, down. When asked about his thoughts on the quality of race relations in the United States, he paused before answering. After some time, he said,

"That's a tough question. Well, if you look at the statistics nothing has really changed since 1894... the employment rate, the mortality rate among Black men. It pretty much hasn't changed in this century."

When I asked him the significance of the year 1894 he explained,

Well its because if you think in terms of the fact that the 1890s was the toughest period in America history for Black men... more of us were swung from trees, shot, or abused in the 1890s... but as far as overall race relations go, Umh, I think that some things might have changed on the surface... like surface things, but they're always offset by a deeper, umh, kind of institutionalized mindset that applies to what they call racism... you've got problems with insurance rates, you've got redlining of urban areas, you've got the decline of Black men in the blue-collar workplace....

Another man, O.S, had the most negative perceptions of contemporary race relations. O.S., who had been married for seventeen years to a Black woman, was now in a relationship of two years with a White woman who was born and raised in Europe. In characterizing the state of current race relations he said:

"They're fucked! They just are. Everybody is a bigot and a hypocrite."

For O.S. the current state of race relations was about as bad as it could get. When I asked him to elaborate on what he saw as specific problems affecting African Americans, and when pressed to suggest ways to improve these problems, he said nothing. I found the interview with O.S. to be somewhat frustrating because of his cynical perspective on just about everything. He was extremely negative and pessimistic about a variety of topics including Black women, children of mixed marriages, and of course, race relations. During the interview, he seemed to be most interested in describing his vision of a great conspiracy that had been systematically carried out against African Americans. He referred to a particular HBO cable movie as evidence of his point. It was challenging getting him to respond directly to my questions.

This was not the case for the interview with W.G., whose wife was White and who prior to his marriage could not have conceived of being in an interracial relationship, let alone married to a White woman. W.G. was somewhat pessimistic about the state of race relations today. He said,

> "Race relations are probably as bad as they have been since I was born... I think that in certain parts of the country they're actually more racist than they were in the 1960s... I wouldn't even take my wife to South Carolina golfing with me... "

As a group, the men more often than not expressed awareness of the continuing existence of racial discrimination. But importantly, where the men tended to differ was in their predictions about the future of race relations and whether it was actually even possible to eliminate racial bigotry. For some, the quality of interaction between racial groups, in particular between African Americans and Whites, had steadily improved. But for others, intergroup relations were at their worse. As evidence, they pointed to the problems of racial profiling and police brutality, among other things.

To some extent, both of these perspectives are accurate. Without doubt race relations between African Americans and Whites are dramatically different from that which characterized interaction between the two groups as recently as fifty years ago. Before the Civil Rights Movement that gathered momentum in the 1950s, "Jim Crow" reigned and African Americans were officially regarded as second-class citizens. So in that respect, progress for African Americans has certainly occurred. Furthermore, the very fact of the respondents' open involvement in an interracial relationship was also clear evidence of at least some of the strides that had been made. Respondents, like BARRY, who cited specific examples of improvement in the workplace and in politics, were right to feel optimistic.

At the same time, however, because most of these men came of age either during or after the civil rights period, they perceived certain things to be their just due. In a society free of racial discrimination, Black men would be no more likely than men of any other race to be overrepresented in the criminal justice system, for example. But unfortunately, reality suggests otherwise. Though African Americans make up less than 13 percent of the population in the United States, they are disproportionately over-represented in prison populations. Consequently, respondents like O.S. correctly regard practices such as the deliberate distribution of inferior treatment and justice to African Americans as a direct violation of the ideals of a democracy. As was the case with the more optimistic respondents, they are also correct.

Where truth lies is in the *actual* quality of race relations and in the extent to which racial discrimination is *real*. An understanding of this truth is often hard to come by and presumably more complicated than the "all or none" positions articulated by a majority of the respondents. However, I think it is useful to conclude this section by returning to a comment made by DAVID, the San Francisco based respondent who was introduced in an earlier section of the text. If any one of the men interviewed fully grasped the contradictions of living in a society that espouses democracy but that continues to discriminate on the basis of race, and if any one of them has actually considered their own double-consciousness as a requisite to being in an interracial relationship, my bet would be on David. His response to the question about the current state of race relations and the continuing existence of racism reflected both of the perspectives articulated by the other men interviewed. In addition, his response also reflected a keen awareness about the way that being in an interracial relationship made one especially prone to making race-based explanations. He said,

> I think at this point, hmm... I think things have changed since the Civil Rights movement... I think that there has been some definite movement towards equality. Still, there is a long way to go before that time comes. Regardless of how things are between the different races, there will always be some animosity or ill will between people. That's just the nature of humans. In any group there will always be some that will tend not to interact

with others, and there will also be a group that will seek out interactions with others...So, I think race relations may be getting better, but I think on some level people will continue to find new ways to separate themselves from others.... .The truth is, you have to know when people are just being people or when their actions have to do with something racial. It gets really complicated sometimes...and even more so when you are interracially involved.

Notes

1.   One such example involves the June 2000 *New York Times* Poll of 2165 adults including 1107 Whites and 934 Blacks. Results of that poll are discussed in *How Race is Lived in America* by the Correspondents of the *New York Times* (New York: Times Books, 2001).

2.   One recent sociological study clarifies just how polarized attitudes are and finds that the difference in attitudes is generally overstated. According to researchers Paul DiMaggio, John Evans, and Bethany Bryson, race differences exist primarily in attitudes about assistance to minorities and aid to the poor. See "Have Americans' Social Attitudes Become More Polarized?" in *American Journal of Sociology 102* (1996): 690-755.

3.   Most public opinion surveys strive to include racially and ethnically diverse samples. These surveys often include responses of Hispanics, Asians, Pacific Islanders, Indians, and others that comprise moderate size minority groups within the United States. However, my discussion here is limited primarily to the responses of Blacks and Whites because the racial division has been most extreme between these groups.

4.   See "*Black Dissatisfaction Simmers beneath Good Race Relations*," by Lydia Saad. Princeton, NJ.: The Gallup Organization, 2003.

5.   See again the study cited in note 2. above.

6.   Interestingly, this view of reality helps to explain why many Whites expressed opposition to former President Bill Clinton's second term decision to initiate a long-overdue dialogue on race, racism, and White privilege.

7.   See the article titled "The Conversation" in the Sunday July 23, 2000 issue of *The Washington Post*, Style section, F1 & F4. Curiously, the newspaper included this article on two women's perceptions about the continuing significance of race in America in the Style section. Presumably, it regarded it as the most *appropriate* section for inclusion of such an article. Placing the article here rather than in the newspaper's first section or even its editorial section was significant. The inference a reader draws in finding an article about so contentious an issue as race, is that one "chooses" to dwell on race, and doing so reflects a certain style rather than the reality about the continuing significance of race in our society.

8.   One well-known example is the conservative spokesman Ward Connerly. Connerly is a Black man who sees the current problems that plague Blacks and their communities as largely self-induced. He is committed to eradicating what he sees as "the new discrimination" through the California Civil Rights Initiative. To date, that policy has effectively reduced the numbers of minorities in most state-subsidized enterprises in the state of California to their pre-civil rights era numbers.

9.   In his 1995 book, Andrew Hacker, who is White, articulates this position. See *Two Nations: Black and White, Separate, Hostile, Unequal (*New York, NY: Simon & Schuster, Inc., 1995).

10.   See p. 24 of *The State of Black America 2001*, Washington, D.C.: The National Urban League.

11. From p. 163 in *The Debt* by Randall Robinson (New York: Plume, 2001).

12. According to writer Victoria Shannon, "the anonymous filter of the computer hides a lot of what we are, including our race." In the article "Networking: When race meets life on-line there's a disconnect," she suggests that the inherent anonymity of online communication contributes to the gradual diminution of racial stereotypes.

13. See the book *Rage of a Privileged Class* by Ellis Cose (New York: HarperCollins Publishers, Inc., 1993).

14. Damon was referring to the tangible outcomes of the Civil Rights Act of 1964 that made racial discrimination in a variety of settings illegal.

15. The administration of the 36th U.S. president, Lyndon B. Johnson (1963-1969) is generally credited with creating a more balanced, equal society. During that time, important civil rights legislation was enacted that made previous forms of accepted discrimination against Blacks illegal and ensured relief for millions of elderly people through passage of the 1965 Medicare amendment to the Social Security Act, among other things.

16. See the report no. 99-191 of the U.S. Department of Housing and Urban Development *What we know about mortgage lending discrimination*. Washington, D.C.: U.S. Department of Housing and Urban Development, September 1999.

17. The case involved White police officer Jeremy Morse who on July 6, 2002, was videotaped beating a handcuffed Black youth. The incident occurred when Morse and his partner confronted the teen and his father while at a gas station ostensibly because of an expired car registration and suspended driver's license.

18. See the report from Amnesty International "United States of America: Race, Rights and Police Brutality" in *Rights for All: Amnesty International's Campaign on the United States of America*. New York: Amnesty International USA, 1998.

19. See p. 31 of *The State of Black America 2001*, Washington, D.C.: The National Urban League, 2001.

20. This is not in any way unique to the men in this study. It occurs at some time or another to almost all Black men. For an in-depth discussion of these affronts see Elijah Anderson's chapter "The Black Male in Public," in *Inside Social Life,* ed. Spencer Cahill (Los Angeles, CA: Roxbury Publishing Co, 1998), 206-213.

21. Not limited to men, I, too, have found it necessary to provide White ATM customers with a wide berth. My failure to do so on one such occasion unduly frightened a similarly aged White woman who almost dropped her belongings in her rush to safely "escape." Ironically, this "courtesy" is not only denied me while I am conducting a transaction, but on more than one occasion while using the machine, I have found White customers hovering about me. In one case, one man who was waiting to use the ATM actually propped his arm and belongings onto the machine that I was currently using.

22. From *The Souls of Black Folks* by W.E.B. Du Bois (Chicago, Ill.: A.C. McClurg & Co, 1903).

23. A recent example to which the reader is referred is the book edited by Gerald Early, *Lure and Loathing*. New York, NY: Penguin Books USA, Inc., 1993.

24. According to the scholar Gerald Early, the first chapter of Du Bois' book was originally written as an essay published in the August 1897 issue of the periodical the *Atlantic Monthly*.

25. For example, see the chapter by Molefi Asante, "Racism, consciousness and Afrocentricity" (pps. 127-143), as well as the one by Ella Pearson Mitchell "Du Bois' dilemma and African American adaptiveness" (pps. 264-273) included in *Lure and Loathing* (see note 23. above).

26.   For most African Americans today, the ultimate offense a White person can perpetrate is to call a Black person a "Nigger." This term, which has recently garnered a fair amount of attention as a result of the publication of Randall Kennedy's (2002) book *Nigger: The Strange Career of a Troublesome Word,* continues to pack a powerful punch when Whites use it to address Blacks.

27.   As evidence of this tendency among an array of disadvantaged groups, see the chapter by Donald Taylor, Stephen Wright, and L.E. Porter, "Dimensions of Perceived Discrimination: The Personal/Group Discrimination Discrepancy," in *The Psychology of Prejudice: The Ontario Symposium*, edited by Mark P. Zanna & James M. Olson, Vol. 7, pp. 233-255 (Hillsdale, N.J.: Lawrence Erlbaum Associates Inc., 1993). Though many studies have documented its occurrence, rarely have researchers adequately explained its underlying cause. An example of a particularly helpful explanation is found in Don Operario and Susan Fiske's article "Ethnic identity moderates perceptions of prejudice: Judgments of Personal Versus Group Discrimination and Subtle Versus Blatant Bias," *Personality and Social Psychology Bulletin 27* (2001): 550-561.

9

Explanations for Challenges That Were Linked to Mates' Race and Ethnicity

Nearly all of the men interviewed attested to having experienced certain challenges because of their interracial relationship. These challenges were multifaceted, and while they sometimes took the form of impolite stares or whispers from strangers, at other times they involved alienation from their own family members. A few of the men attributed these challenges solely to the fact that they were involved in an interracial relationship. Yet some of the other men's explanations tended to go a step further, and their comments reflected specific ideas about the significance of their partner's *actual racial and ethnic status*. That is, whether their partners were White, of Asian descent, Hispanic, or foreign-born was associated with the way the men explained the challenges they encountered. It is safe to say that their mates' skin color and country of origin determined whether they saw the problems they encountered as being a result of the relationship itself, or whether they saw the problems as resulting from their partners' different race or ethnicity.

Of the men I interviewed, more were in relationships with White women than were involved with Asian or Spanish-speaking women. Indeed, seventeen of the men were either married to, divorced from, or dating White women.[1] Consequently, a disproportionate amount of the experiences described to me throughout the interviews were based on the experiences of men who were involved with women who were White. For most of these men, there was a tendency to see the problems they encountered in their relationship as being a result of the *actual relationship* rather than their own or their partner's racial status. In contrast, the other men who were involved with women who were of Asian descent or from Spanish-speaking countries more often than not attributed the challenges they encountered to the specific racial and ethnic status of their partners. Usually, these men saw the couple's problems as being a result of "cultural differences" that they tended to equate with racial and ethnic differences. This section examines the possible reasons the men differed in this way.

Not surprisingly, there were also certain demographic factors that appeared to be associated with the men's perceptions of their experiences. At the outset of the study, it was unclear whether there were any identifiable trends in demographic factors among the men. Following the interviews, several demographic factors became apparent, which seemed to play a role in the actual experiences the men reported having had as well as the way in which the men explained those experiences. These factors included their partner's level of attachment to their families of origin, the men's relationships with their own families, and whether their partners were similarly educated and employed.

Men With Women Who Were White

Those men who were involved with White women, tended to attribute the problems they experienced as a couple to the interracial aspect of their relationship. That is not to say that the men perceived that all of their problems were a result of the interracial nature of their relationship. They did not. But they did believe that the negative reactions from others resulted from the fact that they were in an interracial relationship. These men saw the negative and hostile reactions as being more a result of the interracial nature of their relationship than as a result of the fact that the women they were involved with were White. Admittedly, this is a subtle difference in attribution—that is whether one sees problems as resulting from the race of one's partner (or oneself), or whether one sees them as occurring because the two people in the relationship are simply of different races. However, though it may be subtle, it is a meaningful difference in that those men involved with White women overwhelmingly offered this type of explanation—that the problems that others had with their relationship were a result of the interracial nature of the relationship.

Moreover, none of these men mentioned experiencing the potential problem of "cultural differences."[2] This makes sense and is not especially surprising given that Black and White Americans exist within the same American culture. Those in comparable income categories also share many habits, preferences, and styles.[3] For most of the men involved with White women, the problems they associated with being in an interracial relationship were problems that more often than not had to do with other people's "baggage." These men tended to externalize any and all problems with being in an interracial relationship. In other words, they attributed their problems to outside factors over which they had little, if any, control. As will be seen in a later section, this interpretation represents an important way in which these men differed from the other men whose partners hailed from Asian and Spanish-speaking countries.

It should be clear at this point that one of my motivations in carrying out this project was to determine whether and to what degree the men were in some way similar to one another, or, for that matter, how they differed. Up to this point, I have examined each of the men individually throughout discussions of a variety of topics.[4] Though this strategy falls short of the case study approach in which a smaller number of men would have been described in greater detail for each topic, the strategy employed throughout has been useful, as it has enabled in-depth consideration of each of the men's stories when they have been most relevant. However, by focusing on the individuals, it is difficult to identify trends or emergent patterns among the men, and, consequently, certain questions remain. For example, what else did the men who were involved with White women have in common other than the fact that they more often attributed the negative reactions of others to the interracial nature of their relationship than to themselves or their partners? In order to answer this question, one needs to examine this particular cohort collectively—that is, as a group. A different type of question was also worth considering at this point. Were the men in relationships with White women qualitatively distinct from those involved with women from Asian and Spanish-speaking countries?

The men who were in relationships with White women ranged in age from the mid-twenties (E.M.) to the fifty-eight-year-old actor J.H. A number of the men were in their thirties at the time of the interview (there were six), and eight were in their forties. Almost half of the men were married to their partners while six were divorced and the remaining eight were dating or living with their partners. Given the fact that the number of men was fairly evenly distributed across age ranges and within married and dating categories, these men were not especially distinguishable in this regard. Stated another way, these data suggested that among the men to whom I spoke, those in interracial relationships with White women were no more likely to be married than they were to be single. (Nor were they any more likely to be in their thirties than in their forties.)

Of the 16-17 men who were in relationships with White women, sixteen of them reported having at least bachelor's degrees. In addition to undergraduate degrees, four of them had obtained graduate or professional degrees. Furthermore, three others noted that they had taken college classes or had obtained an associate's degree. Was there a greater than average probability of a college education among these men? Although the number is fairly evenly split between those with a college degree and those without, given current rates of college enrollment and completion[5], there appears to be a slightly greater likelihood of having a college education among these men than what one might expect in a random sample drawn from the general population of African American men.

However, and not surprisingly, having a college degree did not always result in high-income generating employment. Rates of attainment of a college education did not necessarily correspond to a greater likelihood of earning any particular income level. The men were widely distributed across income categories ranging from one man who reported his income as "below the poverty line" to another who indicated that he earned "well over $100,000" each year.[6] Ironically, the one man who indicated that his income was below the poverty line was one of four men who had obtained a professional degree. The men generally reported having higher incomes on average ($\underline{M}$ = $58,071) than their partners' average income ($\underline{M}$ = $37,929). Finally, eleven of the men noted that they were employed in "White collar" jobs, and this number was similar ($\underline{n}$ = 13) to the number reporting that their partners also were employed in these types of jobs.

All but six of the men were living in California. As discussed in an earlier section, the state of California was viewed by a number of the respondents as the "best place for interracial relationships," particularly when viewed in comparison to several Southern states. And as census data indicates, interracial marriages continue to occur more frequently in the western followed by the northeastern states. Given this fact, and the fact that at the time that I carried out this project I, too, was living in California, it is not surprising that a majority of the men included in the study hailed from this state.

What may be more interesting to consider is whether the men as a group reported differences in experiences that were linked to living in California or, as was the case with six of them, elsewhere? Were the six men who lived in Indiana, Missouri, Illinois, Virginia and New York more likely to report having had certain types of experiences than were the others living in California? Were they any more or less satisfied with their lifestyles or their relationships? In short, was this subgroup of men qualitatively different from the larger subgroup of men living in California?

When viewed collectively, the six men who lived in states other than California reported similar experiences with similar rates of occurrence as did those in California. For example, these men were no more likely to report having faced particular challenges with their families or in-laws because of their involvement with a White woman. Nor did they report more negative reactions from strangers, including from African American women. The length of time spent in the relationship varied for each of the men and was similar to those respondents in California. One of the four men outside of California who had married a White woman was divorced, and this was also the case for one of the five men living in California who had married a White woman. Thus, whereas one in four of the non-Californian men was divorced, one in five of those living in California who had married a White woman was divorced. Apparently, the rates of divorce were fairly similar within the subgroups of Californian and non-Californian residents. Living in California was not associated with differences among the sixteen men in intimate relationships with White women.

So what, if anything, distinguishes these respondents from those who were involved with Asian and Spanish-speaking women? And more important, what do these men have in common with one another that they don't share with African American men who marry, date, and love African American women? To be sure, there is no easy answer. However, it may be instructive at this point to consider whether this particular group of men tended to express a preference for physical features that were more often associated with White women. Although a discussion about this tendency as well as a review of existing explanations about why it occurs was presented earlier, revisiting this issue is useful to determine its applicability to the entire cohort of those interviewed who were involved with White women.

With the exception of one person who explicitly articulated his preference for "non-Negroid" features, none of the men involved with White women expressed a preference for physical features that were more often associated with White women. When the men did express a preference for a physical feature, it was more often a preference for a certain height. In talking with each of the men and reviewing the contents of their interview, with one exception, none of the men acknowledged a preference for fair skin complexions, straight hair, or thin noses and lips. Indeed, several of them explicitly decried this particular motivation for being in an interracial relationship.

Given the pervasiveness and subtlety of anti-Black sentiment, to question the veracity of these men's claims is tempting. Were they deliberately misrepresenting their true preferences in order to portray themselves in a particular light? Did they secretly pine for and pursue their partner *because* she was White? Based on the interviews, my answers to these questions would be "No" and "No." Yet, by the same token, I am aware of just how closely representations of beauty in our society are linked to representations of Whiteness.[7] It would be impossible for any one of these men to escape awareness of or exposure to ideals elevating White phenotypes over Black phenotypes, for example. Moreover, it is useful to point out again that the conversations that I had with the men were affected by their individual concerns about appearing in a socially desirable light. For most of them, doing so meant presenting themselves as open-minded and equally as prone to appreciate women of color, in particular African American women, as they were to appreciate White women. Contrary to predictions offered by a number of researchers[8], rarely did the men indicate a preference for light-skinned complexions or features more typical of White women.

Aside from the fact that the men involved with White women may have been slightly more likely to have received a college education, they seemed to have little else in common. One last possibility that might be suggestive of a degree of commonality among the men concerned their previous experiences in intimate relationships. I reasoned that it was useful to examine the relative frequency with which these men had had previous relationships with African American women, or were exclusively involved with women who were not. Recall that this was the case for A.D. who emphasized the importance of cultural similarities in his selection of a mate.

Unfortunately, several of the men did not identify the racial status of their former intimates. Even when I explicitly asked them to do so, these men avoided an exact indication and instead noted that they had been involved with "all kinds of women." Of the sixteen men involved with White women, eight of them explicitly acknowledged having been involved at some time with a Black woman. Two of these men who were divorced from White women currently included African American women within their roster of available dates. Thus, there was no greater propensity for the men to report never having been involved with a Black woman than there was for them to report that they had at some point either been married to or dated such a woman.

Although the men appear to have been as likely to have had relationships with African American women at some time as they were to report never having had them, this state of affairs warrants further consideration. About half of the men involved with White women could not explicitly acknowledge ever having had an intimate relationship with a Black woman. To be sure, there is no precise way of estimating the likelihood that minority persons in a society would interact exclusively with members of the majority group. It is even more difficult to determine whether the situations these men found themselves in were fortuitous and devoid of potential African American mates, or whether they actually avoided these types of interactions. However, the reader is encouraged to speculate about what social and psychological forces would operate so as to result in half of the men in this subgroup never having had a relationship with a Black woman.

Examination of the conditions under which the men first became involved in their relationship revealed similarly varied circumstances. During the interviews, each of the men was asked to describe their first interracial relationship. They discussed the circumstances that led up to it, their age at the time, and whether they or their partner had initiated the relationship. Although there was a great deal of variance in the men's accounts, in a majority of the cases the men revealed that they had pursued their *current* partners. There was considerably more variability in whether they had initiated their first interracial relationship or whether their partner at the time had done so. Moreover, all but two of the men who were involved with White women reported becoming involved in an interracial relationship as early as adolescence.

This fact is worth noting, and it may represent one additional factor that this subgroup of the men actually had in common. Given that most of the men (all but two) described having had their first experience in an interracial relationship during their teen years, becoming romantically involved with someone of a different race at a young age represents an important identifiable characteristic for these men. That is not to say that having an interracial relationship at a young age is necessarily predictive of future involvement in an interracial relationship. The point here is that the two conditions are merely related to one another. Presumably, most people have a greater number of options for friendships and dating during adolescence than adulthood. Consequently, being involved in an interracial relationship at that time in one's life may be more a matter of the desire to be involved with someone from a different racial group than a matter of chance.

To be sure, this latter point says nothing about the ranks of Black men who may have had interracial relationships in their youth but who later exclusively dated and/or married Black women. An understanding of the motives of those men would require further analysis that goes well beyond the scope of the current study. However, the point here is that more men reported that their first involvement in an interracial relationship occurred when they were teenagers than those who said their first interracial relationship occured in later years.

To sum, the men in interracial relationships with White women shared few characteristics. A review of their interview responses and demographic data yielded little evidence of similarities between the men other than the fact of their interracial relationship. Indeed, the men shared only three discernable characteristics. The men in this subgroup tended to attribute outsiders' reactions to the *interracial nature* of their relationship rather than to personal characteristics of themselves or of their partners. There was also a greater proportion of men reporting post-secondary education than what one would expect from a sample within the general population of African American males. A final characteristic that the men shared was the age at which they reported having had their first interracial experience. In most cases, they reported becoming involved during adolescence.

Men with Women of Asian Descent and Women From Spanish-Speaking Countries

Four of the men with whom I spoke were interviewed because they were in an interracial relationship with a woman whose native home was located in Asia or one of the Pacific Islands. Who were these men and where were their partners from? This subgroup of men included one man who married a woman who had recently emigrated from the Philippines. Another man had recently ended his involvement in a long distance dating relationship with a woman he met while living in Japan, and another had recently married and begun a family with an Indian woman from Singapore whom he first met on the internet. Finally, this subgroup also included one young man who though recently married to a Black woman, had earlier ended a serious long-term relationship with a Chinese woman. The four men in relationships with Hispanics ranged from twenty-three to thirty-four years of age, and three of the men were younger than twenty-five years old. Two of the men identified their partners as Mexican, and the other two identified them as El Salvadoran and Puerto Rican. Two of the men were married to their partners. The men reported meeting their partners at work and at school.

As I had with the subgroup of men who were involved with White women, I sought to determine whether these men had anything in common with one another other than the fact that they were in inter-racial relationships with Asian women and Hispanic women. How were these men qualitatively distinctive from the other men in the sample? In order to answer this question, it was necessary to view the men within each of the two remaining subgroups collectively. Admittedly, however, because these subgroups each contained only four people, the information presented here is primarily descriptive rather than quantitative. Therefore, rather than providing the information across each of the two remaining subgroups, I have simply presented the data for each of the four men within each of the groups. The reader is encouraged to keep this fact in mind while attempting to draw conclusions about the distinguishing characteristics of the men.

The men involved with Asian women tended to see others' reactions to them as either being a matter of their partner's racial status (and in some situations their own) or a matter of the cultural differences between the two that became apparent as the relationship progressed. When the men noted having experienced cultural differences with their partners, they tended to attribute these differences to the fact of their racial differences. More often than not, the men attributed the challenges associated with being in the relationship to other people's specific attitudes about their partner's racial status.

In contrast, the men involved with Hispanic women did not make these types of attributions. Indeed, with the exception of one person who spoke at length about his in-laws hostility and prejudice, the men generally did not report very many negative reactions. When they did, they tended to speak more about the reactions of other Hispanic males rather than the reactions of family or friends. As a group, these men noted having particularly negative experiences with their partners in the presence of other Hispanic males who often used language as a way of excluding the men and as a way of expressing a measure of machismo. This reaction represents an important difference between the men in these two subgroups and those men in intimate relationships with White women.

In addition to the possibility of unique cultural influences among the men in the latter two subgroups, I thought it reasonable to consider whether issues of citizenship or immigration had played a role in the formation of these relationships. After inspection of the men's reports, my suspicions about whether this variable was a reasonable concern were confirmed. Only one of the men involved with an Asian woman was also in a relationship with someone who happened to have been born and raised within the United States. In that individual's case, the relationship had ended, and he had since married a Black woman. More of the men in relationships with Asian women were with women who were not presently citizens of the United States, though according to their partners, this goal was one to which they obviously aspired. In this respect, the issue of cultural differences resulting from their partners' racial differences was not only very real in the eyes of these men, but it was also an important characteristic which three of these men shared in common and which distinguished them from the others interviewed who were in relationships with White and Hispanic women.

Because three of these men were involved with Asian women who were not U.S. citizens, and two of these men had married their Asian girlfriends, it is instructive to consider what role their foreign status may have played in the formation of the relationships or in the

men's decision to wed. During the interview with K.F., who at the
time of the interview had not yet married his Phillippino girlfriend, I
cautiously broached this subject by asking him whether he had given
any thought to the possibility that his partner's quest for U.S. citizenship may have played a role in the ease with which their relationship progressed from friendship to dating to discussions about marriage. As evidence that their relationship had nothing to do with her
need for citizenship, he pointed to her date of arrival to the United
States. According to him, she had arrived long before he had ever
met her (almost a year). A local Phillippino businessman with whom
K.F. was acquainted had sponsored her immigration to the United
States.

In contrast, the circumstances surrounding the initiation and pro-
gression of the relationship of another man who was married to an
Asian woman suggest otherwise. In his case, the couple's decision
to wed was tied to his ability to sponsor the woman's passage to the
United States. The two met online and following extensive correspondence and the exchange of photographs, they decided to marry.
The man traveled to Singapore to meet his prospective in-laws, and
shortly after his return to the United States, his fiancée joined him.
The two are as upfront about their feelings of love for one another as
they are about her sponsored status through him.

The men in relationships with Asian women were 34, 35, 37 and
47 years of age. Two of these men, who happened to be in their
thirties, were currently married. Two of the men had bachelor's degrees, and one had obtained a graduate degree as well. The other two
men, one of whom was actually married to a Black woman at the time
of the interview, and the other who was not married, had taken college courses. Among the men involved with Hispanic women, two
reported having college degrees, and at the time of the interview, one
of these men was in the process of applying to medical school.

Did a greater proportion of the men in the smaller subgroups possess a college education than did those involved with White women?
Although half of the men within each of the latter two subgroups
(i.e., two) had obtained a college degree, half had not; suggesting
no greater likelihood that men in relationships with Asian or Hispanic women were college educated. Notably, all of the men involved with Asian women reported some level of exposure to a college education. Within that group, the men who did not have college
degrees reported having taken college courses at various times.

With the exception of the one man who was now married to a Black woman, all of the men involved with Asian women reported incomes that were substantially greater than their partners, though in two of these cases the men's partners were not employed outside of the home. Interestingly, this subgroup included the two men within the overall sample who were professional musicians. The remaining two people in this subgroup noted that they were employed in "White collar" jobs. With the exception of the one person who was applying to medical school and who characterized himself as a full-time student, all the men involved with Hispanic women reported earning more money than their partners. Among these three men who were involved with Hispanic women, one was employed as a health insurance administrator, another as a security guard, and another as an insurance enrollment coordinator. They reported that their incomes ranged from $20,000 to $40,000.

Two of the men who were involved with Asian women were living in Queens, New York, and the other two resided in California and Pennsylvania. Thus, while three of the men were residents of the Northeast, one was not and was a native of the western region of the United States. In the case of the latter person, he not only expressed his enthusiasm at being a native Californian, but also acknowledged that he would have been hard pressed to relocate. As it happens, I learned some time after the interview that he had since relocated to Las Vegas, Nevada, with his wife. Apparently, the prospect of a permanent "gig" as a back-up musician for a well-known country western entertainer was too good a deal to turn down. None of the other men within this subgroup raised any issues about region.

These findings were also the case for those men who were involved with Hispanic women. Each of these men lived in large metropolitan areas that were ethnically diverse and included the New York City area, Chicago, and Los Angeles. This group was geographically spread out, and none of the men expressed any particular concerns about regional influences or constraints.

None of the men who were involved with a woman of Asian descent reported having faced particular challenges with their own families because of their partners' racial status. With one exception, they also did not report having difficulties with their partner's families or in-laws. Indeed, two of the men reported having been graciously received by their partners' families, and one had had no contact whatsoever with his in-laws because his spouse had recently emigrated from the Philippines. Only one of the four men reported problems with family reactions, when he described his long-term dating relationship with a Chinese woman as having been repeatedly stymied by her family's hostility towards him. He suggested that because "the Chinese community is a very tight community" they saw him as an outsider and were unwilling to embrace the couple's relationship. Though he has maintained a friendship with the Chinese woman, he is now married to a Black woman.

Among the men involved with Hispanic women, only one reported problems with family members. This person, who was described in detail in another section of the book, reported negative reactions from his own family, in particular his mother, as well as negative reactions from his in-laws. When viewed together, only a minority of the men within the smaller subgroups reported experiencing problems with family members because of the interracial nature of their relationship.

The length of time spent in the interracial relationship varied for each of the men, and the proportion of those who had married and those who had not was equal within the two smaller subgroups. Two of the men in each of these subgroups had married their girlfriends. The men involved with Asian women whom they had married had done so in a relatively short span of time; one following a passionate nine months exchange via internet, and the other after a dating relationship of about five months. As for the two men who had not married their girlfriends, one had married a Black woman and the other had recently ended his relationship shortly before the time of the interview.

The men who had married Hispanic women had generally done so after a relatively longer courtship than those who had married Asian women. One of these men began dating and subsequently married his friend from high school. The other who married had done so following a dating relationship of a little over a year. Because of the small number of men within these smaller subgroups, as well as the variability in relationship type and length, it is difficult to generalize. However, I see the fact that the two men who married Asian women had done so relatively quickly, and the fact that they had partners who lacked citizenship as related. This may represent a potentially important difference between this particular subgroup of respondents and the others.

What else is unique about the smaller subgroups of men, and what, if anything, distinguishes them from the others who were involved with White women? Were these men any more likely than the others to express a preference for physical features that were more often associated with women of a particular racial status? As was the case with almost all of the other men, the answer to this question was "no." None of the men involved with women of Asian descent expressed a preference for physical features that were typically associated with a particular racial category. This finding was, however, somewhat different for the men involved with Hispanic women. Within this subgroup, one of the respondents had enthusiastically noted his preference for long, straight, silky hair, and another had only recently come to terms with the possibility of there being such a thing as a homely White woman!

I also considered whether it would be useful to examine the relative frequency with which each of the men in the smaller subgroups had had previous relationships with African American women, or were exclusively involved with either Asian or Hispanic women. Within the subgroup of men involved with Asian women, each of the men reported having had past relationships with women from multiple racial groups. That is, when asked, each of these men attested to having had previous relationships with African American, Asian, White and Hispanic women. As was the case with the men who were in relationships with White women, these men were just as likely to report having been involved with a Black woman as they were to report that they had at some point either been married to or dated a woman of another racial status.

In contrast, two of the men involved with Hispanic women whom they had married could not recall ever having had any previous experiences with African American women. Indeed, at least one of these men was quite conscious of this and described a conversation he had had with his mother when he was younger. His mother had asked him while he was in his late teens "when are you going to get yourself a Black girl?"

In answer to the question about the first time that they were involved in an interracial relationship, the men who were involved with Asian and Hispanic women collectively reported first-time interracial encounters with two White women, one Vietnamese woman, and one Cuban woman. The man who described a first-time experience with a Vietnamese woman and who is currently married to an

Asian-born woman, also noted a host of relationships with women from a diversity of racial backgrounds during the intervening time period.

Were the men similar in reporting first time intimate interracial encounters at an early age? With the exception of the person who was not currently married, all of the men involved with Asian women indicated that they had had their first interracial relationship experience during their teenage years. That is, these three men reported relationship experiences at age 8, 14, and 16.

Similarly, three of the four men involved with Hispanic women indicated that they had interracial relationship experiences early during adolescence. For each of these men, the period coincided with their high school experience. The fourth man in this subgroup indicated that his first experience in an interracial relationship occurred when he was twenty-nine, and at that time it was with a White woman.

Taken together, how did the smaller subgroups differ from one another, and what, if anything, distinguishes them from the larger subgroup of men involved with White women? Perhaps, more important, what characteristics do the three subgroups of men share with one another? First of all, the men involved with Asian women tended to be more likely to make cultural attributions for the problems they experienced as a result of other peoples' reactions. These other people included family, friends, and strangers. For example, they were especially likely to make these types of attributions when they described having had specific problems with others. Furthermore, those involved with Asian and Hispanic women were similar in that they both spoke of specific experiences, which they attributed to cultural differences. Recall that those men involved with Hispanic women described having experienced negative reactions from Hispanic males, and these reactions involved these males speaking in Spanish to their partners. Not surprisingly, the likelihood of reporting certain experiences because of cultural differences was greatest among the men involved with Asian and Hispanic women than among those involved with White women.

Second, as was the case with the subgroup of men in relationships with White women, three out of the four men involved with Asian women and three of the men involved with Hispanic women reported having had an interracial relationship at a fairly young age. But, whereas all of the men involved with Asian women reported multiple past intimate experiences with women from a diversity of racial backgrounds, including African Americans, this was not the case with at least half of those involved with White women and half of those involved with Hispanic women. Almost half of the men involved with White women were not able to describe specific relationship experiences with Black women. Although they boasted of having been involved with "all kinds of women," when pressed, they could not recall an actual relationship with a Black woman. Similarly, two of the four men who reported relationships with Hispanic women could recount only having had relationships with Hispanic women.

The three subgroups differed from one another in interesting ways. At the same time when viewed collectively, they shared common characteristics with one another. The fact that the two smaller subgroups each consisted of four men only is an important point to keep in mind and should not be overlooked. Having two subgroups composed of such a small number of men makes it not only difficult to identify common factors among the men but also risky to do so. It is fruitful to remind the reader at this point that attempts to generalize about <u>all</u> African American men involved with women of Asian descent or <u>all</u> African American men involved with Hispanic women on the basis of such a small subgroup would be especially problematic. Nonetheless, it is interesting to consider each of the observed differences and similarities among the men interviewed that account for important ways in which the race and ethnicity of mates matter.

Notes

1. The greater number of men in this sample who were involved with White women is consistent with national trends for rates of Black/White marriages as compared to those between African Americans and others. For example, Census Bureau figures for the decennial 2000 census reveal that there are approximately 365,000 interracial marriages between Blacks and Whites compared to approximately 57,000 marriages between Blacks with Asians and Hispanics.
2. Interestingly, this was also the case for the 2 men (who were referred to throughout as O.S. and A.D.) in the sample involved with White women who were originally from European countries.
3. The eminent cross-cultural psychologist Harry Triandis conducted some of the earliest research attesting to the various cultural differences and similarities between African Americans and Whites. See for example his edited volume *Variations in Black and White. Perceptions of the Social Environment* (Urbana, Ill.: University of Illinois Press, 1976).

4.   The exception to this tendency occurred in conceptualizing a typology of interracial relationships involving African American men in chapter 6.

5.   U.S. Department of Education figures for 2001 revealed that 781,000 Black men were enrolled in U.S. colleges. Findings from that year also show that approximately 15 percent of Black men (and 16 percent of Black women) had obtained a college degree or more.

6.   The respondent "Carlton" who indicated that his income was below the poverty level did so only half seriously. However, it is probably more accurate than inaccurate as he is currently his infant son's primary caregiver, and appears to be enjoying his role as a "stay at home" dad. His wife is the family's breadwinner.

7.   See the article by Jeffrey Yang and Angelo Ragaza, "The Beauty Machine," in *Facing Difference: Race, Gender and Mass Media* edited by Shirley Biagi and Marilyn Kern-Foxworth, 11-15. (Thousand Oaks, Calif.: Pine Forge Press, 1994).

8.   There are a number of examples, but the reader is referred to the following: the article by T. Joel Wade, "The Relationships between Skin Color and Self-Perceived Global, Physical, and Sexual Attractiveness, and Self-Esteem for African Americans," *Journal of Black Psychology 22* (1994): 358-373; and the article by Michael Hughes and Bradley Hertel, "The Significance of Color Remains: A Study of Life Chances, Mate Selection and Ethnic Consciousness among Black Americans," *Social Forces 68* (1990): 1105-1120.

10

The Future, Children and More

Historically in the United States, before full-scale social acceptance of a minority group can occur, a period develops in which large numbers of interracial marriages involving minorities take place. At least, this has typically been the case for the European immigrants, who represent the most heavily studied immigrants to date. More than a few scholars have come up with theories aimed at explaining the process by which minority and immigrant groups become assimilated into American society.[1] As one example, the sociologist Milton Gordon suggested that there were seven stages that an immigrant/minority group passes through on its way to full assimilation within the larger society.[2] Before and after Gordon's analysis, writers have debated about the significance of interracial intimacy as a prerequisite for a minority group's full acceptance in society.[3] These debates have generally focused on the assimilation of White ethnic immigrants, and more recently on Hispanics, who can be of any skin color and racial status.

Fewer researchers have actually taken account of the rigidity of the racial caste system that has effectively subordinated African Americans for nearly 400 years. Among those who have considered that the assimilation experience of African Americans might differ from that of White immigrants, the primary feature that distinguishes the African American assimilation process from that of White immigrants is *time*.[4] The assumption is that assimilation of all groups will eventually occur, but the time period required may take centuries for some groups.[5] According to those who endorse this reasoning, if African Americans as a group have not yet fully assimilated (i.e., are able to move effortlessly throughout society without race-based obstacles in order to achieve success), it is because sufficient time has not yet passed. Presumably, with the passage of the right amount time, African Americans would be no more distinctive than people of German or Italian ancestry; the latter who only became officially "White" within the most recent part of the twentieth century.

So what does the future hold? Do today's interracial relationships involving Black men portend the complexion of America's future? The following section includes discussion of the extent to which Black men in interracial relationships have thought about the way that racially mixed offspring speak directly to the issue of America's future complexion.

The Future as a Melting Pot

Several of the men interviewed offered specific forecasts for intimate interracial relationships and the general quality of race relations in the future. What do Black men in interracial relationships suggest about the future? Can an examination of their responses predict future realities? What are their thoughts about racially mixed children? GARY, the forty-year-old senior telecommunications manager from Virginia, explicitly invoked the notion of the "melting pot" in speculating about the future and the likelihood of interracial relationships.

> It seems to me that the more we become a melting pot, the more we become fragmented with everybody getting into their own separate situations.... .Dealing with the prejudices we have. It seems that it's okay if you're married to someone who is Black, but what if you're married to someone who is White or something else? Then there are problems. These are problems that we as Black people have not gotten past...even though there is the melting pot, there are these fragmented relationships and we are actually going backwards in some ways.

As much as Gary's comment reflects his personal concerns about the quality of race relations, it also reveals the widespread acceptance of the notion that America is indeed a "melting pot." This metaphor of America as melting pot can be traced as far back as the late 1700s.[6] According to this view, the United States was akin to a melting pot in which people from a diversity of ethnic backgrounds and nationalities were added to the mix, became assimilated, and, with time, emerged as "full-blooded Americans." Presumably during this metamorphosis, immigrants would enthusiastically shed their unique cultural idiosyncrasies and loyalties and adopt the behaviors, sensibilities, and customs of the "American" culture.

Not surprisingly, the veracity of this metaphor has been criticized and challenged. One of the most justified criticisms levied at it con-

cerns its tendency to regard the distinctive attributes of ethnic minorities as undesirable, because in the "New World," ethnic minority status was perceived negatively. Assimilation of immigrants was
assumed to have occurred when immigrants no longer retained visible traces of their ethnic ancestry and identity and instead appeared
only as Americans.

A second problem with the melting pot metaphor involves its in-
applicability to the experience of African Americans—one of
America's oldest class of "immigrants." The metaphor does not fit
when applied to the experiences of African Americans. Its inappli-
cability results as much from the highly salient physical feature of
darker skin tone as from the qualitatively different experiences African Americans have had from their forced arrival to the United States
to their status as second class citizens during much of the last few
centuries. Thus, the melting pot metaphor, though extremely popular and well known (witness Gary's comment), implies that ethnic
minority status is undesirable, and perhaps most problematic, it fails
to explain adequately the experiences of African Americans.

W.A., who was from a small town in central Illinois, also brought
up the idea of the melting pot. Unlike GARY, W.A. was openly skep-
tical about the way this particular metaphor could be used to explain
the experiences of African Americans in mixed marriages, as well as
the experiences of the children who were the racially mixed offspring of those marriages.

> I know that there are studies that have looked at how Europeans made it through
> American society when they first got here. There is that whole thing about starting out
> dirt poor as an outsider and then pulling yourself up from your bootstraps, and then
> becoming a full-fledged, accepted person in society. And, of course that idea has also
> come to involve people mixing racially… I mean, think about it, today you can't realisti-
> cally distinguish one group of White ethnics from another, can you? So now, people
> who are descendents of those early European immigrants are in "so-called interracial
> marriages" all of the time. That's what that whole melting pot scenario is about. But, I
> realize that's not what happens for most African Americans who are racially mixed…it
> just doesn't happen that way, and I am not so foolish as to think that it would be that way
> for my own kids who are racially mixed.

While W.A. was fully aware of the idea of the United States as a
melting pot, he remained cautiously realistic, indeed maybe even
pessimistic about its applicability to the experiences of his own offspring who happened to be racially mixed. At the same time, however, he suggested that as the ranks of racially mixed people continue to grow, so, too, will acceptance of them. Their acceptance

will come about not because they have blended into some sort of melting pot, but because after the numbers of racially mixed people have sufficiently increased, they will no longer be distinctive minorities. He comments:

> You know my kids are the future…I'm sure that everyone must think this way, but for us it's especially so. Because even though some people like my neighbor still have hang-ups about interracial marriages, more and more people are doing this. Not just like us, Black and White, but in so many other different ways. At least three of my daughter's friends at school are also racially-mixed. There is one who is Phillipino and Black, one whose mother is from Guatemala and her father is East Indian, and the other I forget, but what you're seeing now in small numbers are these light brown, mixed colored people. But in the future its going to be more common…yeah, I think that down the road, not in my lifetime and probably not in my kids' lifetime, but at some point everyone will look less different from each other…you'll be able to tell that a lot of mixed marriages have occurred at that point… That's it, that's my version of the future.

Racially Mixed Children

Because African Americans typically have darker complexions than Whites and others, children born of interracial relationships involving African American men are more likely than those born of other types of unions to acquire a coloring (however subtle in hue) that automatically affords them the characterization of being "Black." Historians and legal scholars alike have written at length about the way that the "one drop rule" determined that children who were born of at least one parent, grandparent, or even great-grandparent who was Black were also "Black."[7]

Today, this is no longer the case, but what is the case is that there is a visual litmus test of sorts in which those who have any evidence of a certain coloring are more likely to be identified as "Black." However, unlike the practice in earlier periods, the final "say so," or actual identity claimed, rests with the individual. Theoretically, people today can claim any racial and ethnic identity that they want, and this is especially so for people with mixed racial status. Indeed, sometimes when individuals have chosen to claim one identity in lieu of another, they have often found themselves under attack by others who identify with the forsaken identity. Witness the discussions that took place following golf star Tiger Woods' pronouncement embracing his mother's and father's racial identities when he said, "The various media have portrayed me as an African-American, sometimes Asian…In fact, I am both... Truthfully, I feel very fortunate and equally proud to be both African-American and Asian." With that statement, Woods unwittingly incurred the wrath of some of the very people with whom he had wished to demonstrate allegiance. Members of both the Asian and African American communities felt slighted because, rather than identifying fully with their own respective community, Woods had chosen to embrace both.

During the interviews, each of the respondents of this study provided his ideas about the experiences of children of mixed marriages. When the men had children, they spoke about their own children's experiences, and in the case of those who did not have children (there were eleven), they either described people they had known or speculated about others. I reasoned that their responses to this item represented one way of understanding something more about their forecasts for future race relations as well as their own ideas about the experiences of racially-mixed people in the United States.

The respondent CHESTER, who was from Indiana, actually spoke at length about his son's experiences. Some of his son's experiences that he described reflected his biracial status, but some of the experiences also reflected the way that Chester had experienced his own racial status. Though Chester was himself the product of an interracial marriage, he saw himself primarily as an African American man. This was not the case with his children, however. Apparently because his children's complexion was very fair, they had the option of identifying themselves as either "biracial" or "White," but not as "Black." According to Chester, because of his own experiences as a "Black" man, he strongly believed that his children would have an easier life without the burden of identifying themselves as African American. Yet, because of their identification as "White," the children now perceived meaningful differences between themselves and other children who more visibly appeared to be African Americans. This perception was evident in one exchange Chester reported having had with his son:

> Well my kids are still small, but my son he's at that age you know where they chase and harass the girls they like. And the girls, they do the same thing when they like a certain boy…well one day I kind of wanted to know where he was with girls, so I asked him whether he liked them or not. He said, "he liked girls and that there was this one girl in particular." But when I asked him about that one girl, he said "But she's Black." I asked him what that had to do with anything, and I told him that that should have nothing to do with whether he could like her or not…I think that's when I realized that he had an identity problem too…

Chester was clearly troubled by this realization. The fact that he saw his young son as having "an identity problem" was disturbing for him and appeared to resonate with his own experiences as a child of a mixed marriage. What seemed to surprise Chester most about this exchange he had with his son was his son's complete lack of identification with someone who was Black. At the same time, however, he acknowledged having advised his children to identify themselves as "White" and not "Black" or racially mixed in order to avoid potential problems. For better or for worse, there are clearly mixed messages being conveyed to Chester's racially mixed child.

How, then, does the racially mixed child develop a healthy identity? The answer to this question lies in most theories that have been developed by psychologists to explain the process involved in developing a social identity.[8] What most of these theories share is a description of a process that corresponds to specific stages throughout the life cycle. The process of identity development for children who are racially mixed is more complicated and is best studied at the period of late adolescence. During adolescence, individuals strive to establish their own identities, independent of others, and during that time the individual also is confronted by new social (e.g., peers) and biological (e.g., hormones) influences. The development of identity can be complicated for anyone, and for the racially mixed person, even more so.

According to counseling psychologist Joel Crohn whose self-help book on creating healthy "mixed matches" describes the process of identity development for racially mixed children, there are at least four stages of identity development through which mixed children pass, circle back to, or remain.[9] They entail the following:

- Majority group identifiers: Occurs when children primarily identify with the identity of the parent who is from the dominant culture or race.
- Minority group identifiers: Occurs when children primarily identify with the identity of the parent who is from the minority culture or race.
- Universalists/disaffiliates (e.g., neither of the above): Occurs when the child creates its own identity not based in any way on the identities of the parents. May create an alternative identity not related to parents.
- Synthesizers: Occurs when the child is able to bring together and integrate aspects of both of their parents' backgrounds and identities. Acknowledges the importance of both "parts."

Though Chester seems to envision his children as "synthesizers," it is apparent that his son identifies primarily with his mother's racial identity (i.e., she is White). He sees a problem with his pursuit of the little girl who he identifies as "Black."

About the future for racially mixed children, Chester was clearly optimistic. He suggested that with the passage of the right amount of time, his children and others like them would be a lot better off than he was. He said,

> Like I said, I told my kids they'd be better off in the long run if they wrote down that they were White. 'Cause they can pass like that...my kids are real fair. I mean I know first hand what the problems with race are like...I don't want my kids to have to experience the same kinds of things that I had to deal with. You know, it's like you want your kids to have it better than you did, and I know that they will because race won't be as much of an issue for them. They won't have the same strikes against them....

As for the future of race relations in general, Chester was only somewhat optimistic. He saw the interracial relationship as a prerequisite for the elimination of what he called "racial issues." This, he believed, was the only way to "get over it because mixed kids will have a better way to go."

> There are still problems of course, and where I live you see them in certain ways. But I know that after a period of time these problems will disappear. Yeah, they'll be new ones, but the same racial problems that exist today just won't be around in the future, they won't be relevant...I see more and more interracial relationships all the time, and these people are having kids too. So, of course after time there are going to be more and more mulatoes and other racial mixtures around. It's just like a fact of nature, I guess.

The fact is that because Chester's son was as light complexioned as he was, and because he had the option of identifying his racial status as Black, White, "Other," or mixed, he could "pass." Passing, as described in an earlier section, occurs when a minority person (e.g., a Black person) who closely resembles a majority person (e.g., a White person) consciously takes advantage of the social mobility reserved for majority persons. Persons who pass knowingly conceal their "true" identity. Because of his awareness of the continuing effects of racial prejudice in society and because of his own experiences as a "Black" man, Chester encouraged his son to pass. The fact that the child now sees himself as racially distinct from his African American classmate, suggests that Chester's admonitions were taken to heart.

CARLTON, who was introduced in chapter 4, did not have any children at the time of the interview. Since that time, he has married his longtime girlfriend who is White, and the two are now raising their son. When we spoke, he had specific ideas about the future and about the way that the existence of large numbers of racially mixed people would actually contribute to the elimination of certain racial problems.

> Well, of course you can't actually predict what the future holds, but just looking at things that have happened already and the way that interracial relationships have increased in numbers and become more acceptable than they were, you can sort of see that interracial relationships in general will continue to occur. Now I say *in general* because I think that racism will also continue, and given that, then there are still going to be some problems people will have with certain types of interracial relationships. But as far as blatant instances of racism go, you'll see less and less of that in the future.

While Carlton forecasts a future when interracial relationships become increasingly more acceptable and blatant instances of racism decline, he also predicts the continuing aversion many people have to certain types of interracial relationships,—namely, those with Black men and White women. What's more, Carlton also discussed the way that just being a person with a racially mixed status could be problematic for some people. As noted earlier, Carlton was himself a product of a mixed marriage between a White, Jewish woman and an African American man. Carlton's complexion was dark brown, which was also the case for at least one of his brothers. He characterized this particular brother as having been traumatized about the fact of his dark skin and racially mixed status during high school. He went on to suggest the way that being racially mixed can be a serious burden for some.

> Being a racially-mixed person in this country is interesting to say the least. And of course, if you are also a religious minority person, it gets even more interesting. Actually, I think you are able to see more. I mean by definition you have experiences on both sides of the fence. Me, I can interact with most people, but that's not the case for everyone who is racially mixed. Take one of my brothers for example…[he] had a really hard time in high school. I mean he is as mixed as my other brother, but his complexion is dark like mine, and he had a real hard time with it all in high school. It's not the same now of course, but his experience is totally different from mine and my other brother.…

Each of the men to whom I spoke had specific ideas about what the future would entail, where they saw themselves fitting into it, and how racially mixed children would influence the future. R.L., another man in this study, who was from New York, suggested that the future was unclear. Though he acknowledged that the number of interracial relationships and mixed offspring was clearly on the rise, he was pretty pessimistic about how these numerical realities would actually affect the quality of race relations. The latter he saw as bleak.

"I think that things are getting worse. I don't know if things are really getting worse, or if I'm just becoming more aware...It's the White/non-White rift. Racism is something that needs to be addressed in the White community... "

At the time of the interview, R.L. was thirty-five-years old and came to my attention by way of a female family member with whom I had had some contact in recent years. The two had recently married. R.L. was referred to me because of his previous long-term involvement with a Chinese American woman who he discussed briefly during the interview. At the time of the interview, R.L. did not have children. When I broached the subject of racially mixed children, he suggested,

"They have some unique experiences ahead of them, maybe even problems. I know that it gets more complicated for people who are mixed. Personally, I know that mixed people sometimes have different perspectives..."

In an earlier section, I described the remarks of one of the men who was, by far, the least optimistic about the current state of race relations. Not surprisingly, O.S. was similarly pessimistic about the future. Because he saw the future quality of race relations as less than promising, he was particularly pessimistic about what he saw as the likely experiences of racially mixed children. O.S. had had a son with his ex-wife who was Black and had no plans to have additional children. His young son had recently died tragically. The fact that he had suffered so grave a loss probably accounts for at least some of his negativity. About whether he had considered having children with the woman he was involved with who was White, he said:

Umm...I wouldn't want to do it. Why do that to a kid? Not in this day and age. Uh-Unh. Things just aren't right. Like I said before race relations are bad. I see them that way. Look, I may sound negative, but I'm a realist. Here in Los Angeles you've got the Blacks, Whites and Hispanics and the Asians too, and they don't get along. So, then you bring a mixed kid into all of this and what are they supposed to do? I mean who are they going to side with? Because that's what is going to have to happen, at some point that kid is going to be forced to pick a side. It doesn't matter how good things are at home, or how hard the parents have tried to make the kid well rounded, at some point it'll come down to that....

For O.S., the prospect of raising a racially mixed child was too problematic. As he saw it, even though the parents might make every effort to ensure that the child identified with the races of both parents, there were still going to be negative experiences the child would have simply because of their mixed-race status.

Ironically, one of the men who was most optimistic about interracial relationships in general was as pessimistic as O.S. about the future for racially mixed children. According to BARRY:

> You've got to think about it though when it comes to children. Having children definitely complicates the situation. Then you have to decide how the child is going to be raised, who the child is going to be identified as being…I mean what are they going to put down on the census form? It can get really complicated. Believe me, I've seen it firsthand.

Barry then went on to describe the problems he saw that affected a close family friend who was racially mixed. According to him, that friend had suffered. He said,

> "I remember when he got to his teenage years…that's when things really seemed to go out of sync for him. I don't know if he ever really figured out what he was going to be. It was clear that he was confused."

Among the men who had racially mixed children at the time of the interview (E.M., Derrick, Damon, W.A., W.G., Chester, Keith, A.D., D.M., Warren, and Peyton) there were many different impressions about the future of race relations as well as the experience of racially mixed offspring. Though they differed in what they saw as the specific challenges (or in the case of Chester, the advantages) facing their children, they were necessarily optimistic about the future. This attitude is understandable and likely reflects genuine feelings of optimism as much as it reflects the fact that it would have been psychologically uncomfortable for them to think otherwise. What could be gained by any one of these men thinking that their children were going to have an especially difficult time navigating the future? Such thoughts would have been debilitating to entertain. The fact that those men who did not have children were most pessimistic is evidence of this thinking.

Their pessimism is reasonable when one considers how racially mixed people have been treated within the United States. In addition to concerns about identity, individuals who are visibly racially mixed have had to confront the often negative reactions of others. These reactions have been most acute when one parent is African American. Indeed, in his book *Interracial Intimacies*, which argues against race-matched adoption, legal scholar Randall Kennedy reviews several important legal cases initiated *because* of adverse reactions to racially mixed children and interracial parenting.[10] Though his focus throughout this particular chapter on racial conflict is on reactions to interracial parenting, he discusses in some detail the adverse reactions to mixed children who have an African American parent. According to Kennedy, there is a long history of biases in public reactions to parenting of children who appear to be of another race than the parent(s) (i.e., racially mixed).

Based on the preceding discussion and given each of the men's remarks, what can we predict about Black men's involvement in interracial relationships in the future? To be sure, the observed trends in interracial relationship formation involving Black men are likely to continue. Census data suggests that these trends will continue particularly for those regions in the United States that tend to be more ethnically diverse—namely, the northeast corridor and the West Coast. Furthermore, the ranks of people with mixed racial backgrounds clearly will continue to increase. What is less clear is the way this trend will impact the treatment and perception of people of color relative to Whites. In what way, if any, will the racial hierarchy be adjusted? Even less clear is the extent to which the status associated with White skin will continue to outrank that which is associated with the skin color of other racial groups. Do large numbers of people of mixed race signal a shift in the racial hierarchy?[11]

As African Americans integrate formerly racially homogenous neighborhoods, schools, and offices, they are more likely to come into contact with members of other racial groups. Therefore, it is reasonable to assume that as the numbers of interracial relationships involving Black men continue to increase so, too, will those involving Black women. Yet, predictions for rates of Black men's involvement in these types of relationships far exceed those for Black women. The reasons for these predictions have to do with a variety of factors, which have been discussed at various points throughout this text. For example, the stereotypes and cultural representations of Black men tend to be more consistent with beliefs about physical attractiveness than do those associated with Black women. To the extent that popular cultural representations exclude images of Black women from the canon of beauty, Black men will continue to regard non-Black women as most desirable.

Twenty-five men shared their insights about interracial intimacy with me. The information they provided was rich, poignant, and invaluable. But one inherent shortcoming of this type of methodology became apparent to me at the conclusion of the interviews. Though I had obtained a substantial amount of information about each of these individuals, apart from census data, I had learned little about the actual *prevalence* of interracial intimacy among African American men. Consequently, I also carried out an additional, smaller study in order to learn more about prevalence rates and to find out the extent to which African American men were **actively pursuing** intimate interracial relationships.

Although recent census reports provide a useful way of examining current trends in interracial relationships with African American men, I considered the possibility that personal advertisements might also be informative. Personal advertisements provide a reliable medium for singles seeking dating, courtship, and marriage relationships. Researchers within the social sciences have examined the descriptive content of the ads that men and women have placed and have concluded that they permit analysis of at least some of the dynamics inherent to human mate selection. Previous research on the use of personal advertisements by heterosexuals has found that men tend to seek physical attractiveness and youthfulness in a potential mate and offer information about their own financial status. In contrast, women tend to offer physical attractiveness in their ads and seek mature men with financial stability and particular personality traits.[12]

Very little previous research has focused on the usage of personal advertisements by African Americans. One of the few existing studies found that Black male identities in personal advertisements involved more personalized attempts to provide vivid self-portraits, and, similar to mainstream or White samples, they typically included self-portrayals of financial success.[13] By looking at the requests made by African American men who place advertisements for potential mates, one can discern something about the most common and the most desirable features sought in mates as well as the typical ways that individuals represent themselves.

Do Black men request women of other races more frequently than they request Black women in ads? A related question, also of interest here, was the extent to which Black men explicitly state that "race is unimportant" in personal advertisements. In order to answer these questions, I reviewed a small sample of personal advertisements placed by Black men seeking women for dating, cohabitation, and marriage in six of the largest newspapers that contain personal advertisements in the United States.[14] Before doing so, however, I considered the possibility that the men who placed personal advertisements were in some way qualitatively distinct from the general population of Black men. Admittedly, this represents a potential limitation of this type of methodology. However, given that researchers who regularly employ this approach contend that individuals who place personal advertisements do not differ in meaningful ways from other singles, I proceeded with the analysis.[15]

Study of Black Men's Personal Advertisements

Personal advertisements appearing in six U.S. newspapers, which boasted some of the largest personal advertisements sections, were collected and reviewed. The newspapers were regionally distributed and included *The Atlanta-Journal Constitution*, *The Boston Globe*, *The Chicago Tribune*, *The San Francisco Examiner-Chronicle*, *The Washington Post*, and *The Village Voice*. Personal ads were collected from the Sunday editions within a three-month period and included issues released on December 12, 1999; February 13, 2000; and April 16, 2000. All ads placed by heterosexual African American men seeking women were identified and collected.

The analysis revealed 315 personal advertisements placed by African American men during the survey period. Each of the ads was reviewed and coded on the basis of a number of different criteria including the extent to which the advertisers stipulated a particular age, personality type, financial status, or race, among other qualities. I also examined whether the advertiser provided information about his own age, personality, and financial status.

Because I was interested in whether African American men request women of other races at rates comparable to rates of their requests for African American women, the following discussion focuses on the frequency of occurrence of race specific stipulations. An abbreviated table that details the actual number of ads identified in each of the newspapers as well as the frequency in which race specific stipulations appeared is presented below.

As the table reveals, more personal ads were placed by African American men in the Atlanta, Washington, and Chicago newspapers. Furthermore, those papers evidenced the greatest number of ads stipulating Black women as mates. According to these data, 43 percent of the personal ads placed by Black men in the *Atlanta Journal–Constitution* sought Black women, followed by 36 percent appearing in *The Washington Post*, and nearly 31 percent in *The Chicago Tribune*. If the actual newspapers reviewed here are taken as

Newspaper	Ads Placed	Race Stipulated			Race of Person Stipulated			
		YES	NO	B	W	A	L	"Un"*
Atlanta Journal-Constitution	72	37	35	21	8	1	1	6
Boston Globe	42	26	16	5	10	0	4	7
Chicago Tribune	59	31	28	18	8	0	5	0
San Francisco Examiner	23	22	1	5	8	1	3	5
Washington Post	74	46	28	27	8	2	4	5
Village Voice (NY)	41	33	8	6	8	6	7	6

*Un – refers to those ads in which the advertiser explicitly stated that race was unimportant or that women of any racial status should respond; B = African American/Black, W = White/European, A = Asian American/Other Asian, and L = Latina/Hispanic.

proxies for regions of the country or city, then it would be fair to conclude that among the cities included here Black men more often seek Black women in Atlanta, Chicago, and Washington, D.C.[16] It would also be appropriate to go a step further and conclude that no evidence of an "other race" preference in Black men's mate selection is revealed in the personal advertisements because Black women were more often sought than any other group of women in the advertisements placed by the men. Furthermore, the men who placed these ads were no more likely to state that race was unimportant than they were to explicitly request a Black woman.

However, when these trends are viewed in conjunction with those occurring in the remaining three papers included in the analysis, a different, albeit contradictory, picture emerges and suggests that the preceding conclusions may be premature. For example, only 11 percent of the ads placed by heterosexual Black males in *The Boston Globe* requested Black females. This is compared to 24 percent who requested White females and 17 percent who indicated that race was unimportant. Similarly, although 22 percent of the ads placed in *The San Francisco Examiner-Chronicle* and 15 percent of those in *The Village Voice* requested Black women, 36 percent and 20 percent, respectively, requested White women. In the case of, the *Village Voice*, Black men placing personal ads also requested Latino women more frequently than Black women, and the frequency of requests for Asian women was the same as that for Black women. Furthermore, the frequency with which the men explicitly noted that race was unimportant in the ad either equaled or exceeded the frequency of requests for Black women.

To what extent are these findings indicative of Blacks men's preferences for interracial relationships? Which set of findings is most representative of the behavior of Black men selecting mates? Examination of the current trends in personal advertisements appearing in papers in at least three of the cities in which Blacks are heavily concentrated (Atlanta, Chicago, and Washington, D.C.) suggests that Black men are no more likely to pursue women of other races than they are to pursue Black women. But the very same examination of ads placed in papers located in one city (*The Village Voice* is a New York City paper) with a large Black population and in two cities (Boston and San Francisco) with fewer Blacks suggests otherwise.

These findings provide yet another way of looking at and considering current trends in interracial relationships involving Black men. As I noted above, I conducted this study because I thought it represented a novel way of looking at the issue of Black men's involvement in and pursuit of interracial relationships. For me, it suggested an alternative view or perspective about the extent to which African American men *actively pursue* intimate interracial relationships. Recall that a majority of the respondents interviewed described their relationship as being a matter of luck. That is, most of the men in this study did not attribute their involvement in an interracial relationship to conscious pursuit of a woman whose race was different from their own.

As the respondents' testimonies make clear, people in interracial relationships consider many different variables at the outset and throughout their relationship. What is also clear is that no one explanation can accurately account for interracial relationships among

African American men. An explanation of contemporary patterns of interracial intimacy in the lives of Black men requires consideration of individual motives and experiences as well as the social context in which the men live their lives. Without attention to each one of these factors, no real understanding of Black men's involvement in intimate interracial relationships is possible.

While it is true that most of the men to whom I spoke decried any and all explanations for interracial intimacy other than that of happenstance, it is also true that, like all of us, these men exist in a society that provides some very real advantages to people who are more "White" and less "Black." Recall that among the respondents who I dubbed "lonely hearts" there almost seemed to be a note of apology in their stories. These men openly acknowledged having wrestled with the very idea of being in an interracial relationship. Prior to their own relationship, they perceived African Americans' involvement in interracial relationships as a kind of "selling out." Only later, when they had committed themselves to their partners, were they able to resolve the contradiction of their relationship and their beliefs.

Although the decision to be involved in an interracial intimate relationship is an extremely personal one, it is also one that is saddled with all of the baggage associated with race and sex in our society. Consequently, though the decision is at first personal, it is also public. However unwittingly, people in intimate interracial relationships make race and sex issues salient to the rest of us. Moreover, when the particular interracial relationship includes one person whose racial status is markedly different from the other person's, motives are likely to be scrutinized. What does such scrutiny reveal about heterosexual African American men in intimate interracial relationships? Namely, that while some men consciously choose to be involved with their partner because of her race, others do not. As a result of the interviews conducted as well as the content analysis of personal advertisements, it is fair to say that as many African American men can rightfully claim fortuity in explaining their relationship as men who consciously seek women who are not Black.

Notes

1.   Discussions about assimilation have corresponded with waves of immigration. See, for example, the following publications: *Culture and Democracy in the United States* by H.M. Kallen (New York: Boni and Liveright, 1924); *Assimilation in American Life* by Milton M. Gordon (New York: Oxford University Press, 1964); and *Diversity in America* by Vincent N. Parillo (Thousand Oaks, Calif.: Pine Forge Press, 1996).

2.   See Milton Gordon's *Assimilation in American Life* (New York: Oxford University Press, 1964).

3.   Some writers have described what they believed actually to be underway while others have outlined future predictions. Vincent Parillo's text *Diversity in America* makes clear that there are a variety of ideas about the significance of interracial marriage, i.e., intimacy, for full-scale assimilation. As examples, he cites such classics as *Letters from an American Farmer* by J. Hector St. John de Crevecoeur (New York: Albert and Charles Boni, 1925, reprint from 1782); and Ralph W. Emerson in *The Journals and Miscellaneous Notebooks of Ralph Waldo Emerson*, edited by Ralph H. Orth and Alfred R. Ferguson, (Cambridge, Mass.: Belknap, 1977).

4.   For further discussion of this point, see *Race and Culture: Essays in the Sociology of Contemporary Man* by the late sociologist Robert E. Park (New York: Free Press, 1950).

5.   A more extensive discussion of the assimilation process, as it may or may not pertain to African Americans, appears in chapter 4 of this book.

6.   See Hector St. John de Crevecoeur (1782) as cited above (note 1). *Diversity in America.*

7.   The reader is again referred to legal scholar Randall Kennedy's informative text that describes some of the experiences of racially mixed children and the issues that arise in transracial adoptions. See *Interracial Intimacies. Sex, Marriage, Identity and Adoption* (New York: Pantheon, 2003).

8.   For general discussions of identity development, see *Identity, Youth and Crisis* by Erik Eriksen (New York: Norton, 1968); *Black and White Racial Identity: Theory, Research and Practice* by Janet Helms (Westport, Conn.: Greenwood Press, 1990); and *Children's Ethnic Socialization: Pluralism and Development*, edited by Jean S. Phinney and Mary Jane Rotherman-Borus (Newbury Park, Calif.: Sage Publications, 1987).

9.   See the book by Joel Crohn, *Mixed Matches. How to Create Successful Interracial, Interethnic, and Interfaith Relationships* (New York: Ballantine Books, 1995).

10.   See *Interracial Intimacies.* (Note 7, above).

11.   The recently published book by historian Renee Romano examines the extent to which the gradual elimination of the taboo against Black/White interracial marriage signals shifts in the quality of race relations. See *Race Mixing. Black-White Marriage in Post-War America* (Cambridge, Mass.: Harvard University Press, 2003).

12.   There are a number of studies on the analysis of personal advertisements as a way of understanding the factors involved in mate selection. Some examples include the article by Wm. Michael Lynn and Rosemary Bolig, "Personal Advertisements: Sources of Data about Relationships," *Journal of Social and Personal Relationships 2* (1985): 377-383; the article by D.W. Rajeckie, Sharon Bledsoe, and Jeffrey Lee Rasmussen, "Successful Personal Ads: Gender Differences and Similarities in Offers, Stipulations and Outcomes," *Basic and Applied Social Psychology 12* (1991): 457-469; and the article by George Yancey and Sherelyn Yancey, "Black-White

Differences in the Use of Personal Advertisements for Individuals Seeking Interracial Relationships," *Journal of Black Studies 27* (1997): 650-667.

13.   The study is reported in the article by Neal Lester and Maureen Goggin, "'Extra, Extra! Read All about It' Constructions of Heterosexual Black Male Identities in the Personals," *Social Identities 5* (1999): 441-469.

14.   This study was conducted with the assistance of Brandi Cage who served as a research assistant to me at that time. I am grateful for her assistance.

15.   This point is addressed in the article "Personal Advertisements"(See note 12 above). In that paper, the researchers discuss the benefits of using personal advertisements to draw inferences about the formation of intimate relationships.

16.   According to data from the 2000 census, the latter two cities were among the top cities with the largest proportions of African Americans.

Bibliography

Amnesty International. "United States of America: Race, Rights and Police Brutality," in *Rights for All: Amnesty International's Campaign on the United States of America*. New York: Amnesty International USA, 1998.

Andersen, James D. "Literacy and Education. The African American Experience." In *Literacy Among African-American Youth*, edited by Vivien L. Gadsen and Daniel A. Wagner., Creskill, N.J.: Hampton Press, 1995.

Anderson, Elijah. "The Black Male in Public." In *Inside Social Life,* edited by Spencer E. Cahill, 206-213. Los Angeles, Calif.: Roxbury Publishing Co, 1998.

Arias, Elizabeth, and Betty Smith. *Deaths: Preliminary Data for 2001.* Hyattsville, MD: National Center for Health Statistics, Division of Vital Statistics, 2001.

Asante, Molefi. "Racism, consciousness and Afrocentricity." In *Lure and Loathing,* edited by Gerald Early, 127-143. New York: Penguin Books USA, Inc., 1993.

Astor, Charlotte H. "Gallup Poll: Progress in Black/White Relations, but Race Is Still an Issue." *U.S. Society & Values, USIA Electronic Journal 2* (August 1997): online.

Baber, Ray E. "A Study of 325 Mixed Marriages." *Sociological Review 2* (1937): 705-716.

Bell, Derrick. *Faces at the Bottom of the Well: The Permanence of Racism.* New York: BasicBooks, 1992.

Benson, Susan. *Ambiguous Ethnicity: Interracial Families in London.* London: Cambridge University Press, 1981.

Blau, Peter; Terry Blum; and Joseph Schwartz, "Heterogeneity and Intermarriage," *American Sociological Review 47* (1982): 45-62.

Bramlett-Solomon, Sharon & Tricia Farwell. "Sex on Soaps: An Analysis of Black, White and Interracial Couple Intimacy." In *Facing Difference: Race, Gender and Mass Media,* edited by Shirley Biagi and Marilyn Kern-Foxworth, 3-10. Thousand Oaks, Calif.: Pine Forge Press, 1997.

Buss, David. *The Evolution of Desire.* New York: BasicBooks, 1994.

Byrd, Ayanna D., and Lori L. Tharps. *Hair Story: Untangling the Roots of Black Hair in America.* New York: St. Martin's Press, 2000.

Carbado, Devon, W. "The Construction of O.J. Simpson as a Racial Victim." In *Black Men on Race, Gender and Sexuality: A Critical Reader*, edited by Devon W. Carbado. New York: New York University Press, 1999.

Cleaver, Eldridge. *Soul on Ice.* New York: Dell Publishing, 1968.

Coltraine, Scott, and Melinda Messineo. "The Perpetuation of Subtle Prejudice: Race and Gender Imagery in 1990s Television Advertising." *Sex
Roles 42* (2000): 363-389.

Correspondents of the *New York Times. How Race Is Lived in America*. New
York: Times Books, 2001.

Cose, Ellis. *Rage of a Privileged Class*. New York: HarperCollins Publishers,
1993.

Craig, Kellina M., and Karen E. Feasel. "Do Solo Arrangements Lead to Attributions of Tokenism?" *Journal of Applied Social Psychology 28* (1998):
1810-1836.

Crohn, Joel. *Mixed Matches. How to Create Successful Interracial, Interethnic,
and Interfaith Relationships*. New York: Ballantine Books, 1995.

Davis, Kingsly. "Intermarriage in Caste Societies." *American Anthropologist
43* (1941): 376-395.

Davidson, Jeanette R. "Theories about Black-White Interracial Marriage: A
Clinical Perspective." *Journal of Multicultural Counseling and Development 20* (1992): 150-157.

DiMaggio, Paul; John Evans; and Bethany Bryson. "Have Americans' Social
Attitudes Become More Polarized?" *American Journal of Sociology 102*
(1996): 690-755.

Du Bois, W.E.B. *The Philadelphia Negro: A Social Study*. New York: Schocken,
1967.

———. *The Souls of Black Folk*. Chicago: McClurg & Co., 1903.

Dyson, Micheal E. *Race Rules*. New York: Vintage Books, 1997.

Early, Gerald. *Lure and Loathing*. New York: Penguin Books USA, Inc., 1993.

Eriksen, Erik. *Identity, Youth and Crisis*. New York, NY: Norton, 1968.

Fanon, Frantz. *Black Skins, White Masks*. New York: Grove Press, 1967.

Farhi, Paul. A Television Trend: Audiences in Black and White. In Facing Difference. Race, Gender and Mass Media, ed. S. Biagi and M. Kern-Foxworth.
ThousandOaks, CA: Pine Forge Press, 1994, 202-204.

Faulkner, William. *Light in August*. New York: Cape & Smith, 1931.

Feagin, Joseph R. "The Continuing Significance of Race: Anti-Black Discrimination in Public Places." *American Sociological Review 56* (1991): 101-
116.

Fletcher, M.A. "Crisis of Black Males Gets High Profile Look." *Washington
Post* (April 17, 1999): A2.

Gadberry, James H., and Richard A. Dodder. "Educational Homogamy in Interracial Marriages: An Update," *Journal of Social Behavior and Personality 8* (1993): 155-163.

Gaines, Stanley, O., and William Ickes. "Perspectives on Interracial Relationships." In *Handbook of Personal Relationships*, edited by Steve Duck,
197-220. Hoboken, N.J.: John Wiley & Sons, 1997.

Gaines, Stanley, O. & Diana I. Rios. "Romanticism and Interpersonal Resource
Exchange among African American-Anglo and Other Interracial Couples."
Journal of Black Psychology 25 (1999): 461-490.

Goodman, James. *Stories of Scottsboro*. New York: Vintage Books, 1995.

Gordon, Milton. Assimilation in American Life. New York: Oxford University Press, 1964.

Grier, William, and Price Cobbs. "Marriage and Love as Components to Black Rage." In *Black Male/White Female: Perspectives on Interracial Marriage and Courtship*, edited by Doris Y. Wilkerson. Cambridge, Mass.: Schenkman Publishing Co, 1975.

Grier, William, and Price Cobbs. *Black Rage*. New York, NY: Basic Books, 1968.

Hacker, Andrew. *Two Nations: Black and White, Separate, Hostile, Unequal*. New York: Simon & Schuster, Inc., 1995.

Harrison, Paige M., and Allen J. Beck. Prisoners in 2001. Washington, DC: U.S. Department of Justice, Bureau of Justice Statistics: Office of Justice Programs, 2002.

Hauser, Robert M., and David L. Featherman. "Socioeconomic Achievements of U.S. Men, 1962-1972." *Science 185* (1974): 325-331.

Helms, Janet. *Black and White Racial Identity: Theory,Research and Practice*. Westport, Conn.: Greenwood Press, 1990.

Herr, David M. "Negro-White Marriages in the United States." *Journal of Marriage and the Family 27* (1966): 262-275.

Herskovits, Melville. *The American Negro*. Bloomington, Ind.: Indiana University Press, 1968.

Hodes, Martha. *White Women, Black Men: Illicit Sex in the 19th Century South*. New Haven, Conn.: Yale University Press, 1997.

Hohman, Kimberly. *The Color of Love: A Black Person's Guide to Interracial Relationships*. Chicago: Chicago Review Press, Inc., 2002.

Hooks, Bell (1994). Sisters of the Yam: Black Women and Self Recovery. Cambridge, MA: South End Press.

Hughes, Michael, and Bradley Hertel. "The Significance of Color Remains: A Study of Life Chances, Mate Selection and Ethnic Consciousness among Black Americans." *Social Forces 68* (1990): 1105-1120.

Hutchinson, Earl O. *Beyond OJ. Race Sex and Class Lessons for America*. Los Angeles, Calif.: Middle Passage Press, 1996.

Jakoubek, Robert. *Jack Johnson. Heavyweight Champion*. New York: Chelsea House Publishers, 1990.

Johnson, James W. *Along This Way: The Autobiography of James Weldon Johnson*. New York: Penguin Books, 1933.

Jordan, Winthrop. *White over Black*. New York: Norton, 1968.

Kallen, H.M. *Culture and Democracy in the United States*. New York: Boni and Liveright, 1924.

Kennedy, Randall. *Interracial Intimacies. Sex, Marriage, Identity and Adoption*. New York: Pantheon Books, 2003.

———. *Nigger. The Strange Career of a Troublesome Word*. New York: Pantheon Books, 2002.

King, Joyce. *Hate Crime. The Story of a Dragging in Jasper, Texas*. New York: Pantheon, 2002.

Kouri, Kris, and M. Laswell. "Black-White Marriages: Social Change and Intergenerational Mobility." *Marriage and Family Review,* 19, (1993): 241-255.

Kovel, Joel. *White Racism: A Psychohistory*. New York: Random House, 1971.

Lee, Harper. *To Kill a Mockingbird*. Philadelphia: Lippincott, 1960.

Lester, Neal, and Maureen Goggin. "'Extra, Extra! Read All about It' Constructions of Heterosexual Black Male Identities in the Personals." *Social Identities 5* (1999): 441-469.

Levin, Jack, and Jack McDevitt. *Hate Crimes. The Rising Tide of Bigotry and Bloodshed.* New York: Plenum Press, 1993.

Lieberson, Stanley, and Mary C. Waters. *From Many Strands: Ethnic and Racial Groups in Contemporary America*. New York: Russell Sage Foundation: 1988.

Lofland, John, and Lyn Lofland. *Analyzing Social Settings: A Guide to Qualitative Observation and Analysis,* 3rd ed. Belmont, Calif.: Wadsworth, 1996.

Lynn, Wm. Michael, and Rosemary Bolig. "Personal Advertisements: Sources of Data about Relationships." *Journal of Social and Personal Relationships 2* (1985): 377-383.

Madhubuti, Haki. *Black Men: Obsolete, Single, Dangerous?* Chicago: Third World Press, 1990.

Mathabane, Mark, and Gail Mathabane. *Love in Black and White*. New York: HarperCollins Publishers, 1992.

McBride, James. *The Color of Water. A Black Man's Tribute to His White Mother.* New York: The Berkley Publishing Group, 1996.

McCall, Nathan. *What's Going On*. New York: Random House Inc., 1998.

McDowell, Deborah. "Reading Family Matters." In *Changing Our Own Words: Essays on Criticism, Theory and Writing by Black Women*, edited by Cheryl Ward. New Brunswick, N.J.: Rutgers University Press, 1989.

Merton, Robert K. "Intermarriage and Social Structure: Fact and Theory." *Psychiatry 4* (1941): 361-374.

Mitchell, Ella Pearson. "Du Bois' Dilemma and African American Adaptiveness." In *Lure and Loathing,* edited by Gerald Early, 264-273. New York: Penguin Books USA, Inc., 1993.

Moore, Bebe Campbell. *"Hers: Brothers and Sisters." The New York Times* (August 23, 1992): Section 6, p. 18.

Morland, J.K. "Token Desegregation and Beyond." In *Minority Problems*, edited by Arnold M. Rose and Caroline B. Rose, 229-238. New York: Harper & Row, 1965.

Myrdal, Gunnar. *An American Dilemma: The Negro Problem and American Democracy*. New York: Harper & Brothers, 1944.

National Urban League. *The State of Black America 2001*. Washington, D.C.: National Urban League, 2001.

Nielsen Media Research: The 1998 Report on Television. New York: Nielsen Media Research, 1998.

Njeri, Itabari. "Sushi and Grits: Ethnic Identity and Conflict in a Newly Multicultural America. In *Lure and Loathing*, edited by Gerald Early, 13-40. New York: Penguin Books USA, Inc, 1993.

Omi, Michael, and Howard Winant. *Racial Formation in the United States*. New York, NY: Routledge & Kegan Paul, Inc., 1986.

Operario, Don, and Susan Fiske. "Ethnic Identity Moderates Perceptions of Prejudice: Judgments of Personal Versus Group Discrimination and Subtle Versus Blatant Bias." *Personality and Social Psychology Bulletin 27* (2001): 550-561.

Parillo, Vincent N. *Diversity in America.* Thousand Oaks, Calif.: Pine Forge Press, 1996.

Park, Robert E. *Race and Culture: Essays in the Sociology of Contemporary Man.* New York: Free Press, 1950.

Phinney, Jean S., and Mary Jane Rotherman-Borus, eds. *Children's Ethnic Socialization: Pluralism and* Development. Newbury Park, Calif.: Sage Publications, 1987.

Porterfield, Ernest. *Black and White Mixed Marriages.* Chicago: Nelson-Hall, 1978.

Porterfield, Ernest. "Black-American Intermarriage in the Unites States." *Marriage and Family Review 5* (1982): 17-34.

Rajeckie, D.W.; Sharon Bledsoe; and Jeffrey Lee Rasmussen. "Successful Personal Ads: Gender Differences and Similarities in Offers, Stipulations and Outcomes." *Basic and Applied Social Psychology 12* (1991): 457-469.

Robinson, Randall. *The Debt. What America Owes to Blacks.* New York: Plume, 2001.

Romano, Renee. *Race Mixing. Black-White Marriage in Post-War America.* Cambridge, Mass.: Harvard University Press, 2003

Root, Maria M. *Love's Revolution: Interracial Marriage.* Philadelphia: Temple University Press, 2001.

Ross, Sandra I., and Jeffrey Jackson. "Teachers' Expectations for Black Males' and Black Females' Academic Achievement." *Personality and Social Psychology Bulletin 17* (1991): 78-82.

Russell, Kathy; Midge Wilson; and Ronald Hall. *The Color Complex.* New York: Anchor Books, 1992.

Russell, Kathy, and Midge Wilson. Divided Sisters. Bridging the Gap Between Black Women and White Women. New York: Anchor Books, 1996.

Saad, Lydia. *Black Dissatisfaction Simmers Beneath Good Race Relations.* Princeton, N.J.: The Gallup Organization, 2003.

Sanjek, Roger. "Intermarriage and the Future of the Races in the United States." In *Race,* edited by Steven Gregory and Roger Sanjek. New Brunswick, N.J.: Rutgers University Press, 1994.

Schulman, G.I. "Race, Sex, and Violence? A Laboratory Test of the Sexual Threat of the Black Male Hypothesis." *American Journal of Sociology 79* (1974): 1260-1277.

Scott, Patricia Bell. "Debunking Sapphire: Toward a Non-Racist and Non-Sexist Social Science." In *All the Women are White, All the Blacks Are Men, but Some of Us Are Brave,* edited by Gloria T. Hull, Patricia Bell Scott, and Barbara Smith. Old Westbury, NY: Feminist Press, 1982.

Scott, Richard. "Interracial Couples: Situational Factors in White Male Reactions." *Basic and Applied Social Psychology 8* (1987): 125-137.

Shannon, Victoria. "Networking: When Race Meets Life On-line There's a Disconnect." Washington, D.C.: *The Washington Post,* (October 17, 1994).

Shipler, David. *A Country of Strangers. Blacks and Whites in America*. New York: Alfred A. Knopf, 1997.

Smith, Althea, and Abigail J. Stewart. "Approaches to Studying Racism and Sexism in Black Women's Lives." *Journal of Social Issues 39* (1991): 1-15

Smith, Tom W. "Context Effects in the General Social Survey" In *Measurement Error in Surveys*, edited by Paul Biemer et al. New York: John Wiley & Sons, 1991.

Spaights, Ernest, and Harold Dixon. "Socio-Psychological Dynamics in Pathological Black-White Romantic Alliances." *Journal of Instructional Psychology* 11 (1984): 132-138.

Spake, Amanda. "Interview with Yaphet Kotto." *Salon Magazine* (www.salon.com/12nov1995/feature/kotto.html), November 11, 1995.

Spickard, Paul R. "The Illogic of American Racial Categories." In *Racially Mixed People in America*, edited by M.P. Root, 12-23. Newbury Park, Calif.: Sage, 1992.

———. *Mixed Blood: Intermarriage and Ethnic Identity in Twentieth Century America*. Madison, Wisconsin: University of Wisc. Press, 1989.

Taylor, Donald M.; Stephen Wright; and L.E. Porter. "Dimensions of Perceived Discrimination: The Personal/Group Discrimination Discrepancy." In *The Psychology of Prejudice: The Ontario Symposium*, edited by Mark P. Zanna and James M. Olson, Vol. 7, pp. 233-255. Hillsdale, N.J.: Lawrence Erlbaum Associates Inc., 1993.

Terkel, Studs. Race. How Blacks and Whites Think About the American Obssession. New York: Anchor Books, 1992.

Thomas, William Isaac, and Dorothy Swain Thomas. *The Child in America: Behavior Problems and Programs*, 571-572. New York: Alfred A. Knopf, 1928.

Triandis, Harry, ed. *Variations in Black and White Perceptions of the Social Environment*. Urbana, Ill.: University of Illinois Press, 1976.

Tucker, M. Belinda & Claudia Mitchell-Kernan, eds. *The Decline in Marriage Among African-Americans.* New York: Russell Sage Foundation (1995).

———. "New Trends in Black American Interracial Marriage: The Social Structural Context." *Journal of Marriage and the Family 52* (1990): 209-218.

U.S. Bureau of the Census. *Characteristics of the Black Population, Race of Husband and Wife by Selected Characteristics, 2000.* Bureau of the Census, Washington, D.C., 2000.

———. *Current Projections of the Population Make-up of the U.S.* Bureau of the Census, Washington, D.C.,1996. For additional report cited: "Hispanic Origins and Race of Coupled Households." 2003.

U.S. Bureau of Labor. Current Population Survey: Characteristics of the Unemployed. Was., D.C.: U.S. Bureau of Labor Statistics, 2004.

U.S. Department of Education, National Center for Education Statistics, *Profile of Undergraduates in U.S. Postsecondary Educational Institutions: 1999–2000*, Statistical Analysis Report, July 2002,

U.S. Department of Housing and Urban Development. *What We Know about Mortgage Lending Discrimination*. Washington, D.C.: U.S. Department of Housing and Urban Development. Report no. 99-191, September 1999.

U.S. Department of Justice. Bureau of Justice Statistics. *Report on Prisoners in 2001*. Washington, D.C.: Bureau of Justice Statistics, 2001.

Wade, T., Joel. "The Relationships between skin Color and Self-Perceived Global, Physical, and Sexual Attractiveness and Self-Esteem for African Americans." *Journal of Black Psychology 22* (1991): 358-373.

Welsing, Frances, C. *The Isis Papers*. Chicago: Third World Press, 1989.

West, Cornel. *Race Matters*. Boston, Mass.: Beacon Press, 1993.

Whitfield, Stephen *A Death in the Delta: The Story of Emmett Till*. New York: Free Press, 1988.

Wilkerson, Doris Y. *Black Male/White Female: Perspectives on Interracial Marriage and Courtship*. Cambridge, Mass.: Schenkman Publishing Co., 1975.

Williams, July. *Brothers, Lust and Love*. Houston, Tex.: Khufu Books, 1996.

Wilson, Pete. "Securing our Nation's Borders." From Speech at Los Angeles Town Hall Meeting, April 1994.

Wilson, William J. *The Declining Significance of Race*. Chicago: University of Chicago Press, 1980.

Wilson, Yumi. "Interracial Dating Becoming More Common." *San Francisco Chronicle* (1998, July 27): 1 and A7.

Wirth, Louis, and Herbert Goldhammer. "The Hybrid and the Problem of Miscegenation." In *Characteristics of the American Negro,* edited by Otto Klineberg. New York: Harper and Row, 1969.

Wise, Tom. National Opinion Research Center. Chicago: University of Chicago, 1990.

Wright, Richard. *Native Son*. New York: Harper and Brothers, 1940.

Yancey, George, and Sherelyn Yancey. "Black-White Differences in the Use of Personal Advertisements for Individuals Seeking Interracial Relationships." *Journal of Black Studies 27* (1997): 650-667.

Yang Jeffrey, and Angelo Ragaza. "The Beauty Machine." In *Facing Difference. Race, Gender and Mass Media,* ed. Shirley Biagi and Marilyn Kern-Foxworth, 11-15. Thousand Oaks, Calif.: Pine Forge Press, 1994.

Yee, A.H.; H.H. Fairchild; F. Weizman; and G.E. Wyatt. "Addressing Psychology's Problems with Race." *American Psychologist 48* (1993): 1132-1140.

Zuckerman, M. "Some Dubious Premises in Research and Theory on Racial Differences: Scientific, Social and Ethical Issues." *American Psychologist 45* (1990): 1297-1303.

Index

racial status, 155-156
study sample on, 155, 157-161
vs cultural influences, 156
Women (Black)
    interracial relationship of, 5-6, 34-36
    interracial relationship theories, 50-51, 77
    interracial relationships reactions, 50, 120-126
    media and, 76-77
    physical feature concerns, 80
Women (Hispanic) relationship problems
    characteristics shaping, 161-162

Hispanic males, 156
study sample on, 155, 157-161
vs cultural influences, 156
Women (White) relationship problems
    characteristics shaping, 154
    interracial nature of, 148
    study sample and, 149-154
    vs cultural differences, 148-149
    See also "Whiteness" envy
Woods, Tiger, 168

Yang, Jeffrey, 78